TIGER TERRITORY

The Untold Story of the Royal Australian Navy
in Southeast Asia from 1948 to 1971

Presentation of King's Colour at KD *Malaya*

TIGER TERRITORY

The Untold Story of the Royal Australian Navy in Southeast Asia from 1948 to 1971

Ian Pfennigwerth

ROSENBERG

First published in Australia in 2008
by Rosenberg Publishing Pty Ltd
PO Box 6125, Dural Delivery Centre NSW 2158
Phone: 61 2 9654 1502 Fax: 61 2 9654 1338
Email: rosenbergpub@smartchat.net.au
Web: www.rosenbergpub.com.au

The National Library of Australia Cataloguing-in-Publication Data:
Pfennigwerth, Ian.
Tiger territory : the Royal Australian Navy in Southeast
Asia 1948 to 1971 / Author, Ian Pfennigwerth.
1st ed.

Kenthurst, N.S.W. : Rosenberg Publishing, 2008.
ISBN: 9781877058653 (pbk.)
Includes index.
Bibliography.

Australia. Royal Australian Navy--History--20th century.
Sea-power--Australia--History--20th century.
Australia--Military relations--Southeast Asia
Southeast Asia--Military relations--Australia
Australia--Military policy.

359.00994

Cover: HMAS *Duchess* searching suspect vessel (L. Jones)

Printed in China by Everbest Printing Co Limited

Contents

List of Illustrations   6

Acknowledgments   8

Notes and Abbreviations   10

Introduction   12

1 A Decade of Post-War Planning   16

2 The Malayan Emergency   38

3 The Calm Before the Storm   80

4 A Malayan/Malaysian Navy   97

5 Indonesian Confrontation   150

6 The British Withdraw   220

7 The Veterans' Fight for Recognition   247

Epilogue   274

Appendix   RAN Ships of the Far East Strategic Reserve   280

Bibliography   287

Endnotes   294

Index   314

List of Illustrations

Maps and Figures

1-1 Southeast Asia   17
1-2 ANZAM Area   23
2-1 Peninsular Malaya   39
5-1 Command and Control in East Malaysia   153
5-2 Confrontation Command and Control   155
5-3 East Malaysia   163
5-4 Tawau Border Area   167
5-5 Singapore   180
5-6 Singapore Strait Malacca Strait Area   202
Jeff cartoon HMAS *Teal*   *205*
Prime Minister's letter   219

Photographs

page 2 Presentation of King's Colour at KD *Malaya*

Between pages 96-7

HMAS *Arunta* from HMAS *Sydney* (Naval Historical Society of Australia)
HMAS *Warramunga* refuelling from *Melbourne* (Naval Historical Society of Australia)
HMAS *Anzac* (Naval Historical Society of Australia)
HMAS *Tobruk* in Singapore Dock 1955 (Naval Historical Society of Australia)
HMAS *Quadrant* (Naval Historical Society of Australia)
HMAS *Queenborough* (Naval Historical Society of Australia)
HMAS *Quickmatch* in Labuan 1961 (Naval Historical Society of Australia)
HMAS *Voyager* (Naval Historical Society of Australia)
HMAS *Melbourne* with *Voyager* and *Vendetta* (Naval Historical Society of Australia)
HMAS *Quiberon* (Naval Historical Society of Australia)
SEATO Maritime Exercise Group (Naval Historical Society)
HMAS *Sydney* as troop transport (Naval Historical Society of Australia)
Captain Dovers in KD *Mahamiru* (P. Nettur)
Indonesian destroyer (J. Foster)
Indonesian *Komar* Class patrol boat (J. Foster)
Indonesian patrol vessel (J. Foster)

Coastal minesweeper KD *Ledang* (A.N. Dollard)
Inshore minesweeper KD *Temasek* (A.N. Dollard)
HMAS *Yarra* (Naval Historical Society of Australia)
HMS *Mull of Kintyre* at Divisions (P. Procopis)
HMAS *Parramatta* (Naval Historical Society of Australia)
HMAS *Curlew* in Kuching (D. Hiron)
Indonesian prisoners in *Teal* (J. Werner)
RMN Vosper patrol boat (A.N. Dollard)
KD *Malaya* (J. Hume)
RMN Gas Turbine fast patrol boat (P. Nettur)
HMAS *Duchess* searching suspect vessel (L. Jones)
HMAS *Duchess* towing Malaysian vessel (L. Jones)
HMAS *Hawk* interception (J. Foster)
Pig boat alongside HMAS *Duchess* (L. Jones)
HMAS *Duchess* gunnery exercise (L. Jones)
Infiltrators being interrogated in HMAS *Duchess* (L. Jones)
Lookout in HMAS *Duchess* (L. Jones)
Ton Class waist Bren gunner (J. Werner)
Ton Class Bofors in action (J. Werner)
Ton Class messdeck (J. Werner)
Ton Class engine change, Singapore (P. Cooper)
Mobile Clearance Diving Team ordnance disposal (G. Miller)
Prisoner transfer to Singapore Police (1) (J. Werner)
Prisoner transfer to Singapore Police (2) (J. Werner)
Mobile Clearance Diving Team diving party (G. Miller)
Malaysian King at KD *Malaya* with Commander Hume RAN (J. Hume)
Sultan of Johore at KD *Malaya* (J. Hume)
Sultan of Johore takes salute at KD *Malaya* with Commodore Dollard (J. Hume)
Commodore Dollard inspects Guard at KD *Malaya* (J. Hume)
Commodore Thanabalasingham with Malaysian King (J. Hume)
Loch Class frigate KD *Hang Tuah* (A. N. Dollard)
HMAS *Derwent* (Naval Historical Society of Australia)
HMAS *Melbourne* launching Gannet anti-submarine aircraft (Naval Historical Society of Australia)
HMAS *Melbourne's* messdeck, 1958 (Naval Historical Society of Australia)

Acknowledgments

No book, least of all a history book like this, can be written without the willing assistance of a host of supporters. In the creation of *Tiger Territory* some of those have been acting in an official capacity, and I want to thank the staffs of the National Australian Archives, especially in the Canberra and Melbourne reading rooms, the Research Centre of the Australian War Memorial, the Naval Historical Directorate of the Sea Power Centre — Australia, and the Defence Library Service at RAAF Base Williamtown. Amongst them they have successfully and smoothly coped with a continuous stream of requests for open records and monographs, and numerous applications for access to a plenitude of records either 'not yet examined' or 'closed' to public access. Moreen Dee of the DFAT Historical Records Section has also been of enormous assistance on the diplomatic records front, and Alastair Cooper has cast his experienced and critical eye over the naval text.

The Malaysian and Singaporean Defence Advisers in Canberra provided assistance to me in getting in touch with personalities and organisations in their countries. What I learned was useful. The office of the Australian Defence Adviser Kuala Lumpur was similarly helpful.

When I set out on the project I wanted to include the comments and reminiscences of as many FESR veterans as possible, but I wasn't quite sure how I would find them. I therefore owe a debt of gratitude to the 'finders', who heard my call for contributors and then tracked them down for me. So, to Lyn Flett, Darrell Hegarty, Joe Linaker, Peter McGurk, Peter Maher, Keith Markey, Noel Muller, Rick Pengilly, Ken Staff, Alex Stevens and Graeme Thurstans, my appreciation. Special thanks are due to four individuals who really beat the bushes to shake out veterans of interest; Les Dwyer, Marty Grogan, Eric Paul (Macca) McKenzie and John Saywell. Gentlemen, without your efforts this would be a thinner and less interesting volume.

Those who have contributed their recollections and reflections on loan service with the RMN and of the Malayan Emergency and Confrontation rightly get star billing in the book. I list them all here. From the RAN, Denis Appel, Derek Bartholomai, Alex Bate, Bob Bergin, Ray Brown, Jack Callender, Rod Clarey, John Dodson, Allan Dollard, Bill Dovers, Tom Edgerton, Ray Elley, Jock Forbes, Bill Fox, Elizabeth Gordon, Guy Griffiths, Graeme Hanisch, Harry Harkness, Darryl Hiron, James Hume, Peter Humphrey, Laurie Jones, John Lancaster, Hamish MacGowan, Peter McKay, Graham 'Dusty' Miller, Gerry Mitchell, Ken Monk, R.T. Moyle, Phil Mulcare, Bob Nicholls, Michael Olden, Kevin Pickett, Paul Procopis, Pat Spence, Mike Rayment, Alan 'Rocker' Robertson, Ken Schmack, Col Slater, Greg Swinden, Bernard Verwayen, Adrian Wait, John Werner and Ron Whitmore. I was especially delighted to have the advice, assistance and input of RMN colleagues of the era; Hari Arasaratnam, 'Black Joe' Chelliah, Lam Ah Lek, Dick Khoo and Babu Nettur.

If I have managed to render the confusing and complicated series of events depicted in Chapter 7 into a reasonably clear account then it is only because of the unstinting help I had from the veterans of that particular campaign, especially Noel Payne and Bob Gibbs, and other members of the FESR Association.

Allen Atkins, once again, produced the illustrations for the book from my sketchy descriptions. Any errors in the text are mine, but their numbers will have been considerably reduced by the close attention paid to the manuscript by Tony Howland and David Ruffin. And David provided magnificent support to this project by combing though most of the literally hundreds of archival records consulted to glean the information I was seeking for the book, for which I am very grateful.

Finally, my wife Elizabeth has, once again, put up with my preoccupation with historical research and writing, and has been most supportive throughout. I cannot thank her enough.

Ian Pfennigwerth
Port Stephens, November 2007

Notes and Abbreviations

The majority of events in this tale took place at a time when Australia had yet to adopt decimal currency (14 February 1966) and had not yet even discussed a change from the Imperial system of measurements to the metric. The currency in use was the Australian Pound (£1 = $A2), but I have made no attempt to convert values into 2007 prices.

I have elected to use the most common English-language spellings for place names, thus 'Johore Baru' rather than the Malay 'Johor Bahru' and 'Sumatra' instead of the Indonesian 'Sumatera'.

Miles are nautical miles (nm). I have converted other units to metric, except for the calibres of minor weapons and small arms.

ACB   Australian Confidential Book
ALRI   *Angkatan Laut Republik Indonesia* – Indonesian Navy
AMDA   Anglo-Malay Defence Agreement
ANZAM Australia–New Zealand – Malaysia (strategic partnership)
ANZUK Australia–New Zealand–United Kingdom (strategic partnership)
ANZUS Australia New Zealand United States (treaty)
ASEAN Association of South East Asian Nations
AURI   *Angkatan Udara Republik Indonesia* — Indonesian Air Force
AWM   Australian War Memorial
BCOF   British Commonwealth Occupation Force (post-World War II Japan)
CCO   Clandestine Communist Organisation (Sarawak, Confrontation)
CD   Clearance diver/diving
CIDA   Committee of Inquiry into Defence and Defence-Related Awards
CinCFE Commander-in-Chief Far East (British)
CMS   Coastal minesweeper
CNS   Chief of Naval Staff (Australia and Malaysia)
COMFEF Commander Far East Fleet (British)
CT   Communist terrorist (Malayan Emergency)
DEA   Department of External Affairs (Australia)
DOBOPS Director of Borneo Operations (Confrontation)
DoD   Department of Defence (Australia)
DSD   Defence Signals Directorate (Australian signals intelligence organisation)
DVA   Department of Veterans' Affairs

FESR	Commonwealth Far East Strategic Reserve
FOTI	Fleet Operations and Tactical Instructions
FPDA	Five Power Defence Arrangements (from 1971)
HMAS	Her Majesty's Australian Ship
HMMS	His Malayan Majesty's Ship
HMS	Her Majesty's Ship
IADS	Integrated Air Defence System (Malaysia-Singapore)
JIB	Joint Intelligence Bureau
JIC	Joint Intelligence Committee
JPC	Joint Planning Committee
KD	*Kapal di Raja* (His Majesty's [Malaysian] Ship)
KKO	*Korps Kommando*—Indonesian Marine Corps
MALPOS	Orders for Ships Patrolling in Defence of Western Malaysia Seaboard
MRLA	Malay Races National Army (Emergency)
MRNVR	Malayan Royal Navy Volunteer Reserve
NAA	National Archives of Australia
NATO	North Atlantic Treaty Organisation
NGS	Naval Gunfire Support
NGSM	Naval General Service Medal
OPSCO	National Operations Committee (Malaysian)
PKI	*Partai Kommunis Indonesia* — Indonesian Communist Party
RAAF	Royal Australian Air Force
RAF	Royal Air Force (British)
RAN	Royal Australian Navy
RMN	Royal Malayan/Malaysian Navy
RN	Royal Navy
RNZN	Royal New Zealand Navy
RSN	Republic of Singapore Navy
RSS	Republic of Singapore Ship
SEATO	South East Asia Treaty Organisation
SSRNVR	Straits Settlements Royal Navy Volunteer Reserve
TNI	*Tentera Nasional Indonesia* — Indonesian Army
UK	United Kingdom
UKNA	United Kingdom National Archives
UN	United Nations
USA	United States of America
USN	United States Navy

Introduction

When Rear Admiral John Collins, the Chief of Naval Staff of the Royal Australian Navy (RAN) chaired a meeting of the Chiefs of Staff Committee in Melbourne in August 1948, it must have been with a sense of *déjà vu* that he viewed the conclusions — to define an area of strategic and military planning concern named ANZAM, and to establish a planning staff. In June 1941 as a captain, he had been seconded to the staff of the British Commander-in-Chief China to set in motion the much-delayed plans for the coordination of action by the British, Dutch, Australian and (possibly) the Americans in case of a Japanese attack on their Southeast Asian territories. He and his staff had produced and distributed 'Plans for the Employment of Naval and Air Forces of the Associated Powers' just prior to the Japanese attacks on 7/8 December 1941.

Quickly overwhelmed by the power and capability of the Japanese naval air force, the China Fleet ceased to exist, and Collins had found himself in Tanjong Priok, the port of Jakarta, charged with the responsibility of providing naval cover for the troop and equipment convoys being directed to Singapore to bolster the defence against the Japanese land assault down the Malay Peninsula. All too soon, his mission was changed to one of evacuating what could be salvaged from that debacle — and the subsequent Japanese invasion of the Netherlands East Indies — to safety in Australia or India. He himself narrowly escaped destruction in the perilous voyage from Java to Western Australia in the face of Japanese naval task groups that discovered and annihilated less lucky convoys. Collins' association with Singapore and the protective Malay Peninsula was thus both professional and personal.

Before World War II the RAN and the Australian Government were assured by the British that Singapore was 'impregnable' and that a strong force of capital ships would be sent to its defence should the Japanese threaten. This nostrum became the cornerstone of Australian defence strategy and, when the Australians had belatedly become aware that these British claims were not factual, it was too late to do much about it. There was nothing wrong with the appreciation that Singapore was crucial to Australian defence, as the consequences of its fall amply demonstrated. The question that confronted post-war Australian strategic planning was, 'How can Singapore's security be guaranteed?'

In pursuit of this goal, from 1947 onwards Australia and its Defence Force became steadily more involved in diplomatic and military agreements designed to protect Malaya and Singapore from falling under Communist domination. During John Collins' term as Chief of Naval Staff, this involvement moved from staff talks to international treaties and, a few months after he retired in February 1955, to a formal commitment of defence personnel and material to the defence of the two British colonies. The first deployment of RAN ships to this task occurred in July 1955. Collins' successors saw the commitment develop into a continuous naval presence in the region and then into active operations to defend the new Federation of Malaysia against Indonesian aggression after that country's formation in 1963. In the process, the RAN took a key role in the development, training and operations of the Royal Malayan and Malaysian Navies.

At the time of Australia's large-scale involvement in the Vietnam War, there were more Australian naval ships and personnel serving in the waters surrounding Malaysia than in Vietnam, and more have served there, and continue to do so, than ever went to the Vietnamese theatre. Furthermore, the naval campaigns in the

Malayan Emergency and in defending Malaysia against Indonesia's Confrontation, and their aftermaths, were brilliantly successful. Yet a review of the historiography would give the opposite impression: it is difficult to find any account of the RAN's involvement in Malaya, Malaysia and Singapore, apart from the cursory treatment it was given in the official history by Professor Grey.[1] It is also ignored in the official history of the medical aspects of Australia's Southeast Asian campaigns — for the authors, the RAN was just not there.[2]

Why should this be so? Well, first, there is no denying that the Vietnam conflict was a more dramatic and well-reported affair — especially for Australia's land forces — than the steady and unspectacular exercise of maritime power that was taking place further to the south. Not that Indonesian Confrontation of Malaysia was either bloodless or lacking excitement in parts. Second, the campaign took place over a long period, as the subtitle of this book suggests, which made the story less appealing as a subject to the media. Third, the RAN's support of first Malaya and then Malaysia was part of a complex and delicate set of strategic manoeuvres to protect Australian diplomatic, military and economic interests in a volatile region: to appreciate it one had to study it over a long period of time, which most reporters did not have.

In writing this history it was difficult to keep the narrative coherent by employing a chronological approach: too much was happening simultaneously in many different quarters. I've elected, therefore, to describe events within more-or-less discrete silos. This has enabled me to treat each chapter as a single issue, in which the salient features are discussed without excursions to what might have been happening elsewhere or in different arenas. The reader may have to make short leaps backwards and forwards between chapters, but I think the telling of the story will survive this minor inconvenience.

Much of the information which appears in this book is being made public for the first time. RAN veterans of these campaigns took nearly forty years to have the facts of their service accepted and recorded by the Navy and the government departments that sent them there. Some of this unconscionable reluctance to accept the facts was because of the inadequacy of the records; in other cases it was due to simple bureaucratic bloody-mindedness. But there were other reasons. As Prime Minister John Howard said in a letter marking the 2006 unveiling of a memorial plaque to the RAN's 16th Minesweeping Squadron's service during Confrontation:

> Members of this squadron served a country which, due to the sensitive nature of the Confrontation, was largely unaware of their efforts. This is a time to remember and show gratitude for their service.[3]

This is a sentiment with which the many thousands of RAN personnel who took part in the various campaigns in the theatre, including the author, would agree, and it is to recognise their lasting contributions to the peace and stability of the region that this account has been written. Accordingly, in full acknowledgment of the burdens borne and sacrifices made by members of the Australian Army and Royal Australian Air Force during the Malayan Emergency and Confrontation, this book is dedicated to all those naval people who served in Malaya, Malaysia and Singapore, with the hope that the extent and lasting benefits of their service may now be understood, remembered and commemorated by the people of Australia.

1 A Decade of Post-War Planning

Malaya is of strategic importance in the cold war period as well as in a major global war. Retention of Malaya gives defence in depth to Australia. It is the land route leading from Asia to the arc of islands to the north of Australia. Its loss would mean that Communist influence, and power, would come within striking range of Australia; the Allies would lose the focal point for their control of the sea routes between the Indian and North Pacific Oceans and they would be deprived of their best source of supply of rubber and tin.[1]

By any standards, the decade which followed the defeat of Germany and Japan was one of extraordinary change throughout the entire world, but certainly for the continent of Asia and for Australia. The civil war in China resumed following the departure of the Japanese, while French efforts to reassert control over their former Indochinese colonies found resistance from the nationalist forces led by Ho Chi Minh. In the Netherlands East Indies, the Dutch returned to find that the Japanese had fanned the flames of Indonesian independence, and that in many parts of the archipelago they faced a full-scale military insurrection. Burma was racked by violent disorder, leading to the early departure of the British. Even Thailand (then Siam), with its stable monarchy, faced the challenge of combating aggression from a hostile Communist China to its north. India gained its independence in 1947, but the partition of that country on religious

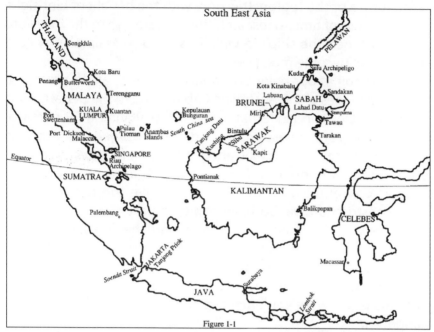

Figure 1-1

lines was to lead to much bloodshed. The British had reoccupied their Malayan and Straits Settlements colonies but unrest was growing.[2] Only in the Philippines had the Americans reasserted their control peaceably and granted Filipino independence in 1946.

To a reader in the early twenty-first century, these foreign affairs and security challenges, and others like them on the other side of the globe in Europe and the Middle East, probably seem as remote as the last Ice Age. As Robert Manne, author of a retrospective article on the Cold War: wrote in 1998; 'It requires an act of historical imagination of one age to understand the unrealised nightmares of previous times. During the Cold War, fears of Soviet totalitarianism were real'.[3] But each of these developments, in their own way, had a direct bearing on the involvement of the Royal Australian Navy (RAN) in Southeast Asian affairs. As one who served there on more than one tour, I realise now that I had little concrete understanding of these events, and even less idea of what the contribution I and thousands like me were making to the future of the region. It is only with the benefit of hindsight, and the luxury of time to research the background to the decisions that despatched the ships in which I served to Malaysian waters, that it has all become much clearer.

This turmoil in our neighbourhood and wider afield presented severe challenges to the Australian Cabinet and to the Departments of Defence (DoD) and External Affairs (DEA). Planning for post-war reconstruction and development had not envisaged that Australia would face any external threat, and yet there were apparent threats to our interests popping up all over the region of this country's strategic concern. Skilled manpower to drive the national post-war reconstruction was to have come, in part, from the ranks of demobilised servicemen and women, and the Treasurer's 'peace dividend' was to have been such that it was anticipated that £A40 million allotted annually to each of the now-depleted three services would be quite sufficient for their needs. However, even before these measures were implemented, the RAN was running short of manpower.[4]

The Government's view, as part of the Labor Party's platform on decolonisation, was that indigenous forces of national liberation ought to be supported. Thus Australia did not back the Dutch in Indonesia (although the ownership of West New Guinea was regarded rather differently) and, accordingly, it noted with approval the departure of the British from India, Burma and Sri Lanka, and the Americans from the Philippines. Australian governments did not support the French efforts to reassert their control in Indochina. Their attitude towards the future of Malaya, Singapore and the British colonies in North Borneo was, again, slightly different.

Prior to World War II, Australian strategic thinking was concentrated on the major naval base being constructed by the British in Singapore. There seems to have been little attention paid to the defence of the Malay Peninsula, down which any land assault against it would be launched: the base was regarded as impregnable from the sea. Some idea of the intensity of feeling the base roused in the minds of successive Australian governments can be gauged by the following comments made by the Australian representative at a meeting of the Committee of Imperial Defence in April 1934:

> Mr Bruce said the question of Singapore was a vital one to Australia ... He commented on the statements in the Report as to the vital importance of Singapore and the difficulty of recapturing it if it was lost. He also emphasised the greatly increased danger to Australia under such conditions. In fact, should the possibility of such a position not be reduced, Australia, failing naval security against invasion, would have to provide for greater land and air forces as a deterrent against such risk.[5]

Mr Bruce's predictions of the threat to Australian security if Singapore fell were, unfortunately, proved true in the war which followed. Remembrance of the Malayan campaign of 1941–42 against the Japanese invaders holds a special place in the Australian psyche. The comprehensive defeat of the British forces — which included significant elements of the Australian Navy, Army and Air Force — by a numerically inferior enemy, whose military prowess had been scorned before the fighting commenced, led to the capitulation of the 'impregnable fortress' of Singapore on 15 February 1942. The Japanese high command had allowed ninety days for this campaign: it had taken only seventy. The Associated Powers — Britain, the Netherlands, the United States and Australia — had lost the strategic initiative, a base from which the advancing Japanese could have been harassed and hindered in their designs, and a considerable, perhaps irrecoverable, degree of 'face'. The white colonial masters had been decisively bested in the field of battle by an Asian nation.

For Australia, the loss of Singapore destroyed the foundations of its pre-war strategic planning and policies.[6] Singapore, and the powerful British fleet that would operate from the great naval base constructed there, was to have deterred Japanese aggression in the first place. If the Japanese pushed their luck too far, it would be from

Singapore that retribution was meted upon their presumption. Australia was willing and eager to provide what men and material it could to bolster the defence of the island and the Malay Peninsula which protected it, and was instrumental in stirring some of the tropical torpor in which the island and its defenders customarily dwelt. The planning exercise referred to in the Introduction is evidence that Australia took the Japanese threat more seriously than some British colonial officials. While Singapore stood, Australia was safe from all but pin-prick attacks — raids by Japanese cruiser forces on Australian shipping and coasts. This was the key to the nation's maritime planning, and the basis for its selection of the order of battle with which it would meet the enemy attacks.

The validity of this belief was demonstrated by the events which followed the collapse of the shield of Fortress Singapore. The Australian 8th Division was marched off into captivity and the rigours of Japanese work camps. None of the Royal Australian Air Force (RAAF) aircraft sent to Malaya survived the campaign, although some personnel were recovered. The RAN reeled back and played its part in the defence of the Netherlands East Indies, making sacrifices in ships and men that were as futile as they were gallant. The Imperial Japanese Navy bombed Darwin with a ferocity just short of what had been visited on Pearl Harbor. Australian outposts in Ambon, Timor and New Britain were overwhelmed. For the first time in its history, Australia found its physical links with Britain all but severed. It was in this atmosphere of shock that Prime Minister John Curtin made his historic appeal for military assistance from the United States in February 1942. The Americans were already on their way, but Curtin's willingness to look beyond the British Empire for help marked an historic lurch towards an independent Australian strategic policy.

Given these clear and recent recollections of how close the Japanese had come, it is not surprising that Australian governments made the security of Singapore and the Malay Peninsula something of a centrepiece of their post-war policies.

Singapore lies at the focal point of the communications in South East Asia. It is directly on the main sea routes between South East Asia and Australia … It is also an essential link on the air route from Australia to India, to the Middle East and to the Western pacific seaboard and beyond. It is evident, therefore, that forces based in Singapore will be required to safeguard our interests in South East Asia. Singapore will be of value only if adequate forces can be made available there.[7]

Australia was as keen to ensure that the Japanese threat would never arise again as it was to take steps to keep the Malay region out of the hands of any other potential enemy that might wish to claim it. The enemy threat on the strategic horizon of the late 1940s was international Communism, and the means of defeating it in Southeast Asia, as conceived by Australian strategists, was to achieve the three related goals of enhancing British Commonwealth defence planning and preparation, supporting the new United Nations (UN) organisation, and developing a series of interlocking regional security arrangements — a security platform with three planks. Later, one other was added — a security treaty with the USA.

The first of these planks — enhancing the level of British Commonwealth defence cooperation — was important to the Government and its strategic advisers alike. However, the British still attempted to call the tune and, despite its appeal to the Australian Chiefs of Staff, the Australian Government was not particularly interested in the British efforts to highlight the importance of the Middle East in Commonwealth defence. The Government directed the Defence Committee that Australia's focus should be in the Pacific.[8] Armed with a Defence 'Appreciation of the Strategic Position of Australia, February 1946', the Prime Minister, Ben Chifley made the point at the May 1946 Prime Ministers' Conference in London that Australia's major contribution to Commonwealth defence should be in the Pacific, in concert with other regional nations.[9]

Chifley also argued, successfully, that a new joint structure of military consultation and planning, in which Britain and the Commonwealth nations should have equal status, should replace the pre-war Committee of Imperial Defence organisation. Britain welcomed this concept as a means of distributing some of its imperial burden to Commonwealth partners, but did not, perhaps, understand fully the Australian desire for a stronger voice in decisions which affected this country's security. At the same time, British strategic attention remained firmly focussed in Europe and on the vulnerability of the Middle East to aggression by the Soviet Union. In strategic terms, the British colonies in Malaya were something of a sideshow, although of intense economic interest as a generator of precious export dollars.

But the British did agree to the concept of combined planning for the defence of areas of Southeast Asia of mutual strategic significance to the UK, Australia and New Zealand—a precedent that had been set by the post-war establishment of the Joint Chiefs of Staff in Australia to oversee the conduct of the British Commonwealth Occupation Force (BCOF) in Japan. The identification of common strategic objectives and the development of plans to achieve them had eluded pre-war conferees on Imperial defence, possibly because the parties spoke from positions of inequality, but there was now an opportunity to learn from the lessons of World War II. And the three Commonwealth nations' interests coincided in Malaya. One outcome was the 1948 conference in Melbourne chaired by the Australian Chief of Naval Staff (CNS), Rear Admiral John Collins, where a visiting British delegation agreed to the setting up of an organisation to plan for the pursuit of common goals in the 'Australia-New Zealand-Malaya' region, abbreviated to ANZAM, and delineated at Figure 1-1. It had originally been intended to include Indonesia in this grouping — creating the acronym ANZIM, but this proposal was dropped because of the potential for misunderstandings that might arise in the emerging independent Indonesia about the purpose of the organisation.

Australia accepted primary responsibility for strategic planning — in cooperation and consultation with the UK and New Zealand —

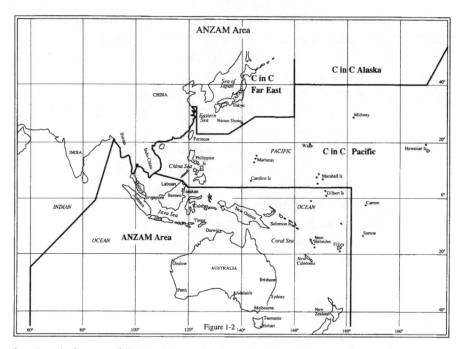

Figure 1-2

for the defence of the ANZAM Area, with Britain acting for Malaya and its other colonial possessions in the region.[10] The defence of Malaya was not included under ANZAM: the British regarded the peninsula as a 'home territory'.[11] Rather, ANZAM was for the overall direction and control of operations in its designated area, but not Malaya itself. Included in this responsibility was defence of the sea lines of communication between the members of the Commonwealth, a factor that influenced the structure and development of the RAN's order of battle for nearly two decades.

> Australia should be responsible for initiating plans for the defence of sea communications, excluding home waters. This planning should be effected by the Australian higher Defence machinery in conjunction with the accredited representatives in Australia of the UK and NZ Chiefs of Staff.[12]

This was a considerable departure from past practice, where the British had taken the lead in all British Empire planning, and it was an area new to Australian Defence. ANZAM was to create an indigenous capacity to undertake maritime strategic planning and a lessening of Australian — and particularly RAN — reliance on the British Admiralty. These issues of sea control in the western Pacific necessarily required the Commonwealth partners to have some form of understanding with the United States. The Australian CNS was not slow off the mark in exploring the delineation of the boundaries of this, essentially naval, responsibility between the Commonwealth and the Americans. In late 1948 Collins visited Hawaii and raised the issue of demarcation of the US and Commonwealth zones of responsibility for shipping in the Asia–Pacific region. It is not clear that he did so with the prior authority of either the Australian Government or its Chiefs of Staff Committee — let alone the British — although there also appear to have been no complaints of his exceeding his authority. By early 1951, the Collins initiative had developed into high-level discussions on coordinating operational naval responsibilities, with Australia representing its other two ANZAM partner navies.

Australia's Foreign Minister, Dr H.V. Evatt, was the principal architect of the second security policy plank — support for the UN. A tireless exponent of the virtues of the UN as a barrier to aggression between nations, Evatt's enthusiasm sometimes led him to take extreme positions, which puzzled and disturbed the British and the Americans. The latter, in particular, became convinced that Evatt's opinions on strategic matters were unsound, and that Australia was being taken to the left of the political centre.[13] Despite the success of the Allies in World War II, American chauvinism found reason enough to doubt Australia's continuing value as an ally. Evatt's foray into international diplomacy as a standard bearer for the UN did nothing to enhance Australia's strategic security and, although Australia continued to be an active participant in and supporter of the UN, that organisation's place in the Australian security strategy rapidly shrank.

The third policy plank — formation of regional security arrangements — was similarly problematical. As has been seen, the period after the end of the war was far from peaceful, and Australia was keen to avoid becoming enmeshed in other countries' colonial wars. The key guarantor of Australian security against attack would be the United States. However, the Americans were occupied with the demilitarisation of Japan, support of the Nationalist Chinese against the Red Army, the rehabilitation of Europe through the Marshall Plan, and the ideological and military struggle with the Soviet Union. They were not anxious to assume more treaty entanglements in the Southwest Pacific. Nevertheless, as the British Chiefs of Staff put it at the October 1948 Prime Ministerial conference in London, if war were to occur, 'Action which may be taken by the United States of America in the Pacific will be of major importance to Australia'.[14]

In September 1951 the outcome of the discussions initiated by Admiral Collins was formalised in what became known as the Radford (US Commander-in-Chief Pacific) – Collins Agreement, the terms of which still apply.[15] The agreement marked US recognition of the existence of ANZAM and the responsibility of the three Commonwealth countries for the defence of shipping within it. Specifically, the Agreement assigned to ANZAM the responsibilities for escorting and protection of convoys, reconnaissance, search and rescue, and anti-submarine warfare (ASW) in its region, and led to the establishment of common procedures in the Pacific, the use of US Navy (USN) publications as the basic doctrinal and tactical sources, and the improvement of signal communications arrangements. While essentially a measure designed to cope with global war, the Radford– Collins Agreement also sanctioned a formal exchange of staff officers between the RAN and USN in peacetime, a major step in cementing relations between the navies and in exposing RAN officers to USN planning and operations.[16] In short, these outcomes were a significant advance in the strategic positioning of Australia — and especially of the RAN — in the Pacific. There was some disappointment in Australian political circles that the agreement did not gain Australia access to US strategic planning, but the longevity of the Radford–Collins Agreement has more than discounted these initial criticisms.

The British were willing to pass this task to Australia because their concentration was on the threat posed to European and Middle East security by Soviet expansionism. As well, in November 1948 they had initiated an independent review of Britain's defence responsibilities and commitments against a set of appropriations for defence expenditure, led by Lord Harwood. The Harwood Working Party's recommendations were shocking. Amongst other bases, Singapore was to be abandoned.

> It would therefore be logical for Australia to provide the Flag Officer to work alongside the Army and Air Force Commanders-in-Chief in the South East Asian Command and we have assumed that this will be done ... We see no reason to keep the general facilities of Singapore Dockyard in care and maintenance for another war, nor can we afford to do so. The base is therefore assumed to be abandoned other than for such facilities as the Australian Navy may need for itself.[17]

Harwood was working on the advice that the British Treasury would not increase the Defence budget, and that the incursions being made by the Soviet Union in Europe required the strongest response from Britain. The British services welcomed the report, not because they agreed in the slightest with its recommendations, but because it effectively demonstrated what would be lost if the Treasury view prevailed. In the end, the views of the British services won the argument. For the moment, at least, the forces based on Singapore would remain predominantly British.

Although not responsible for Malaya's defence, the Australian Government and its strategic planners took a close interest in events in the British possessions in Southeast Asia. From the war's end until it lost power in December 1949, the Chifley Government had reservations about British actions in Malaya, and was particularly concerned when a Communist-led insurgency broke out in 1948. Australian policy makers were inclined to view the uprising as a legitimate indigenous independence movement aimed at removing the British colonial government, rather than an attempt to install a Communist regime in Malaya as part of a worldwide Soviet Union-directed campaign of expansion. In Canberra, the question of the form of Australian assistance to the British authorities in Malaya — if any — became a hot topic. The Chiefs of Staff had recommended in a 1947 Appreciation that Australia should accept responsibility for the Commonwealth scheme of defence based on Singapore, but the Government had banned the export of arms, relenting only to allow limited quantities of small arms to be sent to Malaya in July 1948.

Accordingly, British requests for material and more direct defence assistance from Australia in its struggle against the 'Communist Terrorist' (CT) problem were received cautiously by the Government.[18] In an era of decolonisation, Australia had to tread warily so as to avoid being regarded as a supporter of declining colonial regimes or — worse — as a 'neo-colonialist', picking up the spoils in the wake of departing European imperialists.[19] But there was little doubt in the minds of Australia's defence planners about the importance of Malaya to the defence of Australia.

Having accepted the responsibility for planning the protection of those sea routes to, from and past the Malay Peninsula, the Australian Chiefs of Staff were now receiving intelligence indicating that this would not be an easy task. The major threat to shipping was assessed to be the sea mine laid from submarines in the shallow waters around Malaya and the Indonesian archipelago, and torpedo attacks from those submarines, of which the Chinese were thought to be able to keep two on station from 1950. With a big patrol area to be covered, the operations of the raiders were thought likely to be 'mainly directed against the sea approaches of Malaya'.[20] The Australian force being considered for initial implementation of the plan to defend the ANZAM area was a carrier task group, two AA frigates and one RAAF maritime patrol squadron — a majority of the maritime forces of Australia.

The incoming government led by Robert Menzies inherited

the British request for assistance in Malaya. While it was more philosophically and politically inclined to respond favourably, the new government remained as reluctant as its predecessor to do so. A Cabinet decision of May 1950 showed that the options for providing military forces had been examined, but that the factors militating against committing it lay elsewhere.

> While the present request was for a limited measure of assistance, the obligations which would flow from it would be very likely to increase and to continue for a lengthy period. It was not possible at this stage to be sure that the administration in Malaya was in a position to handle adequately the situation which the presence of the bandits [CTs] had created.[21]

With recent memories of Singapore 1942, the Australian Government was unwilling to commit itself to supporting once again a British regime which might not be able to cope with the responsibility of defending Malaya. But there were other issues to be considered.

> The United States might well lend its support if some Asian movement, as distinct from a Western-sponsored plan, could take form. At the present time discussions were taking place between the Foreign Ministers of United Kingdom, France and United States on Indo-China. An immediate step which might be construed as committing Australia to a militaristic policy in the area might reduce Australia's opportunity to bring about agreement on these wider issues.[22]

That made a lot of sense for a country attempting to make a place for itself in regional councils, but one practical reason why Australian governments were not able to respond to British requests for military assistance was the dilapidated state of the Australian Defence Force. On top of the commitment to the British Commonwealth Occupying Force in Japan (BCOF), all three services were struggling with a re-equipment program approved in 1947. The lack of naval resources was a distinct restraint on government action, and the nature and causes for this are worth examining in closer detail.

Following the 1945 cessation of hostilities, RAN planners were confronted with a conundrum: at a time when its ships were worn out from over six years of warfare and many of its experienced cadres were disappearing back into civilian employment, the political leadership was expecting Australia to 'pull its weight' in regional affairs.[23] A modern and balanced Australian naval force, capable of independent operations in the Southeast Asian region and beyond, had to be created and, as it happened, the British Admiralty thoughtfully provided the visiting Australian Prime Minister with their blueprint for the new RAN in 1946. Including ships in reserve, it should comprise three aircraft carriers, six cruisers, twenty-four destroyers, forty-eight frigates and assorted auxiliaries and mine warfare craft — a much larger force than the RAN order of battle at the end of World War II.

Uncritically, this suggestion was adopted by the Australian Naval Board, but the financial and manpower priorities of post-war Australia soon brought a cold blast of reality to the issue. The introduction of naval air power to replace the ageing cruiser force was endorsed by the Government, as was an initial 1946 plan for the construction of two Battle Class destroyers, with four of the larger and more modern *Daring* Class to follow — an ambitious program, given the limited technological and industrial capability of Australian shipyards.[24]

By June 1947 a consolidated Five Year Defence Program had been presented to Parliament, with a total expenditure of £250 million envisaged, of which the largest individual slice of £75 million went to the RAN. The naval order of battle was to be two aircraft carriers, three cruisers, eight destroyers, ten frigates and thirty-three minesweepers: of this total, sixteen ships would be in service with the remainder in reserve. This significant decision on the RAN's order of battle required the restructuring of the

Australian Squadron, an increase in personnel to man the new ships and aircraft, and the improvement and recommissioning of two former RN airfields on the Australian east coast for use by the new squadrons — a massive staffwork, recruiting and training burden.[25] The British agreed to supply the two light fleet carriers and their air group aircraft on extremely generous terms, and the first — HMAS *Sydney* — commissioned in December 1948.

In February 1948 Admiral Collins became the first RAN College graduate to hold the position of CNS. Despite Admiralty suggestions that Collins was too inexperienced to do justice to the position, the Australian Government held firm in its decision to appoint him in preference to another British officer. Collins' new post was no sinecure: by mid-1949, the RAN's segment of the Five Year Defence Plan was foundering. The problem was not, for once, money. The RAN, along with the other services, was simply unable to attract sufficient recruits into its ranks, or to retain enough of those already serving. By the end of 1949 the Navy was 46 per cent below its planned strength. The Army and RAAF were similarly under target. The inability of the Navy to recruit sufficient manpower forced CNS to decommission three ships.

On top of this, the destroyer construction program was in difficulties, with severe delays in building and fitting out the ships, largely because of the capacity and skill constraints in the Australian shipbuilding industry. This meant that only one of the two Battle Class destroyers could be completed within the Plan's timeframe. The second aircraft carrier would not now be available until 1952.[26] A government's desire to see the RAN committed to any theatre of operations, other than the BCOF in Japan, was thus severely circumscribed by a lack of wherewithal.

In October 1950, the RAN had a July 1951 manpower target of 15,173 regulars and 7580 reserves, with one light fleet carrier and its carrier air group, three cruisers (none operational), three Tribal Class destroyers, two Battle Class destroyers (one incomplete), twelve frigates and thirty-two old corvettes. Four *Daring* Class destroyers were under construction, while five wartime destroyers of the

Q Class were being converted to fast ASW frigates. [27] In a period of post-war boom conditions, the nation as a whole was suffering from a manpower shortage and, to keep even this reduced force in commission, the Navy had a policy of minimum manning for most of its ships. Put simply, ships were not manned and ready for operational service, and to make one ship ready for operations required that the additional manpower be stripped from other ships.

Accordingly, the small number of destroyers available in July 1950 caused the Naval Board considerable difficulties in providing ships for Korean service: only three were in commission, *Arunta*, *Warramunga* and *Bataan*, all of World War II construction. The Australian Government committed the frigate *Shoalhaven* and destroyer *Warramunga* at the outbreak of hostilities, and *Bataan* would replace *Shoalhaven*. The only other destroyer available was the incomplete new Battle Class *Tobruk*, while manpower shortages meant that crewing these ships for active service caused considerable posting turbulence.[28] The RAN was as unready as most of the UN navies for action in Korea, and quite incapable of meeting any other British requests for ships.

If defence chiefs were experiencing difficulties, so were the diplomats. Despite Dr Evatt's enthusiasm for the United Nations, it was clear that the organisation offered no guarantees of collective security for its members. And it was proving very difficult for Australia to kindle any enthusiasm in the United States for its ideas on regional security. On the contrary, Australia's security status continued to slide, particularly when US decryptions of cables to and from the Soviet Embassy in Canberra revealed the existence of a spy network within the Dr Evatt's department, and elements within the US administration determined in 1947 that Australia was a security threat. As a result, an embargo was placed on the supply of classified information to this country. There was some basis to this claim, and it took a major reorganisation of Australia's security arrangements, including the establishment of the Australian Security and Intelligence Organisation in 1949, before the embargo would be lifted. But the event which shifted US opinions in Australia's favour was the Korean War.

The assault on the South by the North Korean People's Army in June 1950 took all Allied governments by surprise. The country least able to respond swiftly was the United States, which had reduced its forces in South Korea to the level of a military advisory group, and whose occupation force in Japan was poorly trained and ill equipped for war. By contrast, Australia and the Commonwealth had elements of the BCOF, especially from the RAN and RAAF, that could be deployed to Korea at short notice, and this was done, although — as explained — it was to cause the RAN particular difficulties to meet the commitment the Government had made. The overall Australian contribution to the UN forces was small, but not insignificant, and the rapidity with which these forces were able to be deployed made a marked impact on American policy makers. Making the most of the opportunity presented, Australia's foreign minister, Sir Percy Spender, had by August 1951 succeeded in bringing into force a treaty of mutual security support — the ANZUS Treaty. Thus, in the space of six years, two of the principal Australian security objectives — a larger role in Commonwealth planning for the defence of the region and a defence treaty with the United States — had been achieved.

The third objective, of a regional security grouping, came into existence because of the fear that a newly 'liberated' China would take an active part in supporting other 'wars of liberation' in Southeast Asia, as it had done in Korea. Yet as late as November 1951, the prospects for forming a defence pact to resist this possibility were viewed as remote by the British and Australian governments.

> Communism, while a threat to South East Asian countries was still internal rather than external. The strategic importance of defending the area required assessment. The conference considered that in a South East Asian defence pact, though unrealistic in the near future, should be an important political objective.[29]

But this issue was fast coming to a head, as the long war between the French and the Communist Viet Minh in northern Indo-China began to shift dramatically in favour of the nationalist forces, and Communism was perceived to be advancing on a broad front. The French had been particularly anxious to convince the other 'European' powers with interests in the region to come to their assistance with a common anti-Communist front, including the use of their armed forces to stave off imminent French defeat. A series of 'Five Power' talks were held from 1953, in which Australians and New Zealanders met with British, French and United States representatives. A Five Power conference convened in Pearl Harbor in September–October 1953 had as its agenda discussion of the provision of sea air and land forces to reinforce the French in Indo-China, the seizure of a beachhead on Hainan Island to deter the Chinese from supporting the Viet Minh, and the provision of ground, naval and air support to the British in Malaya.[30]

This makes extraordinary reading in the twenty-first century, but the threat was regarded as real enough in 1953. The military staff supporting the talks produced a number of reports on what might be required to repel Communist designs on Southeast Asia. In respect to Malaya, it suggested that to save Malaya an enormous naval task force would be required — four attack carriers, two light carriers, eight cruisers, no fewer than sixty-two destroyers, plus supporting lesser craft.[31] A concerted land thrust by the Communists towards the Malay Peninsula would require the pre-emptive Allied occupation of the Kra Peninsula in Thailand, the same premise as lay behind Operation MATADOR, which the British high command had shied from implementing in December 1941. Interestingly, the latter discussion generated the first expression of the concept of a strategic reserve to defend Malaya, and this, unlike most of the matters discussed by the Five Power Staff Agency, was to become a reality.[32]

Despite the apparent threat — the loss of Indo-China was expected to lead to the 'collapse' of Thailand and Burma — none of the five nations seemed willing, or in Australia's case, able to commit themselves to participation in an effort of this size and, as the Battle of Dien Bien Phu raged in 1954, it was only the Americans who were prepared to assist the French militarily. In the end, the French had to withdraw from their northern Indo-Chinese colony while peace talks in Geneva, sponsored by Britain and the Soviet Union, hammered out a ceasefire and the partition of the colony of Annam at the 17th parallel with the rump and the colony of Tonkin to form the Republic of South Vietnam

This second Communist victory in Asia in the space of five years promoted serious discussion on collective security in Southeast Asia. A flurry of diplomatic manoeuvring ensued to develop a regional consensus on the need to present a united front against Communist aggression, and the outcome was the South East Asian Collective Defence Treaty, signed in Manila in 1954 and better known as the South East Asian Treaty Organisation (SEATO). It had eight members, with the Philippines, Thailand and Pakistan joining the 'Europeans' and three 'protocol states', which the treaty members were pledged to support against any Communist advances — Laos, Cambodia and South Vietnam. So in the end, ironically, it was the Communists who enabled Australian governments to finally put in place the post-war security arrangements they sought.

By now, things were also moving on addressing the nation's Defence deficiencies as well. The Menzies Government in 1951 decided that the country had only three years to prepare for hot war with the Communist Bloc, and had put in place a number of measures to strengthen the nation industrially and militarily. National service was introduced, stockpiles of strategic materials were created and strenuous efforts to lift the material capacity of the Australian Defence Force were made. Regardless of the reality of the threat as perceived at the time, this National Security Plan did produce stronger and more capable armed forces, and the Government now had the capability to respond to calls for military assistance that had not been possible beforehand. As the 1953 report of the National Security Resources Board stated:

In the result, the country is in a better position to meet a sudden emergency. A force of nearly 150,000 men, comprising regular and citizen forces, is in being, and the number of men under arms or immediately available has been almost trebled. Arms and equipment have increased considerably; the Navy has more ships, the Army has more tanks and the Air Force has many more planes. Much money is being spent on research and the development of defence production facilities.[33]

The Board noted that the RAN had twenty-three ships in commission, an increase of seven over the three years, and that the quality and fighting power of the Fleet was much greater as it now included two aircraft carriers. These positive figures could not disguise, however, the fact that all this effort had produced only one destroyer, the modernisation of a second, and one Q Class converted to a fast ASW frigate. The Daring Class program had been reduced to three, and one Q Class conversion had been cancelled. The RAN was still desperately short of modern escort ships, although its manpower problems had eased to some extent. This improvement was offset by the large numbers of trained personnel who had been diverted from front line tasks to the training role, a situation which induced more overstretch in the Fleet.

Strategically, the ANZAM planning machinery was activated, with a specific set of responsibilities in relation to 'defence matters of common concern'.[34] Australia sent a joint planning team to Malaya in February/March 1951 to hammer out differences between British and Australian perceptions. No punches seem to have been pulled on either side, the British pointing out that their strategy for hot war required most of their forces defending Malaya to redeploy to the Middle East within three months of the outbreak of hostilities. The Australians, in turn, reiterated their concern over British intentions for its colony:

The Australian planners made it clear to the FAR EAST planners that AUSTRALIA did not wish to be involved in another military disaster in MALAYA. Australian forces were, therefore, unlikely to be made available for the defence of MALAYA unless the combined strength of the Australian forces and United Kingdom forces allocated for that purpose were adequate to deal with the form and scale of attack, both external and internal. If MALAYA is to be held in the event of a full-scale attack by the Chinese communist forces, it will be necessary for both the UNITED KINGDOM and AUSTRALIA to make firm commitments regarding the forces they will provide in Malaya.[35]

Australia was not going to accept any new assurances from the British of a 'Main fleet to Singapore' nature, and tough negotiations were to ensue in the following two years on how the ANZAM nations were going to make firm commitments on forces in Malaya. The outcomes will be discussed in the next chapter.

Thus, at the end of 1954 an Australian analyst of security policy could probably have reflected with some satisfaction on the end result of a hectic decade of negotiation, hot war in Korea, cold war everywhere else, and the outcomes of decolonisation in Southeast Asia. Australia had gained an American security guarantee in ANZUS, it was part of a collective anti-Communist security pact in SEATO, and it was an active partner in a revitalised Commonwealth regional defence arrangement with a major strategic planning role. It had, at last, a seat at the conference tables of the great and powerful when Pacific affairs were discussed. So far as treaties and talking could provide it, Malaya — and the path thence towards Australia — was secure from hostile assault.

Militarily, the nation now commanded a more modern, better trained and better equipped Australian defence force with which to defend its interests and those of its treaty partners. The Government now had a reasonable military option — although with some naval weaknesses — which it could use to support Australian national interests in the region, without having to scrabble together whatever it could, as had happened in Korea. As events transpired, this was just as well, as military demands were about to be placed upon the country that would last far longer than any other commitment previously entered into. Australia was about to be become engaged militarily in Southeast Asia, and 'forward defence' as a concept was about to evolve. Whether the RAN was, in fact, trained and ready to meet the challenges presented by Southeast Asian service will become clear in succeeding chapters.

2 The Malayan Emergency

A long series of historical events, including the capture of colonies held by other European powers, and the extension of protectorate arrangements over Malay sultanates, had resulted in the patchwork of British-controlled political entities which occupied the Malayan peninsula in the 1940s. The Straits Settlements of Penang, Malacca and Singapore lay along the Malacca Strait, while the remaining mainland states — traditional sultanates with a British adviser — were part of the Federated Malay States. A British High Commissioner in Kuala Lumpur was the head of government. Singapore also had a High Commissioner of its own. After 1945, large-scale immigration of labourers from China and southern India to work in the tin mines and rubber plantations, on which Malayan wealth was based, had resulted in a racial demography where Malays were on the point of becoming a minority in their own country. The long-term Chinese and Indian immigrants were generally more entrepreneurial than the Malays, and held much of the country's economic power, but they were denied the right to citizenship. Short-term labourers had come to Malaya simply because their economic prospects were better than in their home countries, and they were only there to make money and depart. The British colonial administration and managerial classes made up a very small proportion of the population of about five and a half million.

The Malay Peninsula is around 800 km long and 250 km wide,

Figure 2-1

with a range of mountains with peaks as high as 3000 m running down its spine. This divides the country into two sections with an 80 km wide coastal plain on the west being the most heavily populated. The land to the east of the central spine slopes away more gently to the South China Sea. In 1948, it was estimated that 80 per cent of the land area was covered with primary or secondary jungle. Living in that jungle were the *orang asli* — aborigines, with little contact with the outside world. On the jungle fringes Chinese 'squatters' had carved small holdings out of mostly Malay land. Otherwise, Malays occupied most of the rural areas, with many Chinese and Indians thronging the larger towns and cities. There were particular concentrations of Chinese on Penang Island in the northern Malacca Straits and in Singapore, at the south of the peninsula, and separated from it by the narrow Johore Strait.

The organisation at the core of the Malayan Emergency, the Malayan Communist Party, had been formed in 1928 and had attracted mostly ethnic Chinese adherents. Taking its lead from the Soviet Union, and drawing its strength from trade union member-ship, the Party soon achieved sufficient political prominence to compel the British to crack down on its organisation in 1931. However, following the German invasion of the Soviet Union in June 1941, the Party had offered to cooperate with the British authorities in the war against fascism. This offer was accepted and, after the Japanese invasion and conquest of Malaya in 1942, the Party was instrumental in founding and providing the organisational structure and leadership for the Malayan People's Anti-Japanese Army. Over the subsequent three years, this group carried out desultory attacks on Japanese installations and forces, while in the latter stages receiving training, material and monetary support from the British through the Special Operations Executive's Force 136. At war's end, the Party had developed cadres experienced in guerrilla warfare, had established *de facto* control of the countryside, had amassed a war chest, and had cached a considerable quantity of arms, ammunition and military supplies.[1] Nevertheless, the Party surrendered its position of considerable strength to the returning British military and civil administrations without a struggle.

The post-war period saw the continuation of trade union agitation by the Party, and outbreaks of rioting and industrial sabotage. However, in June 1947, as moves towards armed struggle were being planned, the general secretary disappeared with most of the Party's funds: it seems possible that he had been a double agent of the British for some years. While the Party regrouped, agitation, strikes, arson, armed attacks on infrastructure targets and the murder of some 'traitors' continued. In May 1948, the British authorities passed legislation aimed at reducing Communist influence in the trade unions, and in June the new leader of the Party, Chin Peng, ordered a mobilisation of his guerrilla organisation to fight the government. Broadly, this comprised former Anti-Japanese Army cadres, with a supporting infrastructure of mainly Chinese civilians — the People's Movement — known by its Chinese title *Min Yuen*.

Chin Peng was greatly influenced by the model of Communist insurrection in China expounded by Mao Zedong. His belief was that the British held Malaya weakly, and that a determined show of force would cause the administration to abandon the countryside and to concentrate in the cities and towns. In the vacated 'liberated areas' he would develop his administrative apparatus and build forces sufficient to confront and defeat government forces in pitched battle. These presumptions were all to be proved wrong; there were marked differences between Malaya and China. In the latter, government administration was weak, especially in the rural areas, and there were considerable masses of peasants who could support and sustain a liberating army with little fear of government retribution. By contrast, Malaya was well governed through a British administration and the traditional prerogatives of the sultans, and these measures were generally effective throughout the country. With a small population, mostly concentrated in towns, there was no peasant mass for Chin Peng and his army to liberate.[2] But it took twelve years of bloodshed before the Party accepted defeat.

Failing to excite a popular rising by an initial campaign of assassination and murder in the urban centres, Chin withdrew his forces into the jungles, and in 1949 renamed his force the Malayan Races Liberation Army (MRLA) in the largely unfulfilled hope of attracting ethnic Malays and Indians into its ranks.[3] The Emergency then settled down to a contest between the government forces and the insurgents — termed by the British 'Communist Terrorists' (CTs) — to attract and retain the loyalty of the urban Chinese communities and the roughly 600,000 Chinese in scattered squatter communities. These had fled to the jungle fringes to escape the Japanese, and they linked the jungles with the remainder of the colony.[4]

The ensuing struggle for control of Malaya was fought almost entirely on the ground, eventually between small units of government forces and smaller groups of CTs, although the British had initially used ineffective sweeps by larger forces to drive the insurgents into the jungles. Extensive aerial bombardment of suspected guerrilla base areas was conducted, but aircraft were most effective in supply and support of ground operations.[5] Naval tasks were the traditional roles of patrol, blockade and naval gunfire support (NGS) to the ground forces. While the northern border of the Malay Peninsula was held, more or less securely, by the anti-Communist Thai Government, the British retained total control of the sea approaches to Malaya and Singapore, to prevent the movement of CTs between base areas by sea or resupply from abroad, and to regulate the activities of legitimate users of coastal waters.

For the British, the Emergency represented an unwanted complication in an already tense international situation. In Europe, the Soviet Union was pressing its military advantages, installing puppet governments in Eastern Europe and challenging Allied control over Berlin. In Asia, it was clear that the Communists were winning the civil war in China, and they would soon be in a position to threaten Hong Kong. Malaya was an important money-spinner of US dollars for the cash-strapped British Treasury, but it showed all the signs of becoming a significant additional military burden. From the inception of the Emergency, the British remained keen to attract other Commonwealth countries to shoulder some of the military and financial burdens of defending Malaya. In August 1948, only two months after the state of emergency had been declared, Australian Foreign Minister Evatt was briefed on the situation by the British Secretary for Commonwealth Relations. Evatt asked for this information to be provided as a paper.

> He wanted this paper to include a full factual statement of the present situation of the forces we have there [Malaya], and of the forces we propose to send; together with a statement of the kinds of help we thought the Australian Government might be able to give.[6]

At this meeting, Evatt parried suggestions that Australia might send military assistance, and the subsequent British briefing paper also failed to produce Australian troops for Malaya. A direct 'suggestion' in December 1948 that Australia should send forces to bolster the garrison in Hong Kong, against any misplaced zeal for conquest by the armies of Mao Zedong, met a similar fate.[7] What were the reasons behind this Australian aversion to helping the British to defend Malaya, or at least to free up British troops from other tasks for that role, if the British colony was regarded as so important to its defence?

While the Australian Government had accepted the responsibility for planning the strategic defence of the sea approaches to Malaya under ANZAM, its reluctance to undertake any commitment to the internal defence of the colony was not just because it was unable to find the forces to back it up. The Labor Party was politically inclined to support decolonisation, as it had demonstrated over Indonesian independence from the Dutch. Put simply, the Australians were unable to determine whether Chin Peng's guerrillas were terrorists or freedom fighters. The Chifley Government's prescription for dealing with unrest and insurgency in Southeast Asia was not military at all; it felt that improving the economic conditions of the population would soon remove the attraction of Communism.

> [T]he primary object of Commonwealth policy should be to

create, in countries exposed to Communist influence, social conditions in which it would be impossible for Communism to flourish. It is by these methods that the advance of Communism must be checked. In Asia, certainly, and possibly in other countries also, military strength was not an effective weapon against Communist encroachment.[8]

This led to embarrassing equivocation over whether to meet British requests for the supply of small arms to arm the rubber planters and mine managers, who were very isolated and vulnerable to MRLA attack. The British were also anxious to have Australia provide a squadron of transport aircraft and a number of Lincoln heavy bombers for the anti-CT campaign. The aircraft were available but, again, the Australian Government procrastinated.

Public opinion appeared to be on the side of intervention. 'Malaya' still rankled in the minds of the man and woman in the street, and there was a sizeable Australian investment in business in Malaya, especially in the tin mining area. Britain's apparent inability to deal effectively with the insurgency was watched with dismay in business circles, and the same groups found the Australian Government's unwillingness to become involved disturbing. In an article written by its Singapore correspondent headlined 'Australia has Vital Interests in Malaya', the Melbourne *Age* made the following points:

Australia should be vitally interested in the campaign against Communist terror and violence in Malaya. This country is the centre of Australia's 'near north' and her well-being is vital to the Commonwealth's security.

For political and economic reasons, as well as her defence — even if not in pure self-interest — Australia must watch and hope the reign of lawlessness will end. One observer said: 'This area is most vital of all to Australia. Let us take the most extreme possibility. If the situation here should blow up, then all South-East Asia will blow up too.' Another stated: 'Should Communism win, then the iron curtain may well reach down to Timor'.[9]

However, the defeat of the Labor Party at the 1949 Federal elections brought the Liberal/Country Party conservative coalition to power under Prime Minister Robert Menzies. While in no rush to embrace foreign military commitments, Menzies and his Cabinet were concerned about the situation in Malaya, where things were not going well for the British. No. 38 Squadron RAAF of ten Dakota C-47 and Skymaster transport aircraft was ordered to Malaya on 31 May 1950. With the Chinese Communist Party now victorious, for the new Australian government the question was not one of the relative merits of the MRLA cause but whether the British were conducting the anti-CT campaign intelligently and effectively. It arranged for a party of Australian military officers, led by Major General Bridgeford, to travel to Malaya to inspect at first hand the situation and the progress being made. But before the Bridgeford Mission, as it was termed, departed on its task, the Korean War erupted. A few days later, on 27 June, an advance party of four Lincoln bombers of No. 1 Squadron RAAF were also sent to aid the British in Malaya: not required in Korea, the bombers had been long sought by the British to augment their air power in Malaya. The first offensive operations by Australian forces in the Malayan Emergency — a bombing mission against suspected CT hideouts — occurred in early August.[10]

The Bridgeford Mission included representatives of each of the Australian services, several of whom were to attain very senior positions in the Australian Defence Force. The membership had obviously been carefully selected. The RAN representative was Lieutenant Commander Anthony Synnot, who was twelve years later to play an important role in the development of the Royal Malaysian Navy (RMN). He was the Australian Chief of Naval Staff from November 1976 to April 1979 before becoming the RAN's third full admiral as Chief of Defence Force Staff from 1979 to 1982. Bridgeford's directive, issued by the Minister for Defence and approved by the Acting Prime Minister, gave the purpose of the Mission as:

Firstly, to study, and obtain information on, the current campaign in MALAYA against the Communist guerrilla forces and subsequently to report thereon to the Australian Government. The following matters of particular importance should be included in the mission's report:-

(a) General policy for the conduct of the campaign.
(b) Planning and control of operations.
(c) Co-ordination of civil, military and police effort.
(d) Organisation, training and equipment.
(e) Conduct of operations and tactical methods at all levels.
(f) The intelligence system.

Secondly, to furnish any advice or assistance which the U.K. authorities or Services in MALAYA may request.[11]

In Singapore and Malaya, Bridgeford and his officers were given a lengthy series of professional briefings and free access to visit units in the field, and their report is a most comprehensive overview of the state of operations in Malaya at the time. The British officials made good use of this opportunity to impress upon Australian service officers the ways in which their country could make a contribution to the campaign against the CTs. On the maritime front, the mission recorded:

Vessels of the Royal Navy are employed to assist Civil authorities prevent illegal seaborne entry into Malaya as their primary task, and in addition provide assistance as may be required.

The Navy is primarily concerned with gun running and illegal Immigration. Checks are also made on fishing licences.

The naval forces appear to be achieving their aim, and there is little or no illegal gun running. The forces employed, however, are barely adequate and could be increased with advantage, and would be essential to achieve an effective blockade in the event of increased Communist activity.[12]

Considering the length of the Malayan coastline, and the

existence of traditional fishing grounds and trading routes between the Malay Peninsula and neighbouring countries, especially Indonesia, it would be wishful thinking to believe that the RN force of two frigates and five harbour defence motor launches, supported by a number of police launches, could possibly have established an effective patrol regime. The Bridgeford Mission also noted that the RN had its difficulties in performing this role, which is why the British were eager for RAN support. The British 'wish list' of Australian naval assistance comprised six harbour defence motor launches, or craft up to the size of diesel-powered minesweepers, equipped with radar, fully manned and supported by maintenance and operational spares, and accompanied by their own maintenance personnel. And the RN would also like a frigate. If the Australian Government preferred, this ship could be sent to Korea to replace one of the British ships of the UN force, which would then be deployed to Malayan waters.

Bridgeford's report met with no favour in the Chiefs of Staff Committee which 'did not wish to make any recommendations'. With its hands full in Korea, the Australian Defence Force was not keen to accept any more challenges, and Minister for Defence McBride agreed.[13] In any case, the RAN had no harbour defence motor launches to send — the last of its wartime fleet had been sent to Hong Kong in response to an earlier British request. Nor did CNS Collins view with any favour the prospect of one of his precious frigates steaming slowly up and down the Malayan coastline.

However if the RAN ships employed in connection with Korea Operations were no longer required for that purpose, or for duty in Japan waters, it would be possible to make a Frigate available for service in Malayan waters. He [CNS] would prefer that any Frigate that could be spared should be employed on exchange in the British Mediterranean Fleet so that it would obtain practical fleet training. If this were done, the Royal Navy exchange Frigate might be used in the Malayan Area.[14]

The Bridgeford Report had noted that there was no evidence that the CTs had received any arms or ammunition from outside sources. There are grounds to question the accuracy of this statement. Chin Peng was certainly aware of the importance of outside support from his wartime experience with the Anti-Japanese Army, and he seems to have arranged resupply across the Johore Strait, at least. Moreover, the threat of outside interference continued to exercise the British authorities. In 1948 it was reported that a CT attack on the coast of Trengganu had been launched from the sea and, again in 1950, it was thought that Chinese People's Liberation Army cadres had arrived in Malaya by boat. Neither report was confirmed, and Chin Peng mentions neither incident, but still the possibility existed of this type of incursion taking place if the patrols were not maintained. In June 1951, the British even extracted a squadron of Sunderland long-range maritime patrol flying boats from Korea in order to bolster coastal surveillance in Malaya.[15] The Bridgeford Mission report saw the situation as follows:

> There is considerable traffic of small vessels, mostly of the junk type, between SUMATRA and the west coast of MALAYA, and to a lesser extent between SIAM [Thailand] and both east and west coasts. The main route for illegal immigrants from CHINA is direct to the east coast, probably transshipping from the larger junks to the smaller boats at some distance from the coast. The North East Monsoon about March is the most favoured time for this. The Navy does not interfere with vessels outside the three-mile limit unless they have reasonable grounds for suspicion.[16]

There is considerable disagreement amongst sources on the question of whether there really was any infiltration of support for the MRLA. In 1950, intelligence from Kedah State suggested that military cadres from China had landed at Songkhla, across the border in Thailand, and had filtered south. This was dismissed out of hand by the British Embassy in Bangkok, and no evidence was found of Chinese nationals personnel fighting with the MRLA. Donald

Mackay, another analyst, stated that, 'the Royal Navy became very good at intercepting most of those [arms smugglers] who tried'.[17] He was backed up by another, E.D. Smith:

> The other reason why so few arms of any significance were brought into the country was due to the constant but unspectacular blockade exerted by the Royal Navy's coastal patrols, backed up by the patrolling of coastal waters by aircraft from the RAF's Far East Flying Boat Wing. [18]

There is evidence to support that statement. For example, in a 1952 report of proceedings, the frigate HMS *Alacrity* recorded that she had carried out a number of patrols in conjunction with harbour defence motor launches and Sunderland aircraft off the east coast. In the process a number of boats had been stopped and searched, but all had been found to have legitimate reasons for being there.[19]

A British intelligence report of October 1951 confirmed — from a surrendered CT — that the MRLA was receiving small quantities of arms and explosives from Thailand. The Party had agents engaged in this activity in the four southern provinces, and the weapons were then smuggled into Perak State by jungle couriers. The same report also referred to rumours that the Party was organising a supply of arms and ammunition across the Malacca Strait from Sumatra using fishing boats, where 'it is not difficult for them to collect arms over there'.[20]

Further concern about infiltration from Indonesia was voiced in an intelligence report from Kuala Lumpur in April 1952.

> There has also been an upgraded report that on the afternoon of 5/3/52 a perahu [*sic*] came in from the sea at TELOK PANCHOR on the Malacca coast. About twenty young men wearing black trousers and loose black shirts landed from the boat. They were wearing round black cloth caps — an Indonesian type of headgear. They carried no arms, equipment or luggage. They

behaved in an orderly fashion, marching off in single file into the rubber. Two days earlier security forces had contacted terrorists in the vicinity of the alleged landing place … It seems possible that this report is true, and that the terrorists were waiting the arrival of these strangers.[21]

However, Chin Peng specifically denied there was any assistance, other than moral, from either the Soviet Union or China, although some arms and ammunition were captured by the Party from Chinese Nationalist guerrillas that the CT displaced in southern Thailand.[22] Certainly, there was nothing like the scale of well-organised and determined Communist resupply operations by land and sea that were encountered by the French, and later the Allied forces, in Vietnam, and on the basis of these conflicting views one can conclude that the efforts of the RN and RAF did prevent any major infiltration of weapons to the CT by sea. The point in belabouring this issue is to highlight the need for anti-smuggling patrolling by the British, a traditional naval role — neither very interesting nor exciting, nor, perhaps, an attractive subject for study by historians, but a necessary support to the efforts of the land forces nonetheless.

Chin Peng further insisted: 'We didn't receive any outside aid … not even a bullet'.[23] However, he clearly overlooked the supply route through Singapore in making this statement. Here was the weakest link in the defence cordon — the Johore Strait, between Chinese-dominated Singapore and the three MRLA divisions initially operating in Johore State on the Malayan mainland. The Singapore Committee of the Party was responsible for this link, and by 1952 a force of eight Singaporean and fifteen Malayan launches patrolled the Strait. A Special Branch report of 22 December stated small quantities of explosives and ammunition had been found in the home of a suspect raided in November 1952 and that 'the Party's sea supply route to Johore has been cut for several months'.[24] So the threat of seaborne infiltration of material and manpower support for the MRLA was real enough, but not sufficient to move the Australian Government or its defence chiefs to provide any assistance to control or to curb it.

Despite this reluctance to provide additional military support to the British, in June 1951, when British fortunes were at their nadir, and there seemed a real possibility that the insurgency might succeed, the Minister for Defence advised a meeting of Commonwealth defence ministers that 'Australia cannot disregard the effect of the loss of Malaya on our future security'. This expression of political direction was reflected in the 'Strategic Basis of Australian Defence Policy' paper released by Defence in January 1953, which stated: 'In view of the effects on the defence of Australia of the fall of Malaya, and the influence this would have on Australia's capacity to deploy forces to the Middle East, it is the Australian Government's view that the aim of the Allies should be to ensure the retention of Malaya'.[25]

That statement marked the end of the fluctuating Australian interest in sending men, ships and aircraft to the Middle East to reinforce British forces in the event of hot war with the Soviet Union. This had been the major role perceived by the British for Australian forces, and it was a strategic and force structure distraction. Now that the Government had firmed up its intentions to put its principal emphasis on Southeast Asia, defence planners could consider how best to reflect this wish. There was certainly more wherewithal to deploy, with operations in Korea now reducing and the Government's defence program beginning to have its effect. And the British remained keen to attract Australian force commitments to Malaya: the Emergency was costing a fortune!

In Malaya it had been recognised that command, control and intelligence were the keys to defeating the CT. In May 1950 the British appointed a Director of Operations to command all counter-insurgency activities conducted by military, police and civil authorities. In 1952 they went further, combining the roles of High Commissioner and Director of Operations as the head of an Emergency Operations Council in the person of General Sir Gerald Templar. The triumvirate arrangement of civil, military and police authority was extended into every state of the Federation through

State and District War Executive Committees. From 1952, there was also established a separate position of Director of Intelligence to coordinate the collection, analysis, and dissemination of all-source intelligence by and to the security forces. This integration of police and military intelligence was a bold and innovative step, and one initially difficult to implement. But it was spectacularly successful, and it was a lesson not lost on the British, who employed similar arrangements in Borneo twelve years later during Confrontation.[26]

During the Emergency, intelligence was principally a matter for the police Special Branch, which steadily extended its authority through the Federation. The Malayan Police were regarded as ineffective in dealing with the initial outbreak of terrorism, and Special Branch was separated from the Criminal Investigation Department in an April 1952 reorganisation. However, Special Branch was initially hampered by the lack of ethnic Chinese members.[27] Its sources of intelligence were informers, defectors ('surrendered enemy personnel') and, later, police agents who infiltrated the MRLA cells. Military sources included information collected by army patrols, and aerial reconnaissance.

Another source of information came from signals intelligence (Sigint). Initially, the MRLA had no radio communications, as it struggled with equipment left over from World War II. Chin Peng was not unaware of the advantages of radio, but, until the Chinese trained one of his cadres in radio maintenance and returned him to Malaya in 1955, there was little he could do to establish a communications network. However, the British could not be certain that a CT radio network did not exist, and a watch was kept by the British–Australian Sigint station in Singapore to identify one should it emerge.[28] The Australian component of operators had begun to arrive in 1950, as part of the responsibilities this country had accepted under the Commonwealth Signals Intelligence agreement of 1946, later formalised internationally by the UK–USA Agreement of 1947. The RAN supplied intercept operators and linguists for this task, and from 1955 small parties of Australian sailors were embarked in British and Australian warships for patrols along the Malayan coast. These were searching for CT transmissions at frequencies and powers not able to be intercepted in Singapore.

As the claim was later to be made that Australian warships were continually involved in seeking out and intercepting CT communications during the Emergency, this is a good point at which to consider its accuracy.[29] If he is to be taken at his word, from late 1956 Chin Peng on the Malayan/Thai border was in regular and apparently reliable, radio communication with China. This would have required transmissions to be at High Frequency (HF) or below, at frequencies easily intercepted by British Commonwealth fixed intercept stations. Besides the jointly manned British station in Singapore, there were Australian stations in Darwin and the Cocos Islands, as well as the British station in Hong Kong. The power of the CT transmitter might have been low enough to make interception at some of these sites problematic, but this gap in reception would have been better covered by a deployed army tactical interception station somewhat closer to the border, rather than occasional coverage by patrolling warships.

In his submission to the 1999 Mohr Inquiry into repatriation benefits (see Chapter 7) Commodore Clarke, who had been the Communications Officer of HMAS *Warramunga* in 1958, made the statement that: 'The "Third Wireless Office" was activated on a continuous basis at sea in the Malayan/Singapore area except in the Singapore Dockyard'. The communications division in *Warramunga* was Clarke's responsibility, but he may not have been privy to the tasking of the Sigint personnel because he lacked the 'need-to-know' qualification. Based on the author's background in the subject, it seems more plausible that the naval operators were tasked on Indonesian or Chinese targets rather than looking for Chin Peng and his CTs. This was a common and routine intelligence collection task for all Australian warships. Therefore, the Far East Strategic Reserve (FESR) Association's assertion that RAN intercept activity was routinely directed at the CTs also seems unlikely to be correct.

A probable solution to this conundrum was provided in a separate submission to the Mohr Inquiry by Allan Moffatt, a tele-graphist posted to HMAS *Anzac* in 1957. He noted that the ship had, on occasion, hosted a two-man special intelligence collection team.

> When they were aboard, they virtually lived in the 3rd wireless office, carrying out whatever duties that was [*sic*] required, i.e. intercept and monitoring. Unfortunately, we were not allowed in there when they were doing this work, and when they left the ship at different times to join HMAS TOBRUK (or some other Royal Navy ship), all their work, some equipment was taken with them. They also if I remember correct would proceed to some place in Singapore on arrival, carrying their analyse [*sic*] by safe-hand ... If my memory serves me correctly, the equipmen in the HF/DF was a FH4 set.[30]

This seems a more likely scenario. The periods during which *Anzac* (and *Tobruk*) were deployed off the Malayan coast coincided with an increase of radio traffic between Chin Peng and his Chinese masters after the establishment of reliable communications, and following an abortive 1955 meeting with Tunku Abdul Rahman. The FH4 referred to by Moffatt was a direction-finding receiver operating in the bands most likely to have been used by the MRLA. The layperson may be excused for thinking that this discussion of signals intelligence minutiae has only passing relevance to the story; in fact it represents the development of an important RAN capability, not just in supporting operations in Malaya but in meeting a wider Australian responsibility in the Asian theatre. It was also the resurgence of a capability the RAN had last exercised in 1938.

Intelligence, whatever its source, was a key factor in under-standing the situation in Malaya and neighbouring countries and in shaping political and military responses to developments. Long before the commitment of its combat elements, the RAN had decided that it needed to have better access to intelligence on the

Malayan situation and what was happening in adjacent areas. In 1953, after discussions with the British Admiralty, an RAN officer was posted to the staff of the Commander-in-Chief Far East Station as Assistant Staff Officer (Intelligence) based in Singapore.[31] This was the start of a long involvement in intelligence in the Far East by the RAN and the other two services.

For the British, as for Australia, the decline of operational tempo in Korea following the Armistice in 1953 allowed for the redeployment of military and naval forces to the Malayan theatre of operations. For the RN this meant that an additional frigate or destroyer could be employed on Malayan operations. A February 1954 report stated that these ships were 'used in the anti-Bandit and anti-piracy operations, or any other requirement in Malayan or Borneo operations'.

However, the pace of collective Commonwealth defence planning for Southeast Asia was accelerated by a June 1953 letter from the British Minister of Defence to his Australian and New Zealand colleagues. He saw the need to take steps to prevent a Korean-style aggression in Southeast Asia and proposed a joint military force.

> We cannot form an adequate Reserve on our own. But if Australia could join with the U.K. and New Zealand it would, I believe be possible to make an arrangement which would effectively safeguard our Commonwealth interests in the Cold War ... The broad conception on which the Chiefs [of Staff] could work might be that the nucleus of the Reserve would be found in the forces in Malaya and in the Australian and New Zealand contingents in Korea as and when the latter can be released by the United Nations Command.[32]

The deliberations of the Chiefs of Staff of the three nations, which found in favour of the proposal, were discussed at a conference of defence ministers in Melbourne in October 1953, which recommended that a military force be created by the three countries. This would be ready to respond to calls for military intervention in the region, and to demonstrate on the international and regional scenes that ANZAM was an alliance in more than name only. Informing these developments were intelligence assessments showing a deteriorating security situation in Southeast Asia. [33] A series of meetings and discussions on the proposal followed. Prime Minister Menzies gave his agreement in principle to the idea in October 1954, and in April 1955 the Australian Government agreed to commit forces to the British Commonwealth Far East Strategic Reserve (FESR). The principal role of the Reserve, as spelled out in the General Directive, was to provide a force-in-being to respond to external threats in the ANZAM region as 'a deterrent to further Communist aggression in South East Asia'.[34] A secondary role was to 'assist in the maintenance of the security of the Federation of Malaya by participating in operations against the Communist Terrorists'.

Australia's naval commitment was for two destroyers and/or frigates continuously in the Far East, and an annual visit of around two months' duration by an aircraft carrier. This was only possible because of a reduced naval commitment to the UN Naval Command in Korea from December 1954. During their time on deployment to the FESR, RAN ships would be assigned to British operational control — that is, they could be employed on a previously agreed range of operations by their British commander, but they remained under Australian Government command. This was a distinct departure form the command and control arrangements that had applied in the past when RAN ships came under RN command. In all, thirteen Australian ships served in this role between 1955 and 1960 during the Emergency period, most more than once, for a total of thirty-five ship deployments.[35]

The Naval Directive under which they were assigned spelled out the conditions under which they could be used by the Commander-in-Chief Far East Station. He was permitted to use them 'for anti-terrorist operations in Malayan waters, and to prevent infiltration by sea of Communist agents or armed bands'. They could also be used 'in the defence of the Federation of Malaya and Singapore and of the sea communications in the Malayan area against external aggression'. They could be rotated through the UN command in Korea as required, and the Naval Board especially asked that they be 'detailed for flag showing duties in South East Asian waters in order that their participation in the Strategic Reserve may be fully appreciated in the countries of the area'. [36] Thus it was through the medium of the FESR that the Australian Government was finally persuaded to allow the RAN to lend a hand in the struggle against the CTs.

The Defence Committee was tasked with preparing an appreciation of what this commitment might mean in personnel numbers and money, and what effects it might have. The Committee reported on 19 May 1955, identifying that the commitment would involve 4735 Australian servicemen, 1502 of them RAN. The Navy would arrive first, followed by the Army in September/October 1955, and the Air Force would follow eighteen months later after necessary work was completed at Butterworth Air Force Base, near Penang. The RAN ships were to undertake nine month deployments — thus not attracting any need for the transfer or accommodation of families — in marked contrast to Army and Air Force. The Committee continued:

> Special allowances to sea-going forces operating on the Far East Station are being examined in relation to those, if any, of the Royal Navy and Royal New Zealand Navy and will presumably also be investigated by the Services-Treasury Team. [37]

Naval common user items would be provided by the RN, while items 'peculiar to Australian ships' would be provided from Australia. The same consideration applied for Fleet Air Arm stores to support the deployment of the carrier *Melbourne*, but this was anticipated to present no problems because of the comparatively short duration, of two months, of the carrier's annual deployment. Rations and fuel were to be provided by British authorities on repayment — that is, Australia would be billed for them later. The Australian Government accepted these views and thus began one of the nation's longest running defence commitments

The RAN met its commitment immediately, with the assignment of HMA Ships *Arunta* and *Warramunga* to FESR duties on completion of an ANZAM exercise in June 1955. It seems that the commanding officers of both destroyers had been advised that this development was possible, as the Prime Minister had made a public statement about Australia's part in the Strategic Reserve on 1 April 1955, but the Government found an unusual way of telling them of its decision.

It was during the fuelling from [Royal Fleet Auxiliary] WAVE VICTOR that WARRAMUNGA passed to me the information that an A.B.C. [Australian Broadcasting Commission] broadcast that morning had stated that the two Tribal Class Destroyers were to remain on the Far East Station as Strategic Reserve. Permission was immediately obtained to break W/T [radio] silence for the day and use the Radio Telephone and despatch Telegrams. Both of these lines were very busy until 2100 that night and the Telegraphists on board and Radio Sydney both did an excellent job of work. Late in the afternoon A.C.N.B.'s [message date/time/group] 160256Z was received officially informing the ships of the official statement regarding the Strategic Reserve. Although this was not unexpected everybody on board wondered why the ships had not been informed or even the Commanding Officers as to what day the radio announcement was likely to be made.[38]

While destroyers and frigates were the ships Australia had to send to honour this FESR commitment, the British requests for smaller coastal patrol vessels dating from the Bridgeford Mission of 1951 were recollected in Navy Office. As evidence of this, in June 1955 the Director of Plans in Navy Office commenced circulation of a minute which was to elicit from the Naval Staff 'what M.D.A.P. [Military Development Assistance Program] aid we should require and bid for' in the event that American intentions to support ANZAM in the defence of Malaya were confirmed. The potential request developed shows how poorly equipped the RAN was, even at that stage, to undertake meaningful operations in defence of Malaya. In the light of subsequent events in Southeast Asia, it is noteworthy that the Navy thought it needed twenty-four minesweepers and a total of eighty-six various patrol craft for the task, a total never achieved — or seriously contemplated — in its order of battle planning.[39]

Ships assigned to FESR did not spend all their time in Malayan waters. On the contrary, they engaged in a very vigorous series of exercises with other British Commonwealth navies and participated in all SEATO naval exercises. As well, they paid port visits to countries in Asia, from Pakistan in the west to Korea in the north. Their activities were purposeful, and must have come as a welcome change from the dreary patrolling of the Korean War. There were new navies to meet, exercise with and get to know: the Indian Navy was particularly active in the western approaches to Malaya, a vital shipping lane for international trade between Asia and the Far East. Veterans will recall the very testing JET series of exercises, commanded by a British admiral, but involving ships from Australia, Britain, Canada, India, New Zealand and Pakistan.

Visits to South Vietnam, Thailand, and the Philippines involved visits to and, sometimes, exercises with ships of those navies. Thailand and the Philippines were included in SEATO exercises as well. And, probably for the first time since World War II, Australian ships began to work again with units of the US Navy: in Korea they had served for the majority of their tours under British command. FESR was different: RAN ships were under British operational control in the Malayan area, but they were under Australian national command. If there was one definable point at which the RAN began to seek a more independent role for itself in its area of prime strategic interest, and to regard and consider the ships, equipment, tactics and methods employed in other navies, the initiation of the FESR commitment has a significant claim to being that point.

In an address to his ship's company in HMAS *Anzac* when the ship sailed for FESR service in November 1955, Captain E.J. Peel made these points in the following words:

> Anti-Communist countries such as Australia, France, New Zealand, Pakistan, the Philippines Republic, Thailand, the United Kingdom and the United States of America have joined together in a South-East Asian Collective Defence Treaty and are pledged to guarantee the integrity of the member nations against open aggression and communist subversion, and to assist the development of the more backward members as much as they can. Educational, practical and monetary assistance is being given by Australia to Asian countries through the Colombo Plan.
>
> It can be seen therefore that we are beginning a policy of trying to understand and assist our Northern neighbours, and also to make them realise that we are interested in their newly-gained freedom and anxious that they should not be overcome by the tide of Communism.[40]

Australian foreign policy was in support of Australia's interests but, at that juncture, Peel's words were very pertinent, and they describe succinctly the role the RAN was to play.

In regard to the Emergency, RAN ships and personnel who served FESR time in the Malayan theatre performed five roles in support of the Commonwealth defeat of the CTs. The first, and most aggressive, of these was in naval gunfire support (NGS) when Australian guns were turned on suspected CT positions. On five occasions between 1956 and 1957, RAN destroyers or frigates undertook NGS missions in Malaya. When the CTs were operating close to the coast, naval bombardment was an effective and stealthy way of disrupting them. But, as Anthony Short, an historian of the Malayan Emergency, observed, the absence of accurate coordinates for the guns to fire on could make the exercise 'more harassment rather than destruction'. There seems to be no clear account of how many NGS firings took place during the Emergency, but records show that thirty-nine were conducted by the RN in 1952 alone.[41]

In September 1956, and in January and August 1957, RAN units bombarded targets identified by British High Command in southern and eastern Johore State. The first occasion was in support of a major security force operation to drive to the north the 400-odd CTs known to be in southern Johore.[42] Ships involved were the destroyers *Anzac* and *Tobruk*, armed with six 4.5-inch (115 mm) guns, to whom bombardment maps of the target area were air-dropped, and whose fire was spotted by an Auster aircraft of the British Army's 1181 Flight. This was not harassment shooting, and the spotter's presence suggests that there were clearly identified targets to be taken under fire. These might have been detected by police intelligence, or by photo reconnaissance carried out by the RAF 81 Squadron, which not only provided tactical prints of areas of suspected CT activity, but also assisted in accurately mapping the whole country.[43]

Hands closed up at Action Stations at 0615 on Saturday 29th [September] to carry out a bombardment of Communist Terrorist positions near the East Coast of Johore State about fifteen miles south of Jason Bay. At 0737 a target indicated by an Army Auster aircraft was engaged successfully. Two more targets were bombarded by both ANZAC and TOBRUK. The air spotter reported that the fire had been most effective.[44]

On the afternoon of 22 January1957, the frigates *Quiberon* and *Quickmatch*, armed only with twin 4-inch (103 mm) guns, were tasked with bombarding a CT campsite in a coconut plantation in south eastern Johore. The operation took place with the ships at anchor — there was no risk of return fire — and forty high-explosive rounds per ship were fired. Again, the shoot was directed by an air spotter. A bombardment damage assessment reported the camp severely damaged and not likely to be habitable for some time. Interestingly, the action was given wide regional publicity the following day on Radio Australia.[45]

In August 1957 CT positions in south east Johore were again

the targets of Australian naval gunfire, this time from the destroyer *Tobruk*, which engaged seven targets indicated by a spotter aircraft and achieved 'good results'. NGS is a traditional role of navies in support of land forces and the Australian ships, with recent experience of the same task in Korea, performed the role with distinction. But after the Johore area was declared clear of CTs there were no further opportunities for destroyers and frigates to undertake NGS to dislodge them. The MRLA directed its regiments to fall back on the Betong Salient in the north on the Thai–Malayan border.

Comparisons of RAN NGS operations in the Malayan Emergency with those conducted only a few years earlier in Korea are not valid: the conditions under which their fire was delivered were totally different. The firings required little planning, there was no threat of enemy retaliation, and they were more a gunnery exercise than a wartime operation. It was, however, a gunnery exercise which claimed the life of the RAN's only operational casualty during the Emergency. On the night of 26 April 1957, during an exercise night encounter between a group led by the British cruiser *Newcastle* and a division of British destroyers, *Tobruk* was hit on the port side forward by the empty casing of a starshell fired by one of the opposing destroyers. Able Seaman R.V. Spooner was killed and Able Seaman J.R. Stevenson seriously wounded. Following emergency surgery, Stevenson was landed in Singapore, while Spooner was buried at sea off the east coast of Malaya near Pulau Tioman. The accident was a reminder to all of the inherently risky nature of sea service, although the Board of Inquiry found that the commanding officer of the British destroyer had

> failed to appreciate that there were ships beyond the target he was attempting to illuminate. He did not appreciate that the order 'Stop Illuminating', given by his Gunnery Officer, was because of the foul range and he ordered 'Star Shell Go On'.[46]

The second role played by the RAN ships was in coastal

surveillance. The directive of 25 April 1956, setting out for the Commander-in-Chief Far East Station the conditions under which RAN ships were allocated for service with the FESR, stated that 'HMA Ships under your operational control may be used, as are ships of the Royal Navy, for anti-terrorist operations in Malayan waters, and to prevent infiltration by sea of Communist agents or armed bands'.[47] Typically, RN ships would carry out patrols in association with motor launches and Sunderland aircraft. It is evident that the British were serious about the blockade and patrolling, which suggests that their government regarded it as worthwhile and necessary.[48]

Thus, immediately on reporting for duty with the FESR in June 1955, *Warramunga* exercised interdiction of coastal traffic off the Malayan east coast. The 'enemy' craft were provided by the Royal Malayan Navy (RMN), the Federation of Malaya Marine Police and Malayan Customs, and the exercise commenced at dusk on 12 June. Weather conditions were poor, with thunderstorms and heavy rain — ideal conditions for a determined infiltrator — and the destroyers were required to sweep an area of 120 miles by fifty miles. Some of the 'enemy' craft were detected and dealt with by night, but most had to wait until morning. It was an interesting illustration of the problems faced in detecting infiltrators, even in an area where small craft were relatively few in number.

In September 1956, HMAS *Anzac* participated in a seaward defence exercise in the Singapore Strait — Exercise NIGHT LIFE — with the destroyer using its radars and operations room plotting facilities to direct Singapore police and customs launches to interceptions of suspect boats. Not unexpectedly, the exercise revealed problems in making radar detections of small craft and complications in plotting caused by the large number of unlit contacts in the area.[49] These were issues which were to recur a few years later in the much more intense environment of Confrontation.

Quickmatch played a central role in Exercise DARK STRIKE in October 1958, the aim of which was to test the seaward defences of Singapore against infiltrators. Acting as an 'island' radar station, she had to compile a plot of shipping movements and to direct her own and 'friendly' boats into interceptions of infiltrating small craft. Presciently, the exercise planners had included attacks on shipping by underwater swimmers: infiltration and attacks by swimmers were both to feature in Confrontation.

We can be almost certain now that of any infiltration attempts from the sea to aid the CTs, few succeeded. To the extent that a relatively few patrolling warships could be said to have prevented these, the RAN played its part in training the police and customs boats that provided the majority of the coastal surveillance, and in developing the procedures and tactics which could be used to deter and to intercept infiltrators.

The third role for the RAN during the Emergency was that of 'showing the flag'. To the observer, and perhaps to some of those participating, this traditional naval role can often seem just an excuse for yet another cocktail party and a round of official visits and entertainment. In fact warship visits to foreign ports are part of a diplomatic offensive, demonstrating solidarity with the hosts, or veiled menace, as the circumstances dictate. During the Malayan Emergency it was especially important to show the flag as often and as effectively as possible. The credit is generally given to General Sir Gerald Templar for the invention of the phrase 'hearts and minds' to describe his campaign to strengthen the resolve of the Malayan community to resist CT pressure and violence, and to foster national identity and confidence. Ship visits to Malayan ports thus had both an immediate and important purpose as part of this campaign.

The Commonwealth security forces were thinly spread, and it was not difficult for a ruthless CT band to demonstrate who held the whip hand to a local community remote from government bases. The presence of a warship — clearly more powerfully armed than a CT regiment — off the coast, or in visits to coastal communities, demonstrated that the Government not only had right on its side but also might as well. *Tobruk* was part of a British force of a cruiser and four destroyers which anchored off Trengganu on the Malayan east coast in March 1956 on just such a demonstration.

The official entertainment which usually accompanied visits, and even short excursions to sea for selected guests to witness warship firepower demonstrations, were effective in stiffening the resolve of community opinion-leaders. The boom of naval guns firing against CT targets reinforced this message.

All the RAN ships were involved in this campaign. West coast ports, such as Penang, Port Dickson and Malacca, were particularly targeted, and visits were also made to Port Swettenham (now Port Klang) and from there to the capital, Kuala Lumpur. To mark the 1957 Queen's Birthday, *Quickmatch* landed an armed party of twenty-four men who took pride of place at the head of the parade through the streets of Malacca to mark the occasion. On Merdeka (Independence) Day on 31 August 1957, *Tobruk* provided a guard to salute to the new nation of Malaya and to witness the lowering of the Union Jack at Fort Cornwallis at Penang after 171 years of British rule. At Port Dickson to the south *Anzac* fired the national salute to Malaya.

However, a typical ship visit was much more than an occasion for ceremonial and an exchange of official entertainment. The October 1955 visit by *Arunta* and *Warramunga* to Port Swettenham involved a full program of activities for officers and men alike.

> Apart from daily Rugby, tennis and soccer matches, large parties of ratings were taken on launch trips, visits to tin mines, rubber plantations, and sightseeing to Kuala Lumpur. 50 ratings from both ARUNTA and WARRAMUNGA were entertained by the Home Guard with a trip to Port Dickson on Wednesday 12th October. In the evening 100 ratings from each ship were entertained at the Mariners' Club with drinks, an excellent supper and a movie program. This event typified the unbounded hospitality shown at Port Swettenham and Klang.[50]

An interesting sub-element of the 'hearts and minds' campaign was directed at schoolchildren in Singapore. The authorities were concerned at the propensity of students at the colony's middle schools — aged between twelve and twenty — to be receptive to Communist propaganda designed to foment unrest, and one solution advanced to lessen these influences in schools was to give pupils a demonstration of British naval power. So on 14 and 15 July 1957, *Anzac* and *Tobruk* embarked thirty students each, boys and girls, and took them to sea for what was termed Operation SHOWBOAT. Joining the carrier *Melbourne*, the destroyers treated their young guests to 'an exhibition of flying, manoeuvring and weapon performance'. Guns and anti-submarine mortars were fired, and simulated rescues were effected by the destroyers' seaboats and the carrier's helicopters. As to the impression this made on the students, the biggest response in *Tobruk* was a rush for the wheelhouse when an offer of the opportunity to steer the ship was made. *Anzac's* commanding officer reported that:

> They seemed interested enough, in the event, and caused no trouble, but the interest aroused in my own Ship's Company at taking boys and girls to sea for a full scale 'Shopwindow' would make it seem necessary that the same privilege be granted their own families at some later date.[51]

Thus, it might be that the Malayan Emergency gave birth to that most popular Australian Fleet institution of Families Day.

A less typical, but not unusual, showing the flag interlude during the Emergency was *Anzac's* hosting of the Regent of Pahang, on the Malayan east coast, in June 1956. The Regent and his entourage were embarked with full military honours and, with an RNM motor launch in company, taken to sea for a firepower demonstration, following which he was landed at one of his outlying fiefdoms, the island of Pulau Tioman, to a rapturous reception. Following a day of festivities, he was taken in the RNM launch to three other towns on the Pahang coast before rejoining *Anzac* the following day for his return to Kuala Pahang. This was probably as close as any RAN ship got to the somewhat feudal nature of traditional Malay society, and it was of some significance that an Australian ship had the honour of conveying the regent around the littoral areas of his sultanate.[52]

Not all port visits received a warm reception. *Queenborough* and *Quickmatch* were visiting Penang in January 1957, and their ships' companies participated in a military pageant organised to celebrate the city's centennial. However, fears of racial rioting between the Chinese and Malay communities caused a curfew to be imposed on the city, which reduced the number of spectators and limited both the scale of hospitality able to be offered and the freedom of libertymen. One sailor recalled:

A civil disturbance, a riot, upset the promising festival week, and caused the cancellation of a large part of the program. I was ashore when the rioting started, and was with a group that took shelter in the British Club. We later returned on board, and a Curfew curtailed all leave for the next two days, any sightseeing or other activities were also cancelled. A special Malayan Riot Squad was stationed in Penang for the celebrations. These Riot Squads were highly trained and well equipped to deal with civil disturbances, even so there was at least one death due to the riots on the first day in Penang.[53]

A rather more direct exposure to the perils of the Emergency was experienced by men of HMAS *Anzac* during a visit to Port Dickson in 1956. Challenged by a British Army unit to a sporting contest, the sports teams were surprised to find that their transport to the camp was to be under armed escort. One of the sportsmen explained why:

One of the soldiers informed us that most of the area was 'black' [not yet cleared of CT bands] ... and that in the week prior to our arrival a convoy of army trucks had been ambushed and burnt and that there were a number of casualties. After travelling some distance we came across the burnt out remains of the convoy where the trucks had been pushed into the jungle to clear the road. On arrival at the camp the first things we noticed was that the camp was surrounded by a high barbed wire fence and there were a number of observation towers.[54]

It is impossible to judge whether the RAN part in showing the flag in Malaya had a significant impact on the population at large, although clearly it did upon the political and business elites. The authorities — British until September 1957 and Malayan afterwards — clearly found them useful, and perhaps this was based on intelligence appreciations. But for many Malayans, the visits would have represented their first encounter with Australians, although older members of the community might have had some wartime recollections of the Army.

The fourth role was in demonstrating a Commonwealth presence, as when insurgencies and insurrections in neighbouring Indonesian Sumatra threatened to spill over into Malaya. This eventuality had been the subject of discussion throughout 1957 between the British naval commander and Australian defence authorities, which resulted in a Supplementary Directive on the Conduct of HMA Ships in Indonesian Waters in December.[55] This was timely policy, for in 1958 there were several insurrections requiring a military response by the central Indonesian Government, and on each occasion, RAN ships were deployed to ensure that there was no interference with the constant flow of trade up and down the Malacca Strait. In March *Voyager* and *Warramunga* were twice stationed in the Strait because of disturbances in Benkulis, close to a major oil terminal. No insurgent activity was noted, although chartered Indonesian vessels taking troops and equipment to the area were encountered.[56]

As part of their FESR responsibilities, RAN ships were also despatched to watch over the passage of Soviet bloc warships transiting the Malacca and Singapore Straits, and on one occasion an Australian destroyer was despatched to investigate reports of an unidentified submarine in the approaches to Singapore.

Again, in May 1959, *Tobruk* was ordered to patrol in the southern Sulu Sea between the Philippines and British North Borneo because of reports of Filipino pirates preying on the copra boats, which traditionally traded between North Borneo and the Indonesian provinces of Sulawesi. The destroyer spent two days in the area intercepting numerous trading and fishing craft, but there were no detections of pirates. Piracy is one of the hazards of that part of the world, and it too was to crop up during Confrontation.

The fifth role played by the RAN was in supporting and training the nascent Malayan naval defence force. The RMN had a few small vessels only, and on many occasions groups of officers and sailors of the RMN and the Malayan Royal Naval Volunteer Reserve were taken to sea in Australian ships from RMN training depots in Penang and Singapore to gain sea experience. They witnessed and participated in evolutions in seamanship and weapon practices, station keeping and manoeuvring, signalling and ship husbandry, and even landing party skills. Their vessels participated in coastal defence and surveillance exercises under RAN direction. The experience was enjoyed and appreciated by the Malayans and their zeal drew favourable comments from the Australians.

A sixth role, unrelated directly to the Emergency, and perhaps only vaguely perceived at the time — the evidence is equivocal — was the development of an Australian understanding of and viewpoint on the affairs of the region. Commanding officers of RAN ships visiting Malayan and North Borneo ports went to great pains to brief their ships' companies on the importance of making a good impression on their hosts, and the necessity of good behaviour ashore. It was as if Australians in general, and the RAN in particular, were learning anew about this area of deep strategic importance, one which had previously been regarded as a British province.

Naturally, ship visits also presented opportunities for Malayans and Singaporeans to inspect and make judgments on Australians. In their monthly reports commanding officers recorded positive comments made about them, their ships and ships' companies, and on Australia in general: it would have been interesting to have some record of negative comments as well. Two examples of the former will suffice. The commanding officers of the frigates *Queenborough* and *Quickmatch* received a harangue from the president of the Penang Municipal Council when they made an official call on him in January 1957. *Queenborough* later reported that:

> He said that in his younger days he, his family and his friend had hated Australians and avoided them where possible. He said that when forced to visit Australia on business, he was treated with the social status of a Chinese Green Grocer as well as suffering severe financial penalties. This of course was years before World War II. Mr Goh said that the hospitality now shown by the people of Australia to those of South East Asia has become well known and many of his relatives have visited Australia through such activities as the Colombo Plan.[57]

Anzac had a similar reaction to her visit to Port Dickson in August 1956. Her commanding officer was invited to a garden party given by the Chief Minister at which

> I had the opportunity of meeting all the Chiefs of Negri Sembilan [State] and leading Malayan Chinese businessmen and Labour leaders. I was struck by the great interest displayed in both the Navy and Australia, and invited four chiefs to come down to the ship the next afternoon before our cocktail party and personally conducted them round the ship. On their arrival on board it was evident that the party had swollen to twice the original number.

The arrival of Australian warships to bolster British and Malayan efforts to protect the sea littoral of the peninsula carried an important message, and this seems to have been answered in a positive manner by the Malayans at whom it was directed. It is interesting to note that Tunku Abdul Rahman, the Chief Minister of the Federation and the first Prime Minister of independent Malaya, took the opportunity of visiting almost all RAN ships during their visits to his country, or at the very least welcomed calls by their commanding officers in Kuala Lumpur. The favourable impression he formed had some bearing on his later request that Australia provide the senior officers for his country's navy, which will be discussed in Chapter 4.

Not related to the Emergency, or to Malaya for the moment, visits by RAN warships of the FESR were also organised to the colonies in British North Borneo. This had been an area of operational involvement for the Australian forces at the end of World War II, but there had been few calls since. In June 1959 *Tobruk* and *Anzac* visited Sandakan in modern Sabah State to show the flag and to renew ties. The ships' companies received a very warm welcome and, in turn, they made a very favourable impression on the local population, as this letter from the Resident attests:

I would like to say how glad we all were to have TOBRUK and ANZAC here over the Queen's Birthday period, and if you can let the contingents know how good we thought they were I should be more than obliged. They put on a very good show indeed … Sandakan and indeed North Borneo people generally have a very soft spot for Australians. Many of them made friends, at considerable risk, with P.O.W.s here during the war and of course North Borneo was finally liberated by the Australian 9th Division. Since the war too a lot of local people have benefited from Australia's generosity under the Colombo Plan. So you can see that a tradition of friendship has sprung up and the TOBRUK and ANZAC crews couldn't have done a better job in cementing this.[58]

Oh, happy the commanding officer with that sort of praise to attach to his monthly report of proceedings! But the sentiments expressed demonstrate the success and value of this sixth role FESR ships undertook during the Emergency.

As for the Emergency itself, once the British had put in place the command, intelligence and food control systems that had been devised in 1952, and the squatter communities came under effective government control through the 'New Villages' resettlement program, the MRLA went into decline. Successively from 1953, areas of the peninsula were declared free from CTs, until only two hard-core areas of MRLA resistance remained in 1959. In fact, truce talks between the two sides took place in December 1955 but broke down. The steady progress being made towards Malayan independence caused the British to do some thinking on the issue of the ramifications of independence on defence arrangements. At that time there was no thought that independence equated to a British withdrawal from the Far East.

> United Kingdom and Commonwealth forces must therefore remain [in Malaya] in order to contribute to internal stability and prevent collapse. In addition our forces must remain in the Area as a manifestation of our concern for the defence of South East Asia and our interests in the Far East.[59]

By Merdeka Day, the Emergency was all but over in most parts of Malaya, although mopping up the CT remnants, who were eventually forced into havens on the Thai side of the border, continued for another two and a half years. The Emergency was officially ended on 31 July 1960, with Chin and a small band of stalwarts isolated in the Thai border region.[60] Over 11,000 lives had been lost in the twelve years of fighting, most of the dead being CTs, but nearly 2500 civilians had also been killed, along with 1865 members of the security forces. RAN deployments to the FESR were maintained throughout the period, but the operational emphasis changed from defeating the CTs to supporting the development of the new nation: the intensity of the training opportunities provided to the nascent RMN illustrates the process.

And the RAN was invited to participate in the parade in Kuala Lumpur on 1 August 1960 to mark the end of the Emergency. Sixteen personnel from HMAS *Quiberon* travelled from Singapore to Kuala Lumpur by train on 27 July to represent the RAN. Accommodated in the Batu Cantonment close to the capital, the contingent trained for three days before taking its place in the victory ceremony.[61] It was a clear recognition by the Malayan Government of the part played by the Australian Navy in the defeat of the CT menace

So much for the RAN's operational involvement in the Emergency: now consider the impacts of this service on the companies of the FESR ships. Conditions on board the older ships caused some concern. *Arunta* and *Warramunga* were veterans of World War II, built to late-1930s British designs. Having fought the Pacific War, their most recent active service had been in Korea, where the major habitability problem had been the intense cold of Korean winters. Now they were serving within a few degrees of the Equator. The majority of operational activities, from the watch on the bridge to manning and supplying the three 4.7-inch (121 mm) twin gun mounts were conducted in the open. Below, in the crowded messdecks, galleys, offices and engineering spaces, without the benefit of air-conditioning, the air was close and fetid. The temperature below decks in Singapore was normally around 30° C and humidity above 85 per cent. It was fortunate that these ships were not often required to close up at action stations: under wartime conditions tuberculosis had become a real threat in Australian cruisers and destroyers. In *Arunta* the demand on the forced-air ventilation fans was such that it was found necessary to run these at only two-thirds speed so as to keep them operable.

Tobruk and *Anzac* were of more modern design, with fully enclosed gun turrets and generally better habitability arrangements. These ships too were veterans of Korea and the contrast with conditions in the Malayan theatre prompted the following comment from the commanding officer of *Tobruk* in 1956:

> Living conditions in the crowded messdecks of a modern destroyer are bad at the best of times, but in a prolonged period in tropical climates, conditions become well nigh unbearable. No permanent solution is possible until we can treat our human machines as the delicate fly plane [gunnery prediction] system is treated and air condition the messdecks and compartments

such as operations and radio control room where men work continuously.[62]

It was not until 1958 that the first RAN ship designed for tropical service, the new Daring Class destroyer *Voyager*, joined the FESR.

The ships particularly found the climate of Singapore enervating, especially when compelled to remain alongside for considerable periods during maintenance periods. In 1958, *Warramunga* found herself in this situation, with an outbreak of minor skin complaints attributed to conditions on board. The commanding officer recommended that means be found to give at least some of the ships' companies a break in a cooler climate and the opportunity to play sport in more temperate climes. This suggestion was acted upon for subsequent maintenance periods in Singapore. In *Tobruk* in August 1957, the conditions on board were cited as a disciplinary problem as well.

> The ship has been two and a half months in Malayan waters and the enervating climate combined with the lack of ports at which the sailor can get out of the ship for the night in congenial company has resulted in a large increase in the number of petty leave breaking offences. There have also been four cases of men missing the ship on sailing. I am certain that this foolishness will cease when Hong Kong is reached and during our next period in Malayan waters I intend to press for visits only to the few ports where all night leave can be given.[63]

But there were other reasons for ships to prefer Hong Kong to Singapore, apart from the generally cooler weather. The naval base at HMS *Tamar* in Hong Kong was situated almost in the centre of the city of Victoria, with easy and convenient access to shopping, services and recreation. Singapore Naval Base was located on the far side of the island from the city with, initially, few entertainment or shopping facilities.

Singapore at that time was also rather unruly. The significant

Communist influence in the city has been described, and this created a hazard for sailors on shore leave. Transport to and from the naval base to the Britannia Club in the city was by naval bus, the windows of which were covered by cyclone wire netting to deflect or limit the damage inflicted by stones thrown by dissidents, and to prevent grenades entering the vehicle. Shore parties were specifically and graphically warned of the personal dangers involved in straying into out-of-bounds areas. Ships in harbour were required to supply a security detail for each bus, led by a petty officer. One RAN senior sailor recalled that:

> The actual title of the duty was 'Security Petty Officer' and two Leading Hands from the Base as detail. I recall being given a clipboard outlining the Duty and Routine, and two sections have always been very clear to me, as follows: a) On leaving the naval base the bus to proceed by the most direct route to Singapore. On no account is the vehicle to stop. On approaching villages and such the door to be locked and all windows to be closed. b) In the event of civil disturbance to proceed to the nearest military or police and leave the area as quickly and safely as possible and to give report to Duty Officer HMS *Terror* on return to Base. The duty finished at about 5 a.m. the next morning, so it was a long and anxious night.[64]

There was also the question of morale. The change of deployment for *Arunta* and *Warramunga* from ANZAM exercises to an attachment to the FESR required a deal of fast footwork from several echelons of the RAN. The CNS, Vice Admiral Sir Roy Dowling, flew to Singapore in June 1955 to brief the companies of the two ships on the reasons for the change. A number of requests for a change of posting ('compassionate postings' in naval terminology) had to be processed, and changes of personnel planned to take effect on the ships' expected return to Australia had to be advanced and personnel exchanged by air. This process seems to have been effected expeditiously, and in August 1955 the commanding officer of *Arunta* was able to applaud the prompt action of the manpower planners and to observe that, 'The majority of the Ship's Company have now settled down to life in the tropics'.[65]

Postings were one thing: food was another. The availability of fresh provisions has always been a problem for warships operating remote from their bases. In the mid-1950s, neither the available food technology nor the physical availability of fresh meat, fruit and vegetables in the Far East met the demands of the Australian ships deployed there. There were deficiencies in the ship's storage facilities as well, as *Tobruk*'s commanding officer made clear:

> Much has been written about the lack of a cool [refrigerated] room in these ships and it is to be hoped that the forthcoming refit will see this remedied. Even when this is done, ships on the Far East Station virtually never get fresh, as opposed to frozen, food, and the best of the frozen food cannot compete with fresh provisions. [66]

One other issue which raised its head was puzzlement over the very different treatment meted out by the Australian Taxation Office to the naval personnel serving in the FESR compared with the privileges enjoyed by Army and RAAF personnel in the theatre. The latter were exempt from income tax, while the sailors had to pay it. Since it was quite obvious from visits to Australian army and air force bases that, except when actually engaged on field operations, the soldiers and airmen enjoyed a far higher standard of living conditions in their barracks and married quarters — the latter provided by the Australian taxpayer with locally engaged servants — than the more than 250 naval personnel crammed into 115 metres of hot steel box that was a destroyer, resentment was inevitable. These and similar issues, such as the denial of repatriation benefits to RAN veterans of the Malayan Emergency, are examined in more detail in Chapter 7.

But despite these difficulties, the Australian sailor always rose to the occasion and the ships performed their duties well. Captain

R.I. Peek, commanding *Tobruk* during her 1957–58 deployment to the FESR, and a man who set stern standards of conduct and performance, made the following comment at the end of his February 1958 report:

> At the end of a second tour of duty in the Strategic Reserve I would record my admiration for our sailors. There are of course occasional bad characters but the overwhelming majority of them make first class ambassadors for Australia, particularly in those ports with smaller European communities where bad behaviour is more noticeable, I have been most impressed with the number of people, locals as well as European, who have told me not only how impressed they are with our men's bearing and behaviour but what decent men they are to meet.

Finally, what did the RAN learn from its participation in the Emergency? There were no RAN staff officers attached to the staff of Flag Officer Malaya to gain experience in the conduct of counter-insurgency operations. In contrast, the Australian Army ensured that its FESR battalions each received experience of anti-CT operations, and that its officers were posted to representative positions on the 28th Commonwealth Brigade staff and in HQ Far East Land Forces. Apart from the development of the 1955 proposed request to the USA for additional naval hardware, it is difficult to identify any Naval Staff action that was rooted in lessons learned from Malaya. For example, despite the demonstrated utility of inshore patrol craft during the Emergency, and the large order of these vessels which was to have been requested of the US in 1955, the RAN procured none that could be deployed either to Confrontation or to Vietnam when this kind of contribution was called for.[67]

A possible explanation for this apparent apathy lies in the fact that RAN eyes were on the main game — defence of Southeast Asian sea lines of communication — rather than on the naval sideshow that anti-CT operations in Malaya were. Under considerable financial and strategic pressure at home, and seriously challenged to play its desired role in Allied military planning in the region, the RAN was content for its ships to slip back into the familiar role of operating under British command in Malaya. Then again, there is the allure to admirals of having 'blue water' warships in their fleets and rather less attraction therefore to the tools of 'brown water' warfare.

The one interesting development in intelligence cooperation that did appear during the Emergency, however, was the embarkation of RAN signals intelligence personnel in ships for the purposes of monitoring possible CT radio transmissions. These men had been sent to Singapore for duty ashore as part of Australia's commitments under the UKUSA agreement, but it has always been difficult to ascertain precisely what their role was and the extent of their contribution to Allied intelligence. Confirmation, by way of the Mohr Review of service entitlements, of a seagoing role for them marked the first essay into this area for the RAN since its Radio Operators Special was withdrawn from its cruisers in 1938.

As Dennis and Grey concluded, referring to both the Malayan Emergency and then later Confrontation with Indonesia:

> the major part of the fighting was borne by the armed forces of the United Kingdom ... and with Australia (and New Zealand) acting in a supporting, and relatively minor, role for much of the time. To say this is not to belittle the Australian involvement, but to place it within the necessary context. An active Australian role was pursued in Southeast Asia from the 1950s onwards.[68]

For the RAN, however, that 'minor' role in the Emergency was a major commitment of ships and personnel, and it was to introduce the navy to the challenges and issues of operating in the region after an absence of more than a decade. New skills were learned — mostly to be forgotten under the imperative of becoming an efficient and effective blue water ASW force. Personal bonds were forged, especially after the RAN became involved in the development and training of the new Royal Malayan Navy, an issue which will be discussed in depth in Chapter 4. To refer back to Captain Peel's words in 1955, much had been done in coming to an understanding of the countries of the region, and the RAN had demonstrated its ability to respond to external aggression and subversion.

3 The Calm Before the Storm

In the 1950s and well into the following decade, Australian perceptions and responses to strategic and defence issues in the region were influenced — some might say dictated — by the attitude of the British Government to its residual interests and obligations East of Suez. The fact is that, notwithstanding the uninformed remarks of the 1948 Harwood Working Party committee about the RAN taking over the Singapore naval base when the British abandoned it, without the British command and control arrangements in the Far East and the communications, maintenance and logistics framework which supported them, no effective Australian involvement would have been possible. So in tracing the development of permanent Australian interests in Southeast Asia, one has first to understand the positions taken by UK governments

When he made his claim that his MRLA campaign against British rule in Malaya had accelerated the process of decolonisation, Chin Peng was speaking with the benefit of much hindsight. In fact, when he met with the leader of the United Malays National Organisation — Tunku Abdul Rahman — in the village of Baling in Kedah State in December 1955, after elections for the first Federation parliament had been held in mid-year, neither he nor the Tunku could have predicted what was about to happen in Malaya's progress towards independence from Britain. Shortly after the Baling meeting Abdul

Rahman flew to London, where he engaged in an intense round of negotiations and discussions at a constitutional conference on the future of British Malaya. In February 1956 he emerged with an agreement that, in a short eighteen months, the British would hand over the Federated Malay States, the Straits Settlements and the Unfederated Malay States to the jurisdiction of a new Malayan government.

Chin and his CTs were only a minor factor in this somewhat startling decision: his forces had effectively been sidelined by that stage. The British Government decided to transfer control of Malaya for reasons more related to events further to the north. The Cold War with the Soviet Union was not going well for the Western governments. Despite its backdown in Berlin in 1949, the Soviet Union maintained the pressure all along the land frontier of the Iron Curtain. Its crushing of the Hungarian uprising in 1956 was an overt example of its determination to maintain control over Eastern Europe. Britain felt obliged to maintain forces in Europe as part of its NATO commitments, and to stiffen the resolve of the Western nations to resist this Soviet pressure. More concerning for Britain, however, was the threat of nuclear annihilation inherent in the growing Soviet arsenal of nuclear-tipped ballistic missiles, and long-range bombers able to deliver nuclear ordnance anywhere in Britain. While the ultimate target of Soviet nuclear weaponry was clearly the USA, the fear was that Britain could be used as a 'demonstration' target.

There was also the issue of Britain's declining influence in Asian affairs. Britain's exclusion from the 1951 ANZUS Treaty, despite the Churchill Government's protests and manoeuvring, is an example. Britain's standing was not helped either when, for sound reasons or not, the government in Whitehall then vigorously discouraged US military involvement in saving the French from military disaster in northern Indo-China, and the felony was compounded — in US eyes — when Britain acted as joint sponsor of the Geneva talks which handed the former French colony to the Communist Viet Minh. Britain's adherence to the Manila Pact, designed to forestall further Communist inroads into Southeast Asia, was a sop to US sensitivities, and to Australia and New Zealand.

It all came down to a question of priorities, especially in a time of financial stringency for Britain. Britain's own independent nuclear deterrent force — principally the V-bombers and a number of missile developments — were expensive to develop, to operate and to maintain, and economies had to be found. While the strategic and defence problems East of Suez were important, they could not rate the highest priority in British thinking. Prosecuting the Emergency had cost more than £550 million in 1954 alone, and the British were looking at how this might be reduced: assistance from Australia and New Zealand was clearly one way savings could be achieved.

There was no question of walking away from the task of defeating the CTs — Britain's continued military support, should the Malayan Government continue to require it, had been agreed at the 1956 constitutional convention. But reductions in the British contribution would be pursued. As an independent nation, Malaya itself would be expected to bear a sizeable proportion of the defence load, and this would also permit the British to concentrate their forces remaining in the region in Singapore. All this was made public in a 1957 British Government White Paper on Defence, known as the Sandys Report, after the minister of the day.

The British were also planning self-government for Singapore, but the minutes of the 1956 Prime Minister's Conference in London made clear why they did not propose to include the colony as a member state of the new Federation.

> The negotiations with Singapore would have been considerably eased if it had been possible to envisage an early link with the Federation of Malaya. This was historically justifiable, but the large Chinese population in Singapore and the extent of Communist infiltration there made the Government of the Federation reluctant to contemplate the inclusion of Singapore in the Federation at this time.[1]

The British perceived that giving Singapore too much independence could result in a Singaporean demand for the closure of the military bases on which British policy in the Far East depended. A worse scenario — as if the first were not bad enough — was that a Communist-dominated Singapore Government might well invite the Chinese to occupy the bases and other facilities vacated by the British. This Singapore independence issue was to resurface a short nine years later in the context of Confrontation: in the interim the self-governing colony gained a limited measure of independence when it negotiated membership terms for joining Malaysia in 1963. As an aside, the 1956 statement provides a wider context to the SHOWBOAT trips to sea for Singaporean schoolchildren that the RAN ships carried out during the Emergency.

Thus, on 31 August 1957, the Federation of Malaya became a newly independent state and was admitted to the Commonwealth the same day. Its army was already involved in the anti-CT campaign: the ships and men which would become its navy were also involved peripherally, but, as will be shown in Chapter 4, they needed a great deal of assistance until they became an effective force. The transfer of political power to the new government under the leadership of Tunku Abdul Rahman also required a realignment of the military arrangements for the defence of Malaya and the prosecution of the Emergency, as the Federation Government did request outside military assistance.

> The Government of the Federation of Malaya is determined that there shall be no relaxation in the conduct of the Emergency campaign, and has now requested Her Majesty's Government in the United Kingdom, and also Her Majesty's Governments in Australia and New Zealand to continue to make their forces available in Emergency operations. [2]

The outcome was the Anglo-Malay Defence Agreement (AMDA), which Australia joined in 1959.[3] The decision to do so was the result of extensive discussions in Australian government and defence circles, which concluded that a presence in Malaya was advantageous to this country.

Prior to independence, there had been discussion among the ANZAM partners over issues such as whether Malaya should become a member of ANZAM and whether the new nation should be encouraged to join the Manila Treaty and thus become a member of SEATO. This compelled a rethink on the roles of ANZAM and the FESR in the post-independence era. The British believed that the original rationale of defending Malaya from external aggression remained current. Australian planners saw the alliance as more than that — a reserve available for deployment to meet any contingency that might arise in Southeast Asia. ANZAM membership was inappropriate for Malaya, which could have no interest in defending Australia and New Zealand. As well, in reality, there was little that Malaya could contribute to ANZAM. The new nation could, however, play a role in the defence of its own region by joining SEATO.[4]

This was not an option that attracted the Malayans. The pace of decolonisation in Asia and Africa throughout the 1950s had led to the development of a Non-Aligned Movement (NAM), largely composed of newly independent states, with the aim of remaining uncommitted to either side in the Cold War.[5] Although some NAM players, such as China and some European Bloc countries, were notably aligned to the Communist side, the Malayans believed there was little to gain and perhaps much to lose by associating themselves with the anti-Communist SEATO alliance. Malaya's defence was to be a matter for discussion and negotiation with the British under AMDA, with Australia and New Zealand informed of the substance of these talks by the British.[6]

So, the new Malayan Government decided to adopt a non-aligned position in relation to ANZAM and SEATO. This meant that it could not be seen to support any activities or operations by ANZAM forces that compromised this independent stance. Thus ANZAM forces stationed in Malaya could not be deployed directly to another country, but had to stage through an intermediate port so as to preserve the appearance of Malayan non-alignment. An ANZAM study of the internal threat to Malaya commenced in early 1958 had, by June of the following year, expanded into a report with the snappy title of 'The Internal Threat to Malaya up to the End of 1961 — Likely Effect of this and Other Developments on the Future of the Strategic Reserve and on the Security and Use of ANZAM Facilities'.[7] The practical effect of the independence of Malaya was to see the majority of British Commonwealth base facilities moved to Singapore, which had not yet gained its independence.[8] There were exceptions: Camp Terendak near Malacca remained as a jungle warfare training establishment and a new camp was built there to house the 28th Commonwealth Brigade, the cost being shared between the ANZAM partners. The large joint airbase at Butterworth opposite Penang Island remained under Commonwealth control, and became a RAAF base in July 1958. One casualty of the reorganisation was the office of the Flag Office Malaya, whose responsibilities were handed to a Commander Far East Fleet.[9]

The Sandys White Paper made it clear, at least to the British, that an even closer integration of Commonwealth forces would now make sense, with a view to having responsibility for the defence of part of Southeast Asia assigned to the Commonwealth under SEATO. This view did not attract the Australian Government, which had recently decided on standardisation of military equipment with the United States, and which had worked hard to cement political and military ties with that country.[10] For Australia, SEATO had greater appeal than ANZAM, as the former held the probability of US assistance. This had already become an important factor in ANZAM planning:

> In global war and war with China, the ANZAM Powers possess the potential, but not the capability in the present circumstances, to meet the threat on land, but considerable assistance in naval and air forces would be required from elsewhere.[11]

Australia also had other strategic concerns, most importantly with Indonesia. Having supported the Indonesians in their efforts to gain independence from the Dutch, Australia had continued its efforts to build substantial links with Jakarta, including the establishment of the position of Defence Attaché Jakarta in 1954, but it was troubled over the apparent instability of its large neighbour. The authority of the Indonesian central government and the territorial integrity of the nation seemed to be threatened by a succession of insurgencies, arising from ethnic, political and religious differences.[12] Moreover, the growing popularity of Communism, especially in Java, indicated that the non-aligned status of Indonesia was steadily being compromised. An unstable, fragmented and Communist Indonesia was not in the interests of Australia or the Southeast Asian region. The looming end of the Emergency seemed set to see the destruction of one Communist insurgency in Malaya while a much larger and more dangerous Communist threat emerged across the Malacca Strait. Additionally, Indonesia had now initiated a campaign to wrest control of West Papua from the Dutch, success in which would result in Australia having a land border with the Indonesians in Papua New Guinea.

There were, however, attempts to establish deeper linkages between the two countries at a military level, commencing with training for Indonesian students in Australian defence schools. This led to the 1957 Indonesian request for places for their officers at the Army Staff College at Queenscliff in Victoria, the Jungle Training School at Canungra in Queensland and the Artillery School at Puckapunyal in Victoria. The Australian Army was keen to accept the Indonesian students and, in a lengthy exchange of correspondence, convinced the Minister for Defence of the proposal's benefits. However, the Army had reckoned without the furore this proposal ignited when the prospect was aired in Parliament. With West New Guinea a sore point, public sentiment was firmly opposed to the idea of accepting the Indonesians in Australian defence schools and, in a display of tact lost on many of their detractors, the Indonesians withdrew the request later in the year. It had been a false start.

But the ties were later renewed, for in January1962 the Minister for Defence advised Parliament that two Indonesian officers were studying at Queenscliff.[13]

For the British — and Malayan — governments there were related concerns with Indonesia's apparent expansionist mood. The British North Borneo colonies shared a land border with Indonesia. There was substantial trade across the sea boundaries between Malaya, Singapore and Indonesia, and ethnic ties across this border also remained strong. Such contact could enable Communist cadres from Indonesia to reignite the enthusiasm of the MRLA and lead to a deterioration of the internal security situation.

While these diplomatic and strategic concerns grew at a planning level, the major issues were how to shape the relationship between the three ANZAM partners and the commitments they had undertaken to SEATO. There seemed to be no let-up in Communist activities throughout Southeast Asia, and intelligence papers of the era spoke ominously of the threat posed by a Sino–Soviet Bloc. In the minds of the planners, the fact that this bloc existed only in name did not lessen its potential for mischief in both SEATO and ANZAM areas, possibly in both at the same time. There were to be specific occasions on which SEATO invited its members to contribute to expeditionary forces being deployed as a counter to Communist activities — in Laos in particular — but for the ANZAM partners the principal concern was the apparent deterioration of control in Indonesia.

Then, in May 1961, the Tunku raised the proposal with the British Government that Malaya, Singapore, Sarawak, Brunei and North Borneo (Sabah) might forge stronger political and economic ties. This could lead to a political union and to the formation of a new nation called Malaysia. Abdul Rahman was not principally concerned with expansion of his country; his worry was that the vigorous Singaporean Government, led by Lee Kuan Yew and the commercially acquisitive Chinese ethnic majority in the island, showed every indication of dominating the economic activity of their Malay neighbour. One means of counteracting this was for

Singapore to join the Federation of Malaya, but this course would tip the ethic makeup of the combined state in favour of Chinese over Malay. This could be counterbalanced by the inclusion of the populations of the three Borneo colonies. While not all ethnic Malays, or Muslims, their populations would at least prevent Malays becoming a minority in the country bearing their name.

Despite this ethnic undercurrent, the idea had considerable appeal. The small, undeveloped and relatively sparsely populated Borneo colonies and the Sultanate of Brunei would, arguably, have a better chance of political survival and economic development as parts of a larger state, and their resources and population would make Malaya stronger as well. The idea appealed to Singapore too; in June Lee Kuan Yew declared his support for the idea, and by August the concept was being considered by the British Government. That month, Australia also expressed qualified support for the Malaysia concept.[14] By October, the British had concluded that the proposal was practical, but that the wishes of the peoples of the Borneo territories would have to be ascertained before it could be taken further. The Malayan Parliament accepted this judgment, appointed a commission of inquiry led by a Lord Cobbold to visit Borneo, and informed the Indonesians of what was planned. In December the Sultan of Brunei endorsed in principal the accession of his territory to the proposed Federation. In the meantime, a union between Malaya and Singapore had been proposed, the terms drafted and the merger accepted by their parliaments.

Strategically, these changes were of great moment for the British East of Suez. Britain had suffered a severe balance of payments crisis in 1960 that continued into 1961. With the prospect of its last Southeast Asian colonial territories being enfolded within Malaysia, and the crown colony of Singapore becoming a part of the Federation, Britain's future defence commitments would be reduced. The end of the Emergency in July 1960 meant that the rundown of military resources to a level commensurate with Britain's ANZAM and SEATO commitments had already begun, AMDA was extended to Singapore in November, and the Malayan armed forces were now expanding to take up a proportionally larger share of the external defence burden. And one could take a reasonably optimistic view of the likely sources of external attack: Indonesia had indicated that it had no objections to the Borneo territories joining Malaysia — subject to the wishes of their peoples being expressed; and the Communist threat might not be as monolithic as had been once thought. October 1961 had seen the enactment of the Cuban missile crisis, with the US facing down a blatant threat by the USSR, and by now splits were being seen in the Sino–Soviet relationship.

This favourable strategic situation, and the probability that Malayan restrictions on the use of Commonwealth bases in that country for SEATO purposes would be extended to Singapore on Federation, led Britain to consider the future of its presence in Singapore.[15] The concept of moving the main part of Britain's Far East forces to Australia was under active consideration for some time, but was not proceeded with because of the huge costs involved, Australian concern over the message this 2000 km withdrawal from its front line of 'Forward Defence' might send to friends and enemies alike, and the conclusion of satisfactory arrangements regarding the Commonwealth use of the Singapore bases for SEATO. Even the United States expressed concern over the power vacuum in Southeast Asia that would be created if the British were to withdraw.[16] However, the writing was clearly on the wall. Britain would, sooner or later, depart the region.

While it was not yet clear what a British withdrawal might mean for Australia and the RAN, it is instructive to look at the effects FESR service had had on the Navy. By 1961, all of the Navy's major fleet units had served at least one tour in the Strategic Reserve, and some had undertaken several. The RAN had become familiar with the oceans, seas and straits of Southeast Asia and with most of its ports. Littoral countries had welcomed visits by RAN units sufficient to enable them to distinguish between the British and Australian sailor. Australian ships and personnel had exercised with the navies of the ANZAM partners, SEATO and the Commonwealth countries of

South Asia. The capability of RAN equipment and the professional skills of its personnel in this potential theatre of operations had been tested and, where they were found wanting, remedial action was in hand.

New ships and equipment were beginning to enter service. The ships were air-conditioned and more comfortable in tropical conditions than their predecessors. Nor was Britain any longer the automatic source of designs and equipment, as the RAN's confidence — sometimes misplaced — in its ability to devise and manage major equipment programs had grown. The new Australian-built destroyers and frigates were more capable than the ships they replaced; submarines were on order from the UK and, in a major shift with multiple ramifications, high-capability missile-equipped destroyers were on order from the USA. These new systems and improved levels of RAN skill in using them gave the Australian Government an enhanced strategic weight in ANZAM and SEATO. Should diplomacy call for it, Australia had some impressive new 'gunboats' to deploy. And the probability that they would be deployed was high should problems arise between Malaysia and Indonesia.[17]

In early 1963 the RAN Directorate of Naval intelligence instituted a formal program of briefing the officers and men of ships deploying to the FESR on the currents stirring in Southeast Asia.[18] The cause of most strategic and intelligence concern was Indonesia's attitude towards its proposed new neighbour, Malaysia. Its decision to 'confront' Malaysia resulted from a complex mix of political, military, economic and racial forces. There have been many attempts to research and explain why the Malaysia proposal excited, after a delay, Indonesian military, economic and diplomatic reprisals. Such explanation is beyond the scope of this book, but a few remarks would be appropriate to set the scene.

A clear factor in the decision was the instability in Indonesian domestic politics, where President Sukarno was implementing his 'guided democracy' form of government. This involved meeting the expectations of disparate influential groups within the Indonesian polity, including religious parties, the powerful armed forces and the growing *Partai Kommunis Indonesia* (PKI). Indonesian foreign policy contributed through Sukarno's ideal of Newly Emerging Forces — essentially members of the Non-Aligned Movement — asserting their superiority over the former and neo-colonialist forces in world affairs. However, deteriorating economic conditions in Indonesia — and a principal cause of instability in the nation — had required Sukarno to seek assistance from the International Monetary Fund at the same time that he continued to place strain on Indonesia's relations with the United States, which was a key member of that body.

Suspicious about the motives for the FESR and SEATO, Indonesia decided to focus on the role of the British in the Malaysia concept, declaring the incorporation of the North Borneo territories as 'encirclement, and a continuation of British colonial policies in a new guise. This was, of course, a serious misreading of the British situation, but it reflected the rhetoric of Indonesian foreign policy at the time. Despite the signing of a treaty of friendship between the two countries in 1959, there were Indonesian misgivings about the conduct of the Malayan Government, and the Tunku in particular, during the various insurgencies which had racked Indonesia. Indonesians believed that the Malayans had not done enough to isolate the rebels, and even that they had offered tacit support for the dismemberment of the Republic. There were groups in Malaya who campaigned actively for the establishment of a theocratic regime in Jakarta — hardly helpful to the government of the largest Islamic country in the world![19] And the Indonesians felt that the Tunku might have consulted them before he made his Malaysia proposal public.

Whatever the reasons for the antipathy, the Indonesian response to the Malaysia concept went from an expression of 'no objection' in June 1961 to the announcement on 20 January 1963 by the Indonesian Foreign Minister that his country intended to 'confront' Malaysia.[20] While it was not clear just what this meant, there had been a foretaste of its potential consequences in a rebellion which erupted in the Sultanate of Brunei in December 1962, in opposition to the concept of Malaysia. Indonesian involvement was suspected, and the Tunku made this view explicit, but the evidence is ambiguous. What is demonstrable is that Indonesia had offered training to various dissident groups, which were predominantly ethnic Chinese in the North Borneo colonies opposed to the Malaysia concept.

The Australian Government watched this deterioration in the Southeast Asian security situation with concern. Anxious to avoid alienating the Indonesian Government by taking too prominent a role in the defence of Malaysia, nonetheless Australia was mindful of its responsibilities towards the new state, whose formation it had supported. To complicate matters further, the security situation in South Vietnam appeared to be spiralling out of control, and SEATO obligations, and understandings with the Vietnamese Government, were calling for an increasingly military response — it had already committed the Australian Army Training Team to Vietnam in 1962. In January 1963, following ANZAM consultation and the introduction of the unified Commander-in-Chief organisation in the Far East by the British, the FESR Directive for RAN ships was amended to include in their secondary role 'to prevent infiltration by sea of communist agents or armed bands [unspecified]' and an appendix covering the rules for their conduct in the vicinity of Indonesian waters was added.[21] It was not long before this appendix came into play because on 26 January the Australian Government agreed that the two ships serving with the FESR could be used for patrol duties in North Borneo waters. The targets were 'rebel elements' associated with the Brunei insurrection.[22]

There is ample evidence that Australian diplomats in Kuala Lumpur and Jakarta made strenuous efforts to persuade the two sides to seek reconciliation, but events had gathered a momentum that seemed unstoppable.[23] Then in July 1963, after Malaya, Singapore, Sarawak and Sabah, but not Brunei, had signed an agreement to federate, Sukarno enunciated his 'Crush Malaysia' policy.[24] A nation of nearly 100 million Indonesians had decided to eliminate an as yet unconstituted neighbour with a population of a little under 11 million.

Indonesian confidence in the power of its defence forces played some role in this. Premier Khrushchev of the USSR had paid a state visit to Indonesia in February 1960 to mark the burgeoning development of relations between the two countries, and in January 1961 this resulted in a massive Indonesian order for Soviet military equipment. The USSR provided the Indonesians with a loan to purchase the arms, but expected this to be repaid. Before long, Jakarta was taking deliveries of equipment that was almost at the cutting edge of military technology, and superior to much that the British or the Australians could field. This cornucopia included long-range 'Badger' bombers equipped with air-to-surface missiles with a range of up to 300 nm, a cruiser mounting 270 mm guns, and a dozen potent little Komar fast patrol boats, equipped with the deadly Styx surface-to-surface missile with a range of 20 nm. As the Flag Officer Second in Command of the Far East Fleet put it in a 1963 report to the Admiralty, 'The real sting lies with the KOMAR, whose speed and weapon capabilities are such that they could only effectively be countered by air strikes ... They would be an early target for destruction'.[25] Destroyers, frigates, submarine chasers, submarines, light bombers and fighter/ground attack aircraft completed the inventory of maritime offensive capability acquired.

While the political and diplomatic wrangling over Malaysia continued, British and ANZAM military planning for the defence of the as-yet unfederated nation had commenced. By May 1963 there existed an Operational Concept for the Defence of Malaysian Area, in which the naval forces of the FESR had been allotted roles, and work was in progress to refine the command and control structure and to apply the lessons learned in the suppression of the Brunei uprising. These led to discussions on the force structure that would be necessary to defend the border between the North Borneo states and Indonesian Kalimantan. Amongst the reinforcements required were four coastal minesweepers and a destroyer.[26] It is clear the British expected Australia to provide these. As to Indonesian intentions, the ANZAM planners had no doubts.

A review in June this year [1963] of Indonesian prospects and intentions concluded that they would continue to campaign against Malaysia with the long term aim of uniting all the Malay speaking peoples of South East Asia into a greater Indonesia.[27]

Diplomatically, the impasse between Indonesia and Malaya and, to a lesser extent with the Philippines, continued. The Philippines asserted a legal right to part of British North Borneo, a claim not supported by Australia or other countries.[28] Although their opposition had resulted in Malaya agreeing to ask the United Nations to conduct a survey of reactions to the Malaysia proposal in the North Borneo territories — and to the discussion of a pan-Malay union of all three countries under the title Maphilindo — the level of mistrust between the Malaysian Prime Minister and Indonesian President grew. Sukarno apparently believed that he had received undertakings from the Tunku at talks in Manila in August 1963 concerning the declaration of the proposed federation. He was therefore incensed when, within three days of the UN's commission reporting that there was general support in North Borneo for the concept, the Tunku proclaimed the formation of Malaysia on 16 September 1963. There had been small-scale infiltrations from the Indonesian side from April 1963 onwards; these were now stepped up in size and frequency. British plans for militarily reinforcing Borneo were activated.[29]

Australian policy makers, especially in the Department of External Affairs, found the development of an appropriate and effective response to Indonesian aggression very difficult. It came down to a question of the lengths to which Australia would be prepared to go to support Malaysia, while recognising that in doing so it might jeopardise its crucial relationship with Indonesia. The ambassador in Jakarta put this question in stark terms in February 1963 by asking, 'Is Malaysia Sacred?' The response from Canberra neatly encapsulated the dilemma in which Australia found itself, which was no less than the possible abandonment of all the work that had been done since 1945 to ensure its security.

> I suppose the question should really be 'Is our forward position in South East Asia sacred?' Could we hope to divorce ourselves from Malaysia and nevertheless maintain that? The problem is that we cannot look only at Malaysia; our strategic reserve and in fact our whole defence policy is involved. All our strategy, as you know, is based on our forward position in South East Asia and we would be cutting our own throats if we were to pull out of Malaysia.[30]

It was clearly necessary for Australia to move cautiously in responding to the new federation, especially as it would be necessary to negotiate a new security arrangement; in March 1963 Cabinet decided to defer any action in that direction until Malaysia became a reality.[31] Australia's delay in making public its military response to Confrontation had attracted some criticism from its ANZAM partners, but Prime Minister Menzies had made clear Australia's support for Malaysia at the end of September 1963 after the new nation had federated, and in the wake of violent anti-British and anti-Malaysian riots in Jakarta:

> We are resolved … that if, in the circumstances that now exist, there occurs, in relation to Malaysia or any of its constituent States, armed invasion or subversive activity — supported or directed or inspired from outside Malaysia, we shall to the best of our powers and by any means agreed upon with the Government of Malaysia, add our military assistance to the efforts of Malaysia and the United Kingdom in the defence of Malaysia's territorial integrity and political independence.[32]

Such ringing declarations of support for Malaysia were diplomatically important, but before making military commitments

Australian decision-makers had directed the development of an intelligence-based analysis of the deteriorating situation. What started in October 1963 as an investigation of the Indonesian threat to Malaysia rapidly became 'Military Implications for Australia of the Malaysian Situation' and finally appeared as 'Possible Indonesian Retaliatory Measures against Australia'.[33] The Indonesian escalation in cross-border raids into East Malaysia pointed to the imminence of Australia needing to make some military response to honour the Prime Minister's pledge.

By November 1963, with the costs of Confrontation rising and causing the diversion of their defence and economic resources from higher priority areas, the British were pressing Australia for military assistance in Malaysia.[34] This escalated, with a direct appeal to the Prime Minister by the British Prime Minister in December, but the request was declined. Australia did not yet believe that the level of hostilities required a substantial reinforcement of British and Malaysian forces; Australian hopes rested on a diplomatic settlement which appeared possible with the involvement of the United States. In early 1964, US Attorney-General Robert Kennedy visited the region to hold talks with all parties to the dispute.[35] However, hopes for a diplomatic settlement foundered on Indonesian intransigence, and the Indonesians increased the pace of attacks across the common border with Malaysia. There was no indication of how resolutely the campaign would be fought by the Indonesians, but a more substantial escalation could not be discounted. British plans for a reduction of forces in the Far East were put on hold, the Malaysian forces commenced a period of rapid expansion — in which the Australian navy was to play a key role — and Britain looked to its ANZAM partners for force contributions. If Malaysia was to survive, Confrontation would have to be resisted by the controlled application of superior Commonwealth force. How that was achieved is described in Chapters 4 and 5.

HMAS *Arunta* from HMAS *Sydney* (Naval Historical Society of Australia)

HMAS *Warramunga* refuelling from *Melbourne* (Naval Historical Society of Australia)

HMAS *Anzac* (Naval Historical Society of Australia)

HMAS *Tobruk* in Singapore Dock 1955 (Naval Historical Society of Australia)

HMAS *Quadrant* (Naval Historical Society of Australia)

HMAS *Queenborough* (Naval Historical Society of Australia)

HMAS *Quickmatch* in Labuan 1961 (Naval Historical Society of Australia)

HMAS *Voyager* (Naval Historical Society of Australia)

HMAS *Melbourne* with *Voyager* and *Vendetta* (Naval Historical Society of Australia)

HMAS *Quiberon* (Naval Historical Society of Australia)

SEATO Maritime Exercise Group (Naval Historical Society)

HMAS *Sydney* as troop transport (Naval Historical Society of Australia)

Captain Dovers in KD *Mahamiru* (P. Nettur)

Indonesian destroyer (J. Foster)

Indonesian *Komar* Class patrol boat
(J. Foster)

Indonesian patrol vessel (J. Foster)

Coastal minesweeper KD *Ledang* (A.N. Dollard)

Inshore minesweeper KD *Temasek* (A.N. Dollard)

HMAS *Yarra* (Naval Historical Society of Australia)

HMS *Mull of Kintyre* at Divisions (P. Procopis)

HMAS *Parramatta* (Naval Historical Society of Australia)

HMAS *Curlew* in Kuching (D. Hiron)

Indonesian Prisoners in *Teal*
(J. Werner)

RMN Vosper patrol boat (A.N. Dollard)

KD *Malaya* (J. Hume)

RMN gas turbine fast patrol boat (P. Nettur)

HMAS *Duchess* searching suspect vessel (L. Jones)

HMAS *Duchess* towing Malaysian vessel (L. Jones)

HMAS *Hawk* interception (J. Foster)

Pig boat alongside HMAS *Duchess* (L. Jones)

HMAS *Duchess* gunnery exercise (L. Jones)

Infiltrators being interrogated in HMAS *Duchess* (L. Jones)

Lookout in HMAS *Duchess* (L. Jones)

Ton Class waist Bren gunner (J. Werner)

Ton Class messdeck (J. Werner)

Ton Class Bofors in action (J. Werner)

Ton Class engine change, Singapore (P. Cooper)

Mobile Clearance Diving Team ordnance disposal (G. Miller)

Prisoner transfer to Singapore Police (1) ((J. Werner)

Prisoner transfer to Singapore Police (2) (J. Werner)

Mobile Clearance Diving Team diving party (G. Miller)

Malaysian King at KD *Malaya* with Commander Hume RAN (J. Hume)

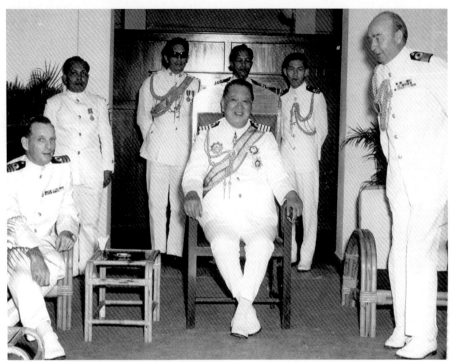

Sultan of Johore at KD *Malaya* (J. Hume)

Sultan of Johore takes salute at KD *Malaya* with Commodore Dollard (J. Hume)

Commodore Dollard inspects Guard at KD *Malaya* (J. Hume)

Commodore Thanabalasingham with Malaysian King (J. Hume)

Loch Class frigate KD *Hang Tuah* (A. N. Dollard)

HMAS *Derwent* (Naval Historical Society of Australia)

HMAS *Melbourne* launching Gannet anti-submarine aircraft (Naval Historical Society of Australia)

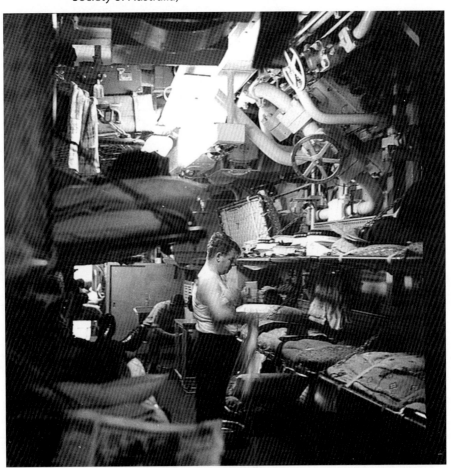

HMAS *Melbourne's* messdeck, 1958 (Naval Historical Society of Australia)

4 A Malayan/Malaysian Navy

The Royal Malayan Navy had its origins in the 1934 when the British began training an auxiliary naval force in Singapore to support the Royal Navy in Malaya.[1] This was known as the Straits Settlements Royal Navy Volunteer Reserve (SSRNVR) and its role was to undertake administrative and logistical tasks ashore and to man auxiliary vessels, such as harbour defence and coastal patrol craft. Officers and sailors were entered, the former almost exclusively European, and the RN provided the permanent service officers and senior sailors. Two weeks of annual sea training for the Reserve were conducted in RN ships. In 1937 two motor launches were commissioned as HM Ships for use by the Reserve for coastal patrols. The name of this group was changed to Malayan RNVR in 1941.

The success of the Reserve encouraged the RN to open a second Reserve establishment in Penang in 1938. This group of volunteers was designated the Malayan Royal Navy Volunteer Reserve (MRNVR) and by 1940 it was manning two additional patrol boats and five minesweepers.[2] At the outbreak of war in 1939 the decision was taken to strengthen the complement at the Singapore Naval Base with a Royal Navy (Malay Section) composed of British officers on loan and locally entered Malay personnel. Known colloquially as the 'Malay Navy', these sailors were employed in seaman and communications duties for service in minesweepers and patrol boats, and the Section expanded from 400 in 1939 to 1420 in 1941.

During the war over a hundred members of the 'Malay Navy' and the RMNVR lost their lives and a similar number were reported missing in the fighting. About 150 escaped from Singapore in February 1942 for service with the RN in other theatres and returned with the British in September 1945. Others served with the clandestine British-funded Force 136 inside Malaya during the Japanese occupation.[3]

Following the Japanese surrender, the 'Malay Navy' was disbanded and the MRNVR languished until the onset of the Emergency and the requirement for sustained patrolling and inspection of minor water craft arose. In December 1948 the Malayan Naval Force was formed under a local agreement by which Malaya was required to raise a military force and Singapore a naval unit to assist the British. Recruitment revived and the British transferred seven motor launches and one landing craft (gun) on loan for use by the Malayans in patrols against smuggling, piracy and terrorists and in naval gunfire support. The force was designated the Royal Malayan Navy in August 1952, although it was financed and administered by the colonial government of Singapore. All the RMN ships saw extensive service during the Emergency, and were included in joint operations with RN and RAN ships supporting land force operations against CT positions.[4]

The 1946 choice of a commanding officer for the Navy was fortunate. Commander (later Captain) H.E. Nicholls RN, who had been born in Pahang State, led the force from the disbandment of the 'Malay Navy' through the Malayan Naval Force days and into the RMN until his retirement just before Malayan independence. It was he who began promoting senior 'Malay Navy' veterans to officers in 1953 and who recruited young men as cadets for officer training in the UK from 1954. These wise decisions were to lay the foundations for the rapid expansion that was to come.[5]

It was not until discussions on the independence of the Malay Federation began in earnest that the nascent new nation's need for a proper navy made itself apparent. To create one in the time available before independence was an impossibility and, while the Royal Malayan Navy contingent paraded proudly at the Independence ceremony in Kuala Lumpur on 31 August 1957, it represented precious little of a seagoing nature. At Independence, the RMN comprised thirty-one officers — all but three of them British, ninety-eight senior sailors (twenty-eight British) and around 500 Malayan junior sailors. Its base was at Woodlands in Singapore, called His Malayan Majesty's Ship *Malaya*. In addition, there were two divisions of the MRNVR, one in Singapore with 183 officers and 529 sailors, and one in Malaya of forty-four officers and 144 sailors, split into subdivisions at Penang and Selangor. It operated a variety of small patrol vessels.[6]

But it remained a part of the Royal Navy while Malaya and Singapore squabbled over the terms under which it would be transferred to the Federation. The major issue was that of rent to be paid by Malaya to Singapore for the use of the base: while Federation officials agreed that the Singaporean figure was reasonable, the Tunku disagreed. While the disagreement continued to fester the British were appalled. Their reasonable expectation was that the Malayan Government would take over the responsibility for normal naval activities after Federation, leaving the additional burdens of the Emergency for the RN.

> The United Kingdom realised that there would now be a gap between what the [Royal] Navy had done before independence and what it would be available to do now. This gap could only be filled by the creation of a Navy under the operational control of the Federation Government.[7]

Tunku Abdul Rahman countered the Singaporean demand with a plan to construct a new base for his navy in Port Swettenham. This was rather a hollow threat, since the costs would be particularly hard for the Federation's budget to bear and the time taken would extend for some years. The Malayan Government hoped to overcome the first problem by asking for a grant from the British. As for the second, it would have to swallow its pride and use the Singapore facilities on Singapore's terms until its own base was ready. As time dragged on into 1958 the Federation's inshore defences comprised around twenty police launches and a clutch of customs boats: the Tunku even suggested at one point that he wasn't sure Malaya really needed a Navy.

The British were having none of that! A review conducted by the Joint Planning Staff in February 1958 spelled out exactly what maritime defence burden Malaya was expected to shoulder.

(i) The continuing rebellion in Indonesia, combined with isolated incidents of piracy, gun running, and illegal immigration dictate in peace a coastwise patrolling capability with an emphasis on the Malacca Straits. The Royal Malayan Navy must also be trained to support the Army in counter-insurgency operations.

(ii) Training for war should be directed towards countering possible enemy minelaying, particularly in the Malacca Straits. In addition, the Royal Malayan Navy must be able to play its part in the Allied control of shipping organisation and be capable of defending its own ports and coastal waters against small scale raids, infiltration by seaborne forces, sabotage etc. [8]

Financial and political pressure was brought to bear, and the Indonesians obligingly provided a face-saving formula for the Tunku by declaring a twelve nautical mile territorial zone. As this brought Indonesian and Malayan territorial waters into close proximity, the Federation decided that it would take over control of the RMN after all. A Bill establishing the Royal Malayan Navy as part of the armed forces of the Federation from 1 July 1958 was introduced into the Malayan Parliament and passed on 18 June, and the British offered over $M20 million in ships and equipment to the new navy, as well as more than $M6 million towards the construction of the new base. Transferred to the Federation Government were seven seaward defence motor launches, two inshore minesweepers, and the base in Singapore, for which Malaya was charged an annual rent of $M400,000.[9] The Malaysian Government assumed full financial responsibility for its navy from 1 January 1959. The naval service's official title was *Tentera Laut Diraja Malaya*, but the English abbreviation RMN continued to be used.

The chain of command was simple. Under the overall direction of the Minister of Defence, the Senior Officer RMN (and other service chiefs) reported to the Chief of Armed Forces Staff. Under them were the respective Staff Divisions. This too was simply organised on functional lines, with directorates of Plans and Operations, Technical, Personnel and Training, and Logistics and Finance.

The Navy Ordinance 1958 stated that the officer commanding the RMN would be appointed by the King and agreed that non-Malayan personnel serving in the RMN on 1 July 1958 would not be required to take Federation citizenship during their current engagements. This sidestepped the issue of Singaporean citizens who had been members of the British-controlled navy and, of course, made it possible for RN officers and senior sailors to continue to occupy positions within the Federation's navy. These did not serve as members of the RMN and were borne on the books of HMS *Terror* in Singapore; they were thus subject to British, rather than Malayan, naval jurisdiction.

The RN had taken responsibility for the development of this element of the Malayan armed forces: command positions were occupied by RN officers, the majority of them on contract. Young Malayan officers had first been recruited into the RMN in 1954 and commenced their training at the Britannia Royal Naval College, Dartmouth, in the UK only in January 1956. But as the 1950s passed, Britain wanted to extract itself from the development commitment, while the Malayan Government had become dissatisfied with the standard of officer being supplied by the RN. Many of these had been passed over for promotion and they were not the dynamic and highly professional people who could tackle the daunting task of creating the new navy. A young Malayan officer encountered this problem directly in his first ship.

My first experience of going to sea in an RMN ship was in 1959 …
I was attached to an inshore minesweeper, or it could have been
an SDML [seaward defence motor launch]. The captain of the
ship was a guy who drank so much gin they called him 'Gino'. He
was a two-ringer. We sailed from KD *Malaya* and I never saw him
again until we reached harbour at Port Dickson. While the ship
went there, there was not a chart on the table and Gino was in
his cabin drinking. The Buffer [Chief Boatswain's Mate], a Malay
sailor, who was a petty officer, took the ship all the way there. So
that shocked me a bit and I passed the word round.[10]

In late 1958, the Malayans rejected the British Government's
nomination to replace the commander of the RMN — now with the
title of Deputy Chief of Staff (Navy) — and turned to Australia and
New Zealand for assistance in providing a suitable officer. They felt
that the RN was too big a force to take the development of the RMN
seriously and that Australia's interests in Southeast Asia were more
in tune with those of Malaya.[11] The Australian High Commissioner
in Kuala Lumpur, Mr Tom Critchley, was keen to help, and supported
the proposal.[12]

So far as the RAN was concerned, this was not an especially
propitious time for such a request to be made. There was a shortage
of officers in the RAN as well as a heavy training program under way
in preparation for the introduction into service of new ships and
new capabilities, such as mine warfare and submarines. However,
this was an important request to which the Australian Government
attached some priority and, while the RAN squirmed for a while
waiting to see what the British could provide, the commitment was
eventually accepted. The Navy agreed to provide the commander
of the RMN, plus other officers and a similar number of senior
sailors to assist in the task of turning the RMN into a navy in more
than name. Australia thus provided the commanders of the Royal
Malayan Navy and led the Royal Malaysian Navy throughout
Confrontation and beyond, as well as the key staff in operations,
supply and training, and the commanding officers of several RMN

ships. Perhaps aware of the shortcomings of the personnel loaned by the RN, the Australians picked their loan officers and sailors with some care, although this might not always have been apparent to, or appreciated by, those concerned.

So little has been recorded about this most interesting and important interlude in Australian naval history that interviews of the surviving personnel who were loaned to the RMN form the major source of information. Yet, as will be shown, this relatively small investment of personnel, professionalism and some capital was arguably the greatest contribution made by the Australian Navy in Southeast Asia during the period covered by this book.

The first encounter most of the new RMN officers had with the RAN occurred at Dartmouth, where they met Australian seaman and supply graduates from the Royal Australian Naval College, and the outcomes of the 'colonial' solidarity thus created were positive. Most of the Australians had three and a half years or more of naval training under their belts already, in contrast with the eighteen months of their British and Malayan counterparts, and were not backward in flaunting their experience. A Malaysian cadet recalled the difference this made in College life.

> We joined [Dartmouth] in 1960 and about five terms later the horrible Australians came and joined us. And the beauty of that was that, for the first one and a half years there were just the three of us [RMN] and a handful of Pakistanis, and we were bullied left right and centre by the RN ... When you came it tipped more towards 50:50 I think, and after that the RN treated us quite well.[13]

Another Malaysian officer recalled that they had more in common with the Australians, including some unflattering observations on the RN cadets.

> It was immediately noticeable that they [RAN] were different from the British cadets. We had a better rapport with them. Until

the Australians arrived we monopolised the showers, as the English cadets hardly used them![14]

Starting at the top, the first Australian officer to head the RMN was Captain W.J. Dovers DSC RAN, a formidable choice. Following a distinguished wartime career, Dovers had held a series of important postings, including command of the RAN College and of the first Australian *Daring* Class destroyer HMAS *Voyager*. He later recounted how unexpectedly his posting to Malaya had come about.

> I got twelve days notice! I was on my way back from New Zealand as Captain of *Voyager* on about 22 December, if I remember rightly. Two o'clock in the morning my Yeoman of Signals woke me up and I bit his head off because I'd only left the bridge a couple of hours before. He said, 'You'd better have a look at this signal, Sir. I think you'll be interested in it.' It said, 'Do you have any personal objection to being in Kuala Lumpur on 6 January to command the Malayan Navy?' And I sent a reply 'No', and went back to bed … I managed to get it put off until 14 January; even so I didn't have any chance to start learning Malay or anything sensible, trying to find out something about the Malayan Navy. I had to go off the deep end, and very interesting it was too.[15]

Dovers took with him to Kuala Lumpur a staff of two RAN officer specialists in operations and administration to assist in the development task, and a determination that the RMN should grow by itself and as quickly as was prudent, rather than continue to rely on expatriates to fill its senior ranks. This was a particular challenge, as the most senior Malayan officer was only of lieutenant commander's rank, and the Dartmouth-trained officers who would form the core of the new navy only began to return from the UK in 1960. For the time being British and Australian officers would have to bear the policy, operational, technical and logistics load. As well, it was necessary to develop a healthy working relationship with the Malayan Government and the other two services to ensure that the

RMN got its share of the Defence pie. Some ground-breaking was required here, as Dovers' RN predecessor had spent most of his time in Singapore, and had visited Kuala Lumpur only occasionally.

> I took the view that the navy should grow by itself, not try to build up a force manned by expatriates and that was the big change I suggested to the Malays. My big asset was my association with the Royal Navy and, having taught at their Staff College a few years before that, I found that a lot of my pupils were manning the Commander-in-Chief Far East's staff at the time. So I had available — not officially by any manner of means — but on the old boy network all the advice I wanted and it was freely given.[16]

With the title Captain of the Navy, and Chief of Naval Staff from 14 July 1960, Dovers began the task of overhauling the administration of the new navy. The Naval Ordinance 1958 had adopted Royal Navy administrative regulations and instructions as an interim measure until Malayan documents covering similar ground could be produced. It is an understatement to say that instruments such as *Queen's Regulations and Admiralty Instructions* were largely irrelevant to the circumstances of the RMN, but little progress had been made in writing their indigenous successor volumes. Dovers ordered the conversion of the hundreds of RN-based temporary memoranda which had governed the RMN into a consolidated book of regulations and instructions.

To fight the Navy's bureaucratic battles in Kuala Lumpur successfully, a system by which RMN files could be created and freely circulated, tracked and actioned within the Ministry of Defence (MINDEF) and its agencies was urgently required, and this was created by RMN personnel in six months of largely weekend work. The system survived its baptism of fire in the intense staffwork campaign that Dovers initiated, and still operates, relatively unchanged, to this day. In a further step to break the RN–RMN nexus, and to generate a new sense of pride in his personnel, he made changes to the RN badges and insignia which had been worn by RMN personnel to make them more Malayan in style and content, such as replacing oak leaves with rice sheaves. In 1961 the prefix 'His Majesty's Malayan Ship' was replaced by the Malay equivalent *Kapal Diraja* (KD)

Meanwhile, Dovers initiated exemplary action as required to rid the new navy of the unacceptable. The Malayan officer with the drunken captain was impressed with the decisiveness of the new policy at work.

> A few months later, this same chap Gino was in Port Swettenham, which is now called Port Klang. Dovers decided, without telling anybody, to visit the ship and when he arrived Gino was drunk in his cabin. This was about 12 o'clock in the morning. So he told Gino to pack all his things, go back to KD *Malaya* and go back to the UK. He didn't want him in the Navy anymore.[17]

It was quite clear that the order of battle of the RMN also needed urgent and radical attention. With a long coastline to protect, the navy needed modern capable craft, able to respond quickly to developing challenges, which its current force could not.

Dovers acted quickly and convinced the Malayan Government to vote the funds to procure a new class of, initially, six high-speed patrol boats from a UK shipyard. Ordered in September 1961, and modified for Malayan conditions with the addition of air-conditioning and stabilisers, the Vosper craft had a speed of 25 knots, a range of 1500 nautical miles and modern radar and weaponry. It was a significant and timely purchase. An increase in the naval personnel strength was required to crew the new ships, including the introduction of short service commissions for officers in May 1962, but, in the meantime, no fewer than nine RMN officers had gained command experience. Dovers also organised the purchase of additional coastal minesweepers of the Ton Class from the UK to bolster his force.

Captain Dovers reverted to the RAN in July 1962 after an exhilarating two and a half years for his adopted navy. For his service to the RMN he was made *Johan Mangku Negara* (Commander of the Order of Defender of the Realm) — equivalent to a British Commander of the British Empire — by the Malaysian King, as well as being awarded the *Pingat Khidmat Berbakti* (Loyal and Devoted Service Medal) by the Malaysian Government. Another award was the *Pingat Peringatan Malaysia* for his contributions towards the formation of Malaysia. His replacement was Captain A.M. Synnot RAN, another offer with FESR experience, and he arrived at a most interesting time. The Malaysia concept was under active investigation and then, in December 1962, there was an armed insurrection in Brunei against the Sultan. Although the RMN was not directly involved, it was a harbinger of what was to come.

Like his predecessor, Synnot took great pains to gain the confidence of his service colleagues and senior public servants in Kuala Lumpur. He had a strong grasp of staff work and was equally as successful in getting resources for the RMN despite the preponderance of the Malaysian Army in numbers, influence and access to senior political figures. His skills and principles rubbed off on his subordinates, as one recalled:

I remember clearly advice that I received from Admiral Synnot was not to exaggerate when asking for additional staff or materials from the Civil staff. He insisted that we always tell the truth. I put this advice to good use when I was later appointed as head of personnel in the Ministry. The Army was in the habit of inflating figures and this was known to the civilians; their requests for additional staff were always reduced by the civilians. We always spoke the truth and if our figures were reduced we refused to accept their decision. After a while we gained their confidence and we had no problems with our submissions. What convinced them was when I showed them the ships' plans and explained there was no point in asking for extra sailors as there were no bunks for them.[18]

In late 1962, just after the delivery of the first Vosper boat, the order was increased to ten. The RMN was also developing its plans to introduce into service an ex-British frigate, the additional minesweepers and landing craft and to develop a base to support its ships patrolling in East Malaysia at Labuan. By July the following year, it had in service a coastal minesweeper, of the same type as the RAN's Ton Class, four inshore minesweepers, two Vosper patrol boats and a dispatch vessel, which doubled as a Royal Yacht. Only one of the motor launches remained in commission, but this change in order of battle required more qualified officers and men. Of the RMN's officer strength in August 1963, of the thirty-eight seconded officers serving, nine were from Australia, with the preponderance at lieutenant commander and lieutenant ranks, and a further nineteen were being sought 'to meet the requirements for the expansion of the Armed Forces necessitated by the formation of Malaysia'.[19]

On Malaysia Day the Singapore Division of the MRNVR became part of the RMNVR and two of its ships were commissioned into the RMN; as well, the Singapore Women's Auxiliary Naval Service also came under Malaysian control. Synnot also strengthened his Naval Staff Division in MINDEF, which now had four sections — Plans and Operations, Technical, Personnel and Training, and Logistics and Finance — almost a mirror image of the Australian naval staff organisation, except that it only had fifteen personnel. The rapid expansion of the RMN in accordance with Plan MAIDEN, a seven year plan devised by Synnot for fleet and shore base expansion, was to place this organisation under considerable strain during the coming decade, especially with the levels of inexperience in junior RMN officers posted to the staff division. There were other issues. In the early 1960s, working in a joint service environment was a novelty to the RAN personnel, a situation that the dominance of the Malaysian Army made almost inevitable in Kuala Lumpur. The Australian officers took their turn at performing as the Duty Staff Officer in MINDEF, which had the virtue of keeping them informed of what was happening on the front line. But naval officers believe that their service's ways of doing things have evolved from experience and the special needs of naval operations, and in Malaysia the most obvious difference of opinion with Army ways was evident in the logistics world. One RAN loan officer scoffed that:

> The Malaysian armed forces all conformed to the Army system, which was a hangover from the British system, whereby every man received a measured quantity of the various ingredients each day, down to '1/16 oz. pepper'. This system went back to the days of the Raj, when officers, unskilled in matters of nutrition simply had to 'follow the book'. But it depended on the rations trucks rolling though the gate every morning, and took no account of climatic conditions or, for that matter, what was held on board. The RN learned back in the days of Pepys that a victualling allowance system was to be preferred, as it enabled ultimate flexibility.[20]

In January 1965 an Australian lieutenant commander joined the Joint Services Staff Division with the task of establishing the Malaysian naval intelligence organisation. Service intelligence was a totally joint responsibility — a strong lesson learned from the Emergency — and the naval intelligence officer attended police special branch briefings, participated in agent-running activities into Indonesia and maintained a strong personal and professional liaison with the Intelligence staff of the Commander Far East Fleet in Singapore. Through this link he was able to advise which cross-strait traffic should be watched and which should not be interfered with, contributing part of the picture used to guide the operations staff in the deployment of their assets. On occasion he was invited to interrogate captured Indonesian Navy or Marine Corps personnel; interestingly, these were almost invariably conducted in English and not *Bahasa*.[21] Naval intelligence was a new skill for all involved, but the development of this Malaysian capability was an important contribution made by the RAN.

Synnot also obtained permission for an increase in the size of the RMN's manpower, a doubling of strength to 2000 officers and men over four years.[22] The new navy not only needed more manpower but also improved specialist skills as it contemplated the additional 1200 miles of coastline it would now be called upon to patrol and protect.

The professional standards of the RMN were of particular concern to its RAN commanders. Dovers had arranged for an Australian officer to be posted on loan in September 1961 to be the seagoing commander of the RMN's ships, with the title Senior Officer Ships and the task of improving the operational efficiency of the force. Lieutenant Commander John Lancaster took over his command on the run.

> On arrival in Singapore/Malaysia, I was at sea within two days as the only European in a 'foreign' ship — a situation that changed little for the ensuing eighteen months. There was no opportunity for either formal language training or other indigenous indoctrination. As far as I can recall there was, in fact, no 'in country training' available, at that time. Without sounding pompous there was not a great need for it for 'Sailors are Sailors' irrespective of their ethnic backgrounds. I was to find, in fact that I had a very good team of both Officers and Sailors. Language was sometimes a barrier and led to a few misunderstandings, which were soon sorted, without acrimony.[23]

This ship's company of KD *Mahamiru* was fortunate in having a strong component of the 'old' RMN sailors, typically with at least five years experience, and the beneficiaries of specialist training with the RN.[24] Lancaster remarked that:

> I had an excellent, experienced Malay Coxswain, an eccentric Tamil-Malay Chief Boatswains Mate, who insisted in calling himself 'Black Joe', an excellent Chinese Malay Yeoman of Signals — who never faltered and, generally speaking my ships company ranging from 'Kampong Malays' to Indian/Tamil, Chinese Malaysians of good education were a reliable hard working team

— who were 'put to the task — watch-on-watch' on a couple of occasions; without complaint. The range of training and experience varied considerably — for which allowances were made. [25]

The main problem was that minesweeping had been neglected because of the demands on the ship's time in patrolling the median line between Indonesia and Malaya. The major task was to act to deter attacks on cross-strait traders and Malayan fishing boats by Indonesian customs launches, which were engaged in a very lucrative piracy and kidnapping for ransom enterprise in the straits. Understandably skills in the ship's primary purpose had deteriorated, but Lancaster was determined to change that, and succeeded. As his chief boatswain's mate recalled:

I served on board KD *Mahamiru*, the first Ton Class minesweeper as the ship's buffer [senior seaman petty officer] under the command of then Lieutenant commander John Lancaster RAN for two years in which time we took part in several minesweeping exercises with different commonwealth navies in the Indian Ocean, Arabian Sea and South China Sea. I would say under his command all the exercises were completed successfully without incident.[26]

Other officers were also requested from Australia to command the ships of the growing RMN, and the RAN responded quickly. This caused some personal upheaval for one of them.

I was bringing back HMAS *Snipe* on her delivery voyage [1962]. Because I was suitably qualified by specialisation [Navigation] and, more importantly, by being single, I was sent at very short notice for two years loan to the RMN. I needed an explanation less than most people because I had just had eighteen months loan service with the Royal Navy minesweepers in Singapore, and I'd been in contact with the RMN quite a bit.[27]

What the Australian officers found was a navy in dire need operational and tactical rigour. One found himself senior officer of a four-ship squadron of inshore minesweepers, only one of which was commanded by a Malayan; the other two had RN captains. The remainder of the ships' companies were all Malayan and, although generally competent, their ships were old and the drills they practised were based on RN doctrine of some years before and were out of date by the naval standards of the 1960s. The basics were the same as in the RAN, but conducted at a lower professional standard, and more slowly. The ships rarely operated in company.

On one occasion — this was before Confrontation: everything was at peace, it was a happy little time to be there — I forecast that all four of the ships in my little squadron [26th Minesweeping Squadron] were going to be out of refit, so I planned an exercise period for two weeks. We sailed up into the Indian Ocean and had four ships playing on constant exercises, which went very well.[28]

At the end of 1963 the RMN had sixteen patrol craft in commission, including the first of the very effective Vosper fast patrol boats, and was expanding towards a target strength of 1700 all ranks by the end of 1964.[29] Apart from the Chief of Naval Staff, the RAN had six other officers and two senior sailors on secondment 'free of cost to Malaysia'. The Staff Operations Officer was an Australian, and four RAN officers were commanding RMN units.[30] However, this rapid expansion was causing problems for the RMN, as one RAN loan commanding officer noted.

The vessel was an ex-RN Ham class inshore minesweeper, about 150 tons, 110 feet in length and a crew of 22 Malaysians. The only other officer, as First Lieutenant, was a Chinese Malaysian midshipman who had been in the RMN for eight months! He had little seagoing experience and was still working towards attaining his bridge watchkeeping certificate.

The crew were all Malaysian of Chinese, Malay and Indian mix. Electrical/communications categories were mostly Chinese or Indian, with the Malay Malaysians occupying seaman, cooks, MEs [marine engineering] and stores category billets. Some spoke little or no English and the expression and understanding of those who did was limited. Some of the more senior sailors spoke and understood English quite well. Their knowledge of naval glossary and jargon was minimal.[31]

Loan officers found that standards of RMN ship husbandry and cleanliness were generally below those acceptable in the RAN. Living and communal quarters were not well kept and this sloppiness extended even to the weapons. The older ships deteriorated rapidly both physically and mechanically, and it was difficult to get spare parts to effect repairs. RMN ships were refitted in a commercial dockyard in Singapore. Their commanding officers, on occasion redeployed to other ships, thus not providing continuity to oversight the progression of the ship's refit and for its timely completion. Commenting on his February 1965 posting to one of the new Vosper craft, which had been in refit for five months, an Australian officer recorded:

The state of the vessel of its age is deplorable, but in view of the fact it has been in refit etc. no CO for ages ... what else?? Parts of machinery/spares etc. are being taken off her at the rate of gunfire. Nobody cares, nobody fusses — 'Take it', seems the attitude.[32]

The Australians made it their business to bring the RMN up to speed as soon as possible, but the use by some of them of Australian modes of speech and the uncompromising way in which their efforts were visited upon the Malaysians were not always immediately appreciated, as one RMN officer recalled.

I mean, he was very good as Staff Officer Operations but he

was very blunt, and I think this is a thing that you learn from Australians. He was very straightforward like that, especially when he thought that ships had to go to sea: whether you had one defect or two defects, he just sent you off.[33]

There were encouraging signs that the Malaysian personnel were keen to learn and apply their improving skills. Prior to Confrontation, KD *Lanka Suka*, an inshore minesweeper under the command of Lieutenant Commander Ron Titcombe RAN, responded to distress calls from a merchant ship in the vicinity of Raffles Light in Singapore Strait. It transpired that the ship was aground, but by skilful use of his small ship, Titcombe and his crew were able to tow the merchant ship clear. This feat demonstrated a high level of RMN seamanship and training and was worthy enough, but Titcombe also pulled off another of more direct interest to all concerned in successfully lodging a claim through Lloyd's of London for salvage money. The money was split amongst his ship's company in the proportions laid down by the Admiralty, which must have made all very happy. This remains the only successful salvage claim in the history of the RMN.[34]

Australia wasn't only contributing manpower to the development of the RMN; there was also a considerable program of defence aid. The naval component of this involved the provision of a variety of small craft, spare parts and other equipment, as well as a number of training aids for the KD *Malaya* schools and courses in Australia. In some cases, these were at least as important as the RAN loan personnel, and this made an impression on the Malaysian officers.

The other thing I remember about the RAN is that just after Confrontation started we had a lot of these problems in Sibu and in the Rejang River and so on — Indonesian Communism, and the RAN gave us about ten or fifteen workboats which we could deploy up the River Rejang. I remember I was commanding a tank landing ship KD *Sri Langkawi*, and we used to go up the river and anchor off Sibu and we'd be the mother ship while these smaller workboats given by the RAN were used to go deeper up to Kapit and all those places which were not navigable by bigger boats. So I think that type of assistance was great then to control the spread of Indonesian Communist influence into those areas.[35]

The Australian commanders of the RMN were well aware of the need for a sound support and training base for the growing fleet. The main RMN base was at Woodlands on the north shore of Singapore Island, and it remained there even after the split of Singapore from the Federation of Malaysia in 1965.[36] It was a large and well-appointed establishment with offices, messes, stores, barracks, classrooms and a large parade ground. Not only did it train and house the majority of the RMN, but the postings of RMN personnel around the navy and fleet were organised from KD *Malaya*. The position of Base Commander was thus an important one and from early 1962 it was filled by an Australian officer for almost ten years. But the major shortage was of experienced and professionally qualified officers and senior sailors to run the establishment and to man its schools. Britain, New Zealand and India agreed to provide some, and others came from the RAN. One who volunteered said:

A signal circulated in the RAN in 1963 calling for volunteers to be loaned to the RMN for a period of two and a half years, and Stores Petty Officer was one of the categories. I had served in HMAS *Parramatta* for just under three years and I was due for a change. There was insufficient time for language training, cultural or ethnic issues etc. I joined KD *Malaya* on 19 September 1963. We completed the draft-in routine and reported to the Clothing Store to be issued with badges and buttons of the RMN, and I reported to the RMN Logistics Officer.[37]

There was a maintenance facility for the RMN's ships at Woodlands, closer to the causeway linking Singapore to the Malayan state of Johore, known as Maintenance Base Johore (MBJ). As will be described later, its capabilities were to develop markedly with the influx of senior maintenance personnel from other navies, but initially the upkeep of the older ships proved something of a problem. Some Australian sailors found themselves 'loaned' to the RMN on an ad hoc basis in an attempt to correct this. In June 1963 two leading electricians from HMAS *Voyager* were sent to join KD *Ledang* in response to an urgent call for assistance from KD *Malaya*.

> Anyway, we arrived there with our tool boxes and everything else, and we were immediately placed on a Ton Class minesweeper, which was going to sea that day but could not join in the minesweeping exercises because nothing worked. They had an EM on board who knew bugger all — I don't know where he got his training from. So we spent a couple of weeks on her and got everything fixed — the sweep generator working again, the radar working, most electrical items working; I think the only things that were working at the time were the lights and the radio. The rest was all cactus but we got it all fixed again.[38]

Having repaired the electrical systems in *Ledang*, on that ship's return to harbour they transferred to KD *Mahamiru* to perform the same service, but remained alongside. This exchange seems to have been arranged on the 'old boy network' because of the absence of official paperwork and the lack of any expression of thanks for their services. The incident does demonstrate deficiencies in RMN training which Australians, amongst others, were expected to correct.

They were not to have much time to do so, as the Indonesian Government decided to 'confront' Malaysia soon after its formation in September 1963. During Confrontation the RMN contributed one frigate and twenty-five smaller vessels to the Commonwealth naval anti-infiltration effort. It was a considerable effort for a small and developing navy.[39] Despite their training and experience deficiencies, the Malaysian sailors proved adept at their principal task — the interception, boarding and interrogation of suspect vessels operating in Malaysian waters. On occasion, these could number up to fifty in a twenty-four hour period. RMN ships commanded by both indigenous officers and by RAN personnel were fully involved in operations during Confrontation. Their principal operating areas were East Brigade in East Malaysia and in the Singapore and Malacca Straits.[40] This chapter is not a history of RMN operations, but it would be an incomplete record were the RAN contribution made to the growth, development, training and operational maturing of the RMN during this critical period in its life not mentioned.[41] The RAN commanding officer of an RMN ship described his ship's routine while on patrol:

> Boarding parties, comprising about five crew, were all carrying rifles and pistols, and all precautions were taken to prevent shots being fired at us, or at the barter boat personnel. I must say the crew were very conversant and familiar with their weapons. They were firm and fair in their dealings with the crew of sampans, barter boats and motor launches. The boarding crew would conduct the entire boarding, talking to the Indonesians and interpreting for me with the replies.[42]

After the curtailment of the barter trade in 1964, when the pressure on the Commonwealth vessels patrolling the Singapore and Malacca Straits eased, RMN ships were often deployed to East Malaysia, and especially to Tawau. Here, as will be explained in more detail in the next chapter, they were facing Indonesian shore defences, which frequently conducted 'harassment and interdiction' fire missions on Commonwealth ships moored close to the national boundary line. A different set of skills was needed here, as one RAN loan commanding officer, explained:

> During one patrol I arranged to conduct an exercise 'Ocean Grove' … to see how quickly my crew could activate action stations, weigh anchor, fire the guns and get speed underway to withdraw the ship away from Indonesian firepower at a time of being in hazardous waterways. Within two minutes of commencing, the

assault boats which lay alongside were away, the anchor was virtually 'home', the ship underway, a rocket flare had been fired, 'A' mounting [forward 40 mm] had jammed, the ship had turned and was proceeding at 1175 revs and the after mount had fired five rounds … Not withstanding some of my thoughts about the efficiency of the RMN crews, it was an event like the foregoing which gave me some confidence that they could do the job, i.e., they were learning.[43]

Captain Synnot relinquished his command of the RMN in March 1965 as Confrontation raged. During his term he had strengthened and developed the themes set in place by Dovers. He had taken the new navy through its first period of large-scale expansion, and led it into its first military conflict, in which it was acquitting itself well. His polished style contrasted nicely with the more extrovert personality of his predecessor, and he ensured that RAN influence on the RMN's organisation, training and operations were well entrenched. He too was made a member of the *Johan Mangku Negara* for his service to Malaysia at a critical time in the nation's development. There is a very typical story told of him by a former RMN patrol boat captain.

Shortly after being appointed as CO of our first patrol craft I had to take Captain Synnot … on his first visit to Penang. On the return journey we had to go through the narrow channel that separates Penang from Butterworth. I was being extra careful as Synnot was on the bridge with me. I was busy keeping the transits in line when Synnot whispered in my ear; 'Babu, how many ferries are there in Penang?' My answer was, 'Three', and then, 'PORT THIRTY!' A ferry was very close and on a steady bearing! Such was the tact of this man no one else on the bridge noticed what had happened.[44]

Synnot was succeeded by the third and last of the RAN commanders of the RMN, Commodore A.N. (Ed) Dollard.[45] The RMN at the time was assisting in dealing with the massive increase in infiltration attempts by the Indonesians while, at the same time, passions between Malaysia and Singapore were on the rise. As is explained in more detail in Chapter 5, these were to culminate in the secession of Singapore from the Malaysian federation in August 1965, leaving the RMN's main base in 'foreign' territory. It was a difficult situation, and one which called for a high order of calmness and negotiating skills to ensure that the RMN weathered the storm in good order. Dollard succeeded in forestalling the Singaporean zeal to withdraw its nationals from the RMN immediately — as happened with its ground and air forces — in favour of an orderly separation to be completed by early the following year. On 1 February 1966 the Republic of Singapore Navy was established, with the personnel of the RMNVR Singapore Division becoming the Singapore Naval Volunteers. All of its vessels were recommissioned as Republic of Singapore Ships (RSS), except for the patrol boat *Panglima*, which continued to serve with the RMN under Malaysian command and colours until October 1966.

Meanwhile, Confrontation continued. Demonstrating a growing capability in Malaysian commanding officers, in July 1965 while on patrol near St John's Light in Singapore Strait, the Vosper patrol boat KD *Sri Selangor*, with Lieutenant P.K. ('Babu') Nettur RMN in command, detected a darkened contact moving from the Riau Archipelago towards Singapore at high speed. Nettur ordered his crew to action stations and closed the contact, challenging it to stop when it was close ahead. The intruder craft responded with its identity as 'KKO'— the Indonesian Marine Corps — and opened fire on *Sri Selangor* with automatic weapons, killing one sailor and wounding two others. The Malaysians replied with fire from their 40/70 Bofors and machine-guns, killing the five marines and sinking their boat. It was a spirited action pressed home with determination, for which Nettur was awarded a Commendation for Brave Conduct.

Then, on 5 September 1965, the Vosper patrol Boat KD *Sri Kelantan* commanded by Lieutenant James Buchanan RAN intercepted an Indonesian sampan, again in Singapore Strait. When the ship closed to investigate, the occupants of the sampan lobbed two grenades towards it, fortunately missing their target. Buchanan then took the sampan under fire, killing two Indonesians and sinking their vessel.

As befitted an officer with a distinguished record of taking the fight to the enemy in Korea, CNS Dollard, apparently with the backing of the other Malaysian service chiefs, was in favour of a vigorous response to Indonesian incursions, possibly including retaliatory or even pre-emptive strikes against the bases from which the infiltration attempts were launched. They were not, however, able to gain the support of the British for this. Dollard recalled:

> Our plans to pursue *Konfrontasi* in a more aggressive manner were frustrated in many respects by the British in Singapore. I knew the British navy there and I met them often during the period and we were on friendly terms, but they did not see eye to eye with us on our position on *Konfontasi*. Vice Admiral McNicoll [Australian CNS] remarked approvingly upon my disagreement with the British naval command in Singapore, which I was pleased to hear, because I was treading on pretty delicate ground.[46]

However, following an attempted coup in Jakarta in September 1965, the pace of Confrontation relented somewhat, but the drive to impress upon RMN personnel the need to master all aspects of the naval profession continued unabated. Exercises embarked on included operating in company with other ships — something the RMN rarely did — manoeuvring and station-keeping, and familiarisation with the associated tactical signals. In the coastal minesweeper KD *Jerai*, a ship similar to those in RAN service, which had been commissioned in the UK in April 1964 and been delivered to Malaysia by an RMN crew, the RAN loan commanding officer and his RMN first lieutenant put the ship's company through a series of seamanship and shipboard evolutions — laying and recovering marker buoys, exercising fire and emergency parties, conducting transfers with other ships, and giving his junior officers experience in manoeuvring the ship.

Utilizing my previous time serving in [HMAS] *Snipe*, I was able to contribute towards the review and update of the Ship's Standing Orders for the Ton Class ships of the RMN, but more particularly the writing of the Minesweeping Departmental Orders. Up to early/mid-1966 virtually no minesweeping tasks had been performed, hence when loop, displacer or hammer sweeps were streamed upon activation they would not work or else 'burnouts' would occur shortly thereafter. Minesweeping was an innovation for the RMN.[47]

These new-found skills were to be tested in April 1966 when *Jerai* represented the RMN in a Commonwealth five-day mine countermeasures exercise off Langkawi Island. *Jerai* and her crew performed well and the ship was subsequently awarded the Cormack Cup for minesweeping.

Confrontation officially came to an end in August 1966, but the modernisation and upgrading of the RMN order of battle put in place by Captain Synnot continued. The RMN ordered a new frigate and introduced into service a new class of gas-turbine powered fast patrol boat, also of British design. Dollard took a close interest in these craft.

They were already on the drawing board, and I followed up the work of my predecessor. I was fairly well acquainted in the end with Vospers, and I trialled the first of the fast patrol boats. We had some problems with that. They would heel over unexpectedly and unsatisfactorily in a quite frightening way in a sharp turn. To overcome this we set the adjustable trim ramp at the stern in a permanently horizontal position. This extended the waterline length of the boat, giving it added stability, which overcame this problem, while not detracting from its manoeuvrability. So they came out like that and were beautiful boats — the fastest boats in the world at the time they were launched.[48]

With the end of Confrontation came the strong desire to see all senior positions in the Malaysian Armed Forces filled by indigenous officers. An important challenge was presented to two RAN officers — the commanding officer KD *Malaya* and Commodore Dollard — in early 1967, when the question of who should replace the latter as CNS came up. It had to be a Malaysian officer, but which one? The Minister of Defence had made it clear that he wanted to Malaysianise the position as quickly as possible but without putting anyone at risk. As Dollard put it:

> The selection of my successor involved three Malaysian officers, one of Malay, one Chinese and the other of Tamil origin. The Defence Minister clearly preferred to have a Malay national in the post of CNS, but my recommendation that this officer, while of excellent ability, was at the time too young and inexperienced was accepted, leaving the choice between the other two, of whom I recommended Lieutenant Commander Thanabalasingham. Again, the defence minister's preference was for the Chinese, but the Tamil won the day on general assessment of ability in all areas of naval activities.
>
> Thanabalasingham served successfully as CNS for some eight years and the Malay officer previously rejected on the grounds of youth and inexperience then became CNS and served successfully in that post. This decision to make a Tamil officer the first Malaysian CNS could only have been a severe disappointment for the Chinese officer and for others who had aspirations for high command, but it was accepted stoically. [49]

So, the thirty-two-year-old Lieutenant Commander Thanabalasingham Karalasingam, popularly known as 'Thana', who had just twelve years naval service, was selected to become Chief of the Malaysian Navy. Following a six month stint in command of the frigate KD *Hang Tuah* and a month's tour of Australian naval training establishments and dockyards, he relieved Commodore Dollard as RMN CNS on 1 December 1967.[50] It was a significant step for Malaysians, and ushered in a complete change in the RAN-RMN relationship.

Dollard's tenure had been marked by a number of delicate transitions for the nation and its navy, building on the work of his predecessors but also dealing with the separation of Singapore, the intense Indonesian activity of 1965 and the end of Confrontation, British plans for a withdrawal of forces (see Chapter 6) and the rising tide of Malaysianisation. Less flamboyant than his predecessors, he had nevertheless steered his command to a successful conclusion of all these endeavours, and had played a major role in the selection of his successor. Not without cause, he too was admitted to the Order of Defender of the Nation, with a *Johan Mengku Negara*.

With a Malaysian officer now as chief of the RMN, the unusual task of Adviser to the CNS, also in the rank of Commodore, was assigned to Captain G.R. Griffiths RAN.

> I was fitted out with an office in MinDef, introduced to Thana, and so on. There were no particular terms of reference for the Adviser; there was nothing that had been pre-discussed, so to speak, about the relationship between the Adviser and CNS. And I guess it would have been a little difficult to do it, but I don't think it would have been impossible to draw up some guidelines, even for discussion between the Adviser and CNS. But we were basically left to our own devices, and with the fact that we met on a solid basis, so to speak, I think we worked it out pretty well in our mutual acknowledgment of each other's position.[51]

In fact the situation was anomalous for both officers. Thana was conscious of the need to establish himself as CNS, in deed as well as word, with his political masters, within the Ministry of Defence, with his fellow service chiefs and, most importantly, with his navy. To be seen to be dependent on a foreign adviser would not have advanced this cause. Yet, at the same time, access to the advice of a more senior and experienced officer was a benefit for a young and relatively inexperienced service chief. The relationship was complicated by the fact that Thana already had one such officer integrated into his chain of command in the form of an RN captain fulfilling the duties of chief of staff. It was not Griffiths' place to interpose himself in the chain of command, let alone be the sounding board on which Thana could test his Chief of Staff's opinions.

> The more Thana put his feet under the desk, the less inclined he was to discuss things with me that he had already, obviously, discussed with his Chief of Staff. Why go to Griffiths before he discussed it with his Chief of Staff, [who] would have been giving him quite sound advice? What was the point? Also, I think, within his local hierarchy, not only within the RMN but in the Ministry of Defence, he couldn't be seen, in their culture, appealing, often, to his Adviser. He wanted to gain his own confidence and do his own thing — as we all remember in the Service — and, as I've said, he wanted to establish his position of authority over the RMN.[52]

Not that the CNS did not consult his Adviser, but this was done informally and often not within the confines of the Ministry of Defence. He was a welcome dinner guest in the Griffiths' home, and the occasional round of golf also provided opportunities for Thana to sound out Griffiths on ideas that he was considering and developing. This was not, however, full-time employment for a senior RAN officer and Griffiths looked for an opening in which he could employ his skills and experience to assist the CNS and the RMN.

> Now I think it was probably after this had rolled on for six or seven months, with both of us finding our feet — and he certainly was, I suggested that he might like me to look into personnel and training. He was delighted, actually, because he hadn't really had the time to do anything about training or to review it, and he didn't really have a chief of personnel. He had a training cell, but that was directly under the Chief of Staff and didn't come to

Thana. So I said; 'Would you like me to look at training?'[53]

Within the Naval Staff, training and personnel matters were the responsibility of a training cell headed by an Indian officer while, as mentioned, postings were made by KD *Malaya* in Singapore. The post-Confrontation need for training for the future fleet and the expansion of the RMN to meet this task was a topical and important issue in need of expertise and coordination. Despite Thana's endorsement of Griffiths' proposal, the Adviser had to take great care not to interfere in the RMN system. Instead, he began a series of visits to the fleet and to training schools to discuss training needs and equipment and to develop suggestions for formal RMN consideration.

So you had to weave your way into this quite carefully, without saying; 'We're going to do this, that and the other', but eventually I went to talk to [KD *Malaya*] about their training facilities and training equipment, and the trainers, I think, were delighted to have somebody they could talk to in some detail about training. And that seemed to work out pretty well.[54]

Until 1967 the position of Training Commander had been filled by a loan officer who held that rank or was given acting rank for the duration of his postings. The schools under his command took RMN recruits from their initial entry training through to training in many specialist categories. The staff of these schools was a mixture of loan and RMN officers, assisted by experienced senior sailors from the RN, RMN, RAN, RNZN and the Indian Navy in both managerial and instructional roles. The organisation had coped well with the strains of Confrontation, but there were deficiencies in the syllabi and the training aids provided. As well, the Malaysians were keen to reduce the number of loan personnel in the RMN, which led to a loss of experience. Finally, there had been some interesting decisions taken on appropriate training. The RAN commanding officer recalled one example.

One of the problems that I had was that MINDEF in an absolute aberration decided that the Cookery School should be disbanded and all the cooks should train with the Army. So off they packed them … and from the first draft I got back I sent one of these cooks to a patrol boat, and the patrol boat came in and said, 'Please send me a cook'. They had taught them how to cook in the jungle in a field kitchen and, given a patrol boat's modern galley, he didn't know what to do.[55]

Another school at KD *Malaya* with strong Australian involvement was the Radio School, which taught the principles and practicalities of radio and radar to RMN maintenance personnel, officers and sailors. From September 1966 the senior instructor was an Australian chief petty officer.

I was in charge of all the instructors, plus I did some instructing myself. I had one Australian petty officer, two Indian petty officers from the Indian Navy, and two RN chiefs and petty officers, who did not react all that well to Australian domination. The RN sent their chiefs and petty officers out there, and I imagine they briefed them as well as our blokes briefed us, and so when they set up the Radio School they were teaching the Malaysian Navy blokes about the stuff that was in British ships, which they didn't have.[56]

Lack of practical skills by the RMN students was a major concern, so that senior sailors were still doing basic equipment training. Fortunately the RMN had purchased additional items of their electronic equipment in ships for use as training spares, and the Australian defence aid program had provided an electronics trainer for the school. When unpacked from the delivery crates in which it had been sitting for two years, the students were able to apply their classroom lessons with practical electronics experiments and demonstrations. Advanced courses for officers were provided by the RN in the UK, but the failure rate by RMN students was alarmingly high, an apparently necessary price for the young navy to have to pay. The RAN senior instructor took up the issue at the highest level.

> I said to Commodore Thanabalasingham; 'How come you still promote these blokes when they come back?' He said; 'Well, we operate on the system that the ones who have been to England know more than the ones that haven't'. That's true too; they might not have been up to our standards, but they were better than they had been.[57]

Outside the KD *Malaya* boundaries and closer to the causeway linking the island to Malaya was Woodlands, the main RN ammunition depot and site of the RMN maintenance and logistic support base. RMN logistics were interesting — to say the least. The Logistics Depot had been established to provide technical and supply services to the fleet, but it was not always in a position to do so. Victualling of ships, for example, was the responsibility of the Malaysian Army, which posted an officer to the base for the purpose, and rations were issued to ships on the same basis as army formations.[58] Common use items were also supplied through the Army, which was sometimes reluctant to supply them. The major challenge was supporting the ships. Petrol oil and lubricants could be obtained from RN sources and older vessels could also be supported by indents on RN stores, but the new Vosper patrol boats proved an engineering and logistics challenge, as one RAN loan officer explained:

> They got twelve patrol boats, six of them Vospers and those six had Mercedes engines made under licence by Bristol Siddeley and the other six had engines made by Maybach in Germany. They were 99.9 per cent compatible, but the spares were all different … so if we wanted a valve which was out of a Maybach we didn't know if the British spares would fit. What they did is take a complete engine down, piece by piece and try it bit by bit, and got a cross-over then.[59]

The storekeeping system used by the RMN also left a lot to be desired in comparison with RAN practice. While the RMN staff were very familiar with their job, because there was nothing like the posting turbulence experienced in the RAN, their level of understanding of the task was not high in the opinion of their Australian officers.

I don't think that there was such a thing as a book of reference, whereas we had ABR 4, the Naval Stores Handbook … It was a hybrid mixture of the RN system and the Malaysian Army system — a bit of both. Mostly it was the old RN ledgers; computers were in their infancy and we had nothing at all — it was all handwritten in ledgers … My main thing with logistics was trying to get what was in the store equal to what was on the ledger.[60]

During Confrontation there was little emphasis placed on manuals or paperwork; the main task was to keep the patrol boats operational. But this was not a sustainable concept for establishing logistics support of the RMN on an ongoing basis. Proper doctrine and procedures were required, as an RAN senior sailor on loan observed.

Towards the end of my loan service I had the notion of taking the ABR 4 RAN Storekeeping Manual and rewriting it to suit RMN conditions. It would be rebadged MBR4 Malaysian Storekeeping Manual, just like we did to the Admiralty publication BR4. Maybe the idea went the way of the Army relevant publications also! I compiled my own notes for the logistics lectures — based on getting the right supplies to the right people in the quickest possible time available.[61]

But some paperwork was essential and the logistics staff members were integral parts of the refit planning process, with the responsibility of identifying the sources for the spares required by the maintenance staff and arranging for their delivery. This involved the compilation and updating of establishment lists for ships and other relevant technical publications, a task generally undertaken by RAN loan personnel with experience in this area.[62] This exercise revealed an unexpectedly high usage of some spare parts, which puzzled the RAN loan staff.

> We could not understand why we had an unusually high turnover in supplying Jabsco pump impellers to the fleet. It came to pass that the predominantly Malay technical seamen, when the need arose, started the pump to disperse water from a compartment, etc. On completion of the task, they would forget or deem it unnecessary to turn off the pump. In failing to do so the impeller blades were worn out. *Tidak apa* — no matter; tomorrow is another day.[63]

Another issue to arise from having the RMN base located in an independent Singapore was that of the import of weapons and ammunition through the Singaporean customs controls, which listed these as prohibited imports. There were ways to circumvent these, but RAN loan personnel had to use patience and experience to find them.

> If you got spare [armaments] parts, to get them unloaded in Singapore was hell of a job. Both the Malaysians and the Singaporeans adopted the British bureaucracy right to the nth degree. I suppose it was the same anywhere — the reddest of red tape. You had to know the right way around it or you were done. You had to wait for Mr So-and-so to put his chop on it, or he was at lunch, or had gone home. That was one of the things we sorted out over time.[64]

The Maintenance Section at MBJ had the responsibility for operational maintenance of the RMN's ships. Major refits were conducted in commercial yards in Singapore, but the section did all the work on weapons and minesweeping systems. The staff comprised a mixed bag of RMN, RN, RAN, RNZN and Indian Navy senior sailors, all very experienced and competent. One of the Australians remarked:

> Whatever they wanted you to do, you did. The ordnance we had up there were 40/70s — they were Bofors but a different type of Bofors, so there was a real learning curve. When we got them they were brand new from Sweden and everything had to be translated from their language to ours. Someone had done it before I got there, but everything was metric and I wasn't. And there were a lot of acoustic displacer and acoustic hammers for the minesweepers, which I hadn't seen before, but they were easy — really farm machinery. They used to work though.[65]

Keeping the older ships running was a trial, but the big challenge for the Maintenance Section were the new Vosper boats, shipped from the UK as deck cargo on merchant ships and delivered to Woodlands still in their shipping cradles. Divers then were sent down to detach the cradle and to manoeuvre it clear of the vessel.

The RMN had patrol boats deployed in both East and West Malaysia and, as will be explained in more detail in Chapter 5, in East Malaysian waters there were plenty of floating hazards against which the boats could and did damage their propellers. While removing the damaged propeller and replacing it was relatively straightforward — provided there had been no distortion of the shaft — to do so required the boat to be slipped. This may have taken the boat out of service for several weeks even if a vacant slipway could be found, and therein lay a problem. So there were big advantages to be gained, including a quick turnaround and the saving of thousands of ringgits by not having to use a civilian shipyard if a way could be found to effect propeller changes with the boat still in the water. An Australian senior sailor did just that.

> This is why the Base Engineer encouraged me to develop underwater prop changes. I started off just a couple of days a

week diving, and in the end I was in and out of the water all the time because they kept bringing these boats back to MBJ with bent propellers. The diving team had pretty good stuff, there was some RN gear but it was mostly commercial Siebe Gorman gear. BR I55 — the Diving Manual — was our bible.

For the screw changes I made the withdrawing gear and when I broke the first one, I had to remodel it and make it stronger, and it worked from that time on. So a Chinese guy — Peter Chua — who was very strong, and I had to crack these boss nuts like you wouldn't believe.[66]

There is, of course, a big difference between training and experience. For a service undergoing the rapid expansion that the RMN was, only time could supply the second, but there were plenty of ways in which its training syllabi and equipment could be enhanced. Augmentation of in-house capabilities was one and, where the cost or small numbers involved made a Malaysian course uneconomical, access could be requested for RMN students in foreign training establishments. Griffiths headed a team of RMN officers who visited Australia in 1968 to look at opportunities in RAN schools, and this later resulted in formal arrangements for RMN apprentices to be trained in HMAS *Nirimba* from July 1969.[67] RMN clearance divers had been training at HMAS *Rushcutter* since 1965.[68] One Malaysian recalled how he came to be selected for the RAN course.

So I did my shallow water course in Plymouth; it took up four weeks of my summer leave, and I only had three weeks to travel round Europe. So I'd made a sacrifice and I was very happy once I qualified. I was breathing pure oxygen all the time, which is what clearance divers use in their course. When I came back to the Malaysian Navy, Ron Titcombe [RAN commanding officer], of course, was a clearance diver and he encouraged me, so I said I'd like to apply for a course. The first two of us were sent here in 1965, and I did a year of that.[69]

From this small beginning the RMN Diving branch was to grow. Basic skills training was done in Malaysia, then the divers went to Australia for specialist courses. Training and procedures were based on RAN doctrine. From May 1967 the Branch was led by RMN officers trained in Sydney while, in country, RAN assistance was also provided.

> I trained a few of the divers; I wasn't supposed to. In our navy I would have had my knuckles slapped but there they used to get me to go down with these young fellows to see if they were game enough. They'd stand on a ladder in their diving gear and you in your diving gear and you'd encourage them a bit, and they'd step down one rung and be up to there in water. 'OK?' 'Yes', and then down another rung. 'OK mate?' 'Good'. If you call that training, that's what I used to do.[70]

The RAN Hydrographic Service at HMAS *Penguin* was also training RMN survey recorders. In fact, in 1968 the RAN was also considering RMN requests for sea training for midshipmen, hydrographic officers as well as mechanician training and photography courses. Most of these requests were honoured. The apprentice and artificer training load was accepted by the RAN despite the fact that the commitment was viewed as 'being to the detriment of RAN training in this area'.[71]

Later on, the Malaysian armed forces hosted visits by the RAN School of Training Technology to apply the latest training methods being used in the Australian Navy to train instructors, as one of the school's personnel related.

> Well, in 1971–72 or thereabouts the Navy was doing a lot of things for the Malaysian Navy, as you're aware. Part of that was that they didn't have trained instructors. And we went up there to run instructor courses. We stayed at the Johore Baru Government rest house, and went across the Causeway every day to the Malaysian Navy base in Singapore, KD *Malaya*. I think we ran two

courses there, and finished on a Saturday. On Saturday night we took the train to Kuala Lumpur and then set up the course on the Sunday and then started training at the military base there — I think it was an air base, more than anything else — and we ran a couple of course there.[72]

The team of RAN officers and senior sailors spent five weeks in Malaysia, and were very impressed by the enthusiasm of their Malaysian students and the speed with which they assimilated and applied the new information.

I still remember one sergeant from the armoured corps; I suppose he'd be in charge of a tank. He couldn't speak English, but he gave his presentation using visual aids, and I understood every bit of it. He had drawings of gunsights and how they lined up, and I could understand what he was talking about.[73]

While there were clearly deficiencies in the RMN training system, the conclusion that Griffiths reached was that much was going very well in the area of operations. He was impressed by the efficiency of the organisation of the RMN's Eastern Command based in Labuan in Sabah state, perpetually on alert to defend a difficult coastline against infiltrations by Filipino pirates from Zamboanga, and by the competence of the Malaysian Navy's patrol boat force.

Then I came back and went to sea in a patrol boat from Penang down to Singapore, an overnight patrol. That was interesting; it brought home to me the difficulties they had in guarding the coast. The environment wasn't easy from a national security point of view because there was so much floating about there. Anyway, the overnight patrol and passage was conducted well. And the other time I went to sea was with Lieutenant Commander Babu Nettur, in his gas turbine Vosper high speed boat rushing around the Straits at 40 knots in the middle of the night, with Babu down below looking at his radar screen, as happy as a sand boy, totally professional and confident.[74]

By the time Griffiths' posting to Kuala Lumpur ended there was no further need for Advisers for the Malaysian CNS. In his own words, Griffiths had overseen 'the cautious and sensitive development to ensure that the CNS was in complete control'. It is noteworthy that at the end of a relationship which could have been fraught with complications and ended in disappointment on both sides, Thana said in his report on Griffith's performance of this, in his own words, 'curiously difficult role':

> He has undertaken a considerable number of studies on my behalf, particularly in the training field, and they have resulted in great improvements to the administration of the Navy ... I have greatly benefited from the unstinting help always at hand and have been fortunate in enjoying both the advice and friendship of such an able officer.[75]

Thus ended the RAN's control of or influence over the top job in the RMN. It had been an interesting decade of development, not only of the RMN but of a relationship between two navies that was to continue well into the future.

Official responsibilities aside, and there seems little doubt that these were discharged fully and well by RAN loan personnel, there was also a person-to-person dimension to their period of service with the RMN. The Australians, with few exceptions, had little preparation for their service in Malaysia, apart from some exposure through previous FESR deployments. Most were encountering Malayan society, mores and standards and the demands of the Muslim religion for the first time. They were more familiar with dealing with ethnic Chinese and Indian Malaysians during port visits — especially as many Chinese, in particular, had attended English-language schools. In the remainder of this chapter I have attempted an assessment of how the RAN loan personnel responded to four big issues of their service — RMN professionalism, the Muslim religion, food, language and ethnicity — as they attempted to adjust to their temporary membership of the RMN.

As some of the quotes extracted from interviews have already suggested, mixed impressions about the level of Malaysian naval administrative and operational professionalism were registered by the Australians. Typical of the pre-Confrontation RMN is the following observation by an RAN loan officer:

> The rules were the same: we still used the same tide tables, we still used the same methods of conducting professional affairs within the navy as in our own. It was just at a slightly lower standard, and it tended to be a little slower, unless one made it quicker, in which case one wasn't always appreciated.[76]

However, the goad of active service in Confrontation, the efforts of the loan personnel sent to improve the standards of RMN professionalism, and the return to Malaysia of the young officers from British training, had all assisted in changing Malaysian attitudes towards the need for professionalism, to the satisfaction of the Australians.

> The ships at sea were very enthusiastic about what they were doing. They didn't like the idea of Indonesians attacking their country. *Konfrontasi*, as the Indonesians called it, started off with paratroopers landing in the state of Malacca, and this became primarily, of course, an army operation. Occasionally, the Indonesian police boats caused difficulties by darting towards the Malaysian side and then going back and, occasionally, people shot at each other in the Singapore Straits. The ships at sea were keen and, for the most part, so were those who were ashore.[77]

By the end of Confrontation, and with newer and more capable ships coming into service, the RMN's operational professionalism had reached a very high standard, including in areas which were outside normal RAN operations.

> Well I think for a very young Service, they were quite impressive. Not all the chaps were experienced, but they were gaining experience; they were learning and I think they were learning very fast. From gaining independence in 1957, in ten years they'd come a long way. So I think they were in good shape; you can't do anything about a lack of experience other than acquire it as the years go by. At that particular time [1969] there was an exercise against the Far East Fleet coming down the Strait with *Victorious* and destroyers, and Babu [Nettur] weaved his way in at high speed carried out a good attack on *Victorious*, and they didn't have the faintest idea who he was or where he was.[78]

Somewhat surprisingly, especially in the light of present day efforts by Islamists to suggest the incompatibility of Islam with other faiths, the observance of their religious duties by Muslim Malaysians created few problems for the Australians. Friday was mosque day and in a routine that had strong connections to RAN practice, ceremonial divisions would be held on Friday mornings after which Muslims were free to attend the mosque. At KD *Malaya* buses were provided for the purpose.[79]

> We all worked pretty happily together. Like on Friday afternoons would be mosque day. They would all trot off to the mosque with their little *songkoks* [traditional Malay brimless caps] on and we would go wherever we wanted to go. But we had to make up for it on Saturday mornings. It was one of the best parts of my naval career, I would say.[80]

The religious faith issue was of particular importance to the commanding officers of KD *Malaya*, who had to be even-handed in their observance of the customs of their multi-faith ship's company.

I wore a *songkok* if I went to essentially religious Islamic functions, and my wife wore Malay dress on those occasions. I don't know if I told you that all my children went to Malay schools. That meant that we were very much closer to the families of the more senior Malays. But for weddings and other things, I was invited by the Imam on a number of occasions to go to a mosque with them. Fundamentally, I was invited to Buddhist ceremonies, Malay ceremonies and Hindu ceremonies, and I went to them all.[81]

Respondents noted only three other incidents affiliated with religious belief, one to do with the practice of the ritual killing of animals for food, one with food considered by Muslims as 'unclean' and the other to do with personal cleanliness.

[An RAN commanding officer] One of the things I first found I had to get used to was that when we parked our little ship, for example, in Port Swettenham, which was the port nearest to Klang and Kuala Lumpur, there was only one person on board, and I think in my case I think it was the coxswain, who was allowed to butcher the chooks. And the victualling sailor, whoever that was — probably also the coxswain — would go ashore and buy live chooks, which only he was allowed to behead on the quarterdeck and then be plucked.[82]

[An RAN commanding officer on food at sea] Before my second patrol I went into a supermarket to get some food and I got a tin of Aussie sausages; they turned out to be pork sausages, but I didn't realise it. So the steward asked me what I'd like to eat second or third night out. I said that I'd like to try some of those sausages out of the can and pointed. He obviously had some problems with that and he obviously could read English, and the next thing the cox'n was at my ear pointing out that it was unclean and, if I insisted on having them — which I didn't — they would have to throw the plates overboard, so I backed away from that. I respected the prohibition and taking them on board was my fault, albeit one done in ignorance.[83]

[An RAN chief petty officer] The only problem was that a couple of the Muslims didn't like communal soap in the showers. I remember one of them saying to Les [RN loan petty officer] one day; 'Oh, PO: when we shower can we have our own soap, not share?' 'Why's that, Zukifli?' 'Well, it's our culture.' Les said, 'That's okay; no problems'.[84]

Food is of no less importance with the personnel of any navy than with the population at large, but in the close confines of a warship catering to the needs of at least three different culinary traditions, it can loom even larger, especially when you do not come from any of those three traditions. Some Australians embraced and enjoyed the opportunity to eat Southeast Asian food, but others were more firmly wedded to the 'meat and two veg' tradition inherited from the British. It should be observed here that Australians generally found the food served by the RN inedible.

[A Malaysian officer's comments] The fellow I liked very much was a chap called 'Basil' Rathbone, a Supply Officer I think. He loved Indian food. Funnily enough, you know how it is when you're a bachelor in the mess, having a few drinks and you say: 'Let's go to Singapore and have lunch'. He'd say: 'Oh, go to this restaurant in this road or that road'. He seemed to know the location of Indian restaurants more than we did. Also he had the capacity to eat very hot food; he was very good. Basil Rathbone.[85]

[An RAN Chief Petty Officer on food] You just had to carefully observe the regulations in the mess with eating habits — no bacon sandwiches. I remember I was warned when I first got there that if you ever did go sea riding with them you wanted to take some bully beef or stuff like that, but to take the label off first. Otherwise they'd rat around in the dirt bin and they could make things unpleasant for people if they wanted to. It never happened to me; we just knew what we were supposed to do. We never ate in their Mess. We used to bring our own lunches and so forth.[86]

[An RAN CO on messing habits at sea] When I was on board my ship I had a steward, just for me, which was pretty grand. He had other jobs to do but that was his primary function. They are very hierarchical the Malay race, and this fitted in well with the Raj attitude. And I would have for breakfast eggs, a piece of toast, marmalade and a cup of tea. For lunch I always had the ship's company *makkan*: for that ship I must have been the only CO who actually deigned to eat the local food, which I adored: it was gorgeous stuff. I didn't ever like when I did rounds smelling the ghee that the food was all cooked in, because it smelt terrible. But I adored the food, and the crew were very pleased that I would eat their food. At night I would have something like lamb chops.[87]

[An RAN leading seaman 'crash-drafted' to an RMN ship] When we arrived on board, she was already singled up ready to go and the lieutenant [RN commanding officer] called us up and said, 'We can't go because we're waiting for your victuals to arrive on board'. 'What victuals, sir?' 'You don't eat curries and that stuff; you'll die.' Because that's what those ships were victualled for. So we waited for about two hours for this stuff to arrive.[88]

At first glance, the language issue in small ships could have been a considerable problem. Some effort — but not much — was made to send RAN loan personnel on a course offered by the Army at Camp Terendak, but short-notice postings and the urgent need to get loan commanding officers to sea to cover for a lack of qualified RMN officers, illness and the increasing operational tempo, did not allow this for most. The situation in their ships varied, but most had the advantage of the leavening of experienced senior sailors who had been trained in the MRNVR and in RN ships, and whose English was very good.

> The sub-lieutenant spoke pretty good English, and the Coxswain was pretty good at English too, but the remaining Malayans in the armed forces and indeed in the police forces of Singapore and Malaya/Malaysia were predominantly Malay race, and not very confident in English.[89]

As the RMN expanded the British-trained senior RMN sailors' numbers diminished relative to the new entrants, and there also commenced a program of encouraging the use of *Bahasa Kebangsaan* — Malay — as the language of government agencies. This had some interesting outcomes for loan personnel. At the trivial level this meant that they had to learn at least some Malay, as a senior RAN sailor recalled.

> Everything — Daily Orders and so forth — used to be in Malaysian; I might have a copy somewhere. So you learned the language that way. I remember the in-tray was *Masok* and *Keluar* was out. *Awas* meant caution; things like that you picked up. And the Pay Office was *Pejabat Wang* — it didn't pay us to forget that expression! [90]

At an instructional level, especially in technical subjects, it was less trivial. Equipment handbooks, technical manuals and instructional material were all in English, to the amazement of the RAN officers.

> When I arrived there I said; 'Where are the Malaysian manuals? These kids' basic English is very basic, and we're trying to teach them in English'. I set some people about translating the various BRs [books of reference — naval manuals] into Malay, but that was difficult too, because the Malay language doesn't lend itself to technicalities at all.[91]

In many contexts the use of English texts was necessary as there were, at that stage, no Malay words to describe some of the concepts and physical interactions of the equipment. When it came to the selection of RMN personnel to undertake overseas training, a thorough grasp of English was essential if the candidates were to stand some chance of success. This was especially so at the junior officer level, where 'back-classing' at the British naval college seriously disrupted RMN plans to man their growing fleet.

As the Malaysianisation program expanded into the 1970s there were some quite bizarre practices imposed on loan personnel arising from the use of the Malay language. A loan staff officer provided an example.

> To send a proposal to MINDEF for approval I had to have the proposal translated from English into BM [*Bahasa Melayu*] and forwarded to Kuala Lumpur, where it would be received by an RN officer, who immediately had it translated into English. He would then take the necessary staff action, write his decision in English and have it translated into BM. Upon studying the response I would have to contact the MINDEF staff officer and tell him I could not understand what he was approving. The loss of sense from all the translations would have been frustrating if it was not so funny. [92]

If there was one feature of the RMN which proved the most irksome to many Australians — as it undoubtedly did for many non-Malay Malaysians — it was the imposition of quotas on the basis of ethnic origin. It is not difficult to understand why the Malaysian Government might have felt that members of the Malay race had to predominate in the armed forces, but it had the unfortunate effect of denying the principle of 'the best man for the job', which had been the feature of the Dovers and Synnot administrations of the RMN. A loan commanding officer remembered that:

> Some of the Chinese officers went to see Tony Synnot and said:

'We can't help but notice that in the Malaysian Army if you're not Malay you don't get promoted. If you're Chinese or Indian, forget it. Is that going to happen in the Malaysian Navy?' Because this was the first group of officers who had risen to the rank of lieutenant commander; slowly they'd come through and they were therefore in command of the ships as senior lieutenants or lieutenant commanders. Admiral Synnot's answer to them was that while he had anything to do with the running of the Royal Malaysian Navy, officers would be promoted on merit.[93]

In a small organisation like the RMN, which was struggling to catch up to the technological sophistication of the equipment it was procuring, discrimination in favour of Malays meant that the best qualified candidates were not always accepted for the training courses on offer. In the late 1960s and early 1970s Australia was not necessarily as 'multicultural' as it has since become, but it did seem to many of the RAN loan personnel that the Malaysian Government's policies were the antithesis of the 'fair go' which lies at the heart of Australian values. Racial hurdles were regarded by RAN personnel as fundamentally unfair and professionally inefficient.

Despite very good standards of Instructional Staff, the final trained sailor was limited in his effectiveness. Considerable on board experience was needed to give confidence in his ability to cope with operational and maintenance tasks. With the reduction of experienced Loan personnel, I had severe reservations on how the RMN would cope in the short term. The Government edict on division of jobs in racial proportions did not help in improving the standard of recruits to solve the above problem. Any Malay who had above average get up and go was already firmly employed in another Government sponsored job. Therefore, meeting a 7:2:1 ratio of Malay/Chinese/Indian was doomed to failure before starting.[94]

This might have been an Australian viewpoint, but it was not that of the Malaysian Government — their current employer, which had introduced its *Bumi Putra* (sons of the soil) policy as a perceived means of redressing the relative lack of education and opportunity which had commonly been the lot of ethnic Malays. RAN loan personnel, in general, had little background understanding of this issue, or of the resentment felt by ethnic Malays towards the privileged position they believed Indian and Chinese Malaysians had gained at their expense. It is very likely that their RMN hosts thought it impolite to air this dirty laundry in public in the presence of their RAN guests, who went about their tasks oblivious to the differences between their subordinates or students, praising, rewarding and encouraging whoever showed initiative.

Most of my fellows were Chinese and Indian, and it was certainly so in the diving branch, although the 2ic PO was a Malay fellow. His name was Tawab Khatib and he was eventually commissioned and took over as the CO of the diving team at MBJ. But yes, I suppose that was the way, a bit like it was in the Army. Everybody at the top was Malay. The thing was the Chinese and Indians were more switched on; whenever people were selected to go to Australia for these courses, we'd always select a preponderance of Chinese first, Indians second and Malays last, but the admin people changed that around, and put a majority of Malays first.[95]

The whole issue was put in stark relief by the events of May 1969, when serious and deadly inter-communal riots erupted in Kuala Lumpur, with Malaysians of Chinese and Malay ethnic origins embarking on an orgy of violence and murder. This shocked most, and perhaps the RAN loan personnel most of all, because it permanently changed the relative value of the Malaysians they were training according to their racial origins.

And then, of course, we come to May '69 and the riots, and the head hunting and the friction between the Malays and the

Chinese, and the statement by the Minister for the Interior on about night 1 or 2 of the riots; 'Democracy is dead in Malaysia'. That fixed a different world for the future and that world, I guess, is in place now. So the good Chinese that we had were obviously not going to be promoted up to the top echelons in Defence, and nor were the Indians.[96]

Still, some RAN loan personnel were prepared to go to some lengths to register a strong protest vote against racial discrimination, as they saw it. Selecting the RMN personnel to go for apprentice training at HMAS *Nirimba* was the task of a board headed by the Training Commander at KD *Malaya*.

I was once provided with 16 candidates for 14 Apprentice places ... the ethic breakdown was 14 Chinese and 2 Malays. Subsequent interrogation by the board members showed the standard of Chinese applicants was exceptionally high ... the 2 Malays could not understand any board member's questions. The board decision was to select the 14 Chinese and reject the non-English speaking Malays ... I was told that I should alter the recommendations, I refused and suggested that if they did not like my decisions they should remove me from the Board. So they did![97]

This was gallant but inappropriate, missing the significance and the intent of the Government's policies, which held that it was essential that the Malays be offered the chance of attending the course, regardless of their apparently suitability. The RAN loan officer was doing his best to assist in the creation of an excellent navy, but that admirable professional sentiment overlooked the Government's political and ethnic imperative that the RMN should be a Malay-dominated navy.

There was another ethnic issue which caused RAN loan personnel some difficulty — the importance to Asians of the concept of 'face'. The most common manifestation of this phenomenon was in the reluctance of many less-confident RMN officers and sailors to admit that they did not understand what they had been told or what was expected of them. The response to the question 'Do you understand?' was often an automatic 'Yes', leaving the Australian questioner unsure whether this was true. Another manifestation was in the Malaysian etiquette of not giving offence, so that a report of an incident or occurrence likely to cause blame to be levelled was delivered in very roundabout language. 'Face' could have other manifestations, though, as the following example cited by an RAN officer demonstrated.

> I remember I had one kid who deserted. He went home but he had lost 'face', so he had to come back. I came to work one morning and I said to the shore patrol at the gate; 'I think whatever his name was is at Sembawang'. They went out and apprehended him and put him in the slammer for a few days. When they let him out I was still his divisional chief, and I was having a little word with him about what had been going on and I said, 'What made you come back?' 'Oh', he said, 'It's as plain as day. I've come back to kill Sub-Lieutenant Huddinutt because I failed, and I've lost face with my family.'[98]

Notwithstanding the above, based on respondents' responses the majority of the RAN sailors and some of the officers enjoyed their loan service very much. The conditions of service were good and the job was challenging and rewarding; they appreciated the opportunity of offering their knowledge and expertise in the development of the new navy. This was not an exchange limited to professional matters. There were examples to be set in personal conduct and in broadening and deepening the understanding of Malaysians about how a navy really operates and the roles and responsibilities of all in making it work.

At that time they were trying to get some of the senior Chiefs in the Malaysian Navy to become SD [Special Duties — sailors promoted to officer ranks]. They had no Special Duties officers; none of them had ever come up through the ranks and become officers, like we did and the RN did. So they had a class of half a dozen, and I spoke to them about three or four times a week in the afternoon about what they might expect. I was fortunate enough to get a syllabus from HMS *Royal Arthur* through Jimmy Hume, I think. I used to talk to them about what the duties were and what it was like to be an SD officer in the Royal Australian Navy and where they were likely to be posted and what they would have to do over there. That was quite rewarding for a couple of months: it was only a part-time job.[99]

Not all the Australian loan personnel went to the lengths of some in becoming assimilated into Malaysian life but they all tried to become team players in working alongside their Malaysian RMN colleagues, as the following comments demonstrate.

[An RAN senior sailor on integration] We got on well with RMN sailors better than we did with RN sailors. We were often invited to Malay weddings, for example. We were the only Europeans present. Some RAN personnel attempted to learn Bahasa Malay but it was rarely used at work because English predominated.[100]

[An RAN officer on RAN–RMN integration] Well, I don't think there was any animosity, but cultural differences were fairly prominent at that stage. I mean, to their credit, most of the Malays were true believers in Islam, and standing around a bar in the mess drinking alcohol was not their bag, whereas the Europeans thought that this was quite a natural thing to do — to have a couple of beers or whatever. Most of the Malays would not touch alcohol, and they had their own attitudes towards women and dress, of course. But in my recollection, most of them were nice people.[101]

[A Malaysian officer on an RAN commanding officer of KD *Malaya*]

Jim Hume was known as 'Haji' Hume because he tried to use his knowledge of Islam to deal with defaulters at the Captain's Table. I remember on one occasion as I, as Accused's Friend, managed to get a petty officer cook charged with slapping a leading cook off the hook by pleading that the leading cook, after being required on board for duty, later went home to sleep with his wife and returned on board to handle food without the proper Islamic ablution.[102]

[An Australian chief petty officer] I actually played badminton in the Navy team and we toured all over Malaysia and that was great. They didn't quite know what to do with me when we got to some of these places, because here was one white guy and all these brown fellas. We had to stay at an Army mess one night, and they wound up putting me in the wardroom.[103]

A striking finding of the research for this chapter has been the number of genuine friendships that were formed between RAN and RMN personnel at all levels and have survived the years since. Even forty years on, Malaysians and Australians alike seem to have no trouble remembering each other and the roles each played in the development of the RMN, and a surprising number of ex-RMN personnel of that period either emigrated to Australia or maintain strong links to this country. The number of reunions that take place regularly, especially between the former senior sailors of both navies, is impressive. That in itself is one measure of the impact the loan personnel had on their contemporaries, and vice versa.

As far as can be determined, the last RAN loan personnel left Malaysia in August 1974, when services for the RMN at the former RN radio station at Kranji in Singapore transferred to the RMN's own station.[104] The relationship between the two navies did not end at that point, as will be discussed in the Epilogue, but it had changed significantly over the fourteen tumultuous years since Captain Dovers took up his posting in Kuala Lumpur. It has not been possible, unfortunately, to develop an accurate count of the numbers of

Australians who served with the RMN but it was in the order of fifty all ranks. Of course, not only Australia provided loan personnel to assist in the development task, but there is no denying that the RAN example set in those days has been an enduring feature in the growth and maturing of the RMN.

Yes. I would say that at a very critical time leading up to, during and probably after — although I can't comment on that — Confrontation, we, with some support from the RNZN, were responsible for improving their procedures and their attitude towards their professionalism, which sounds like I'm being critical of the RN. I'm not being critical of the RN: I am critical of the RN's choice of officers whom they sent to the Malaysian navy as some sort of out-of-the-way colony, over there and they didn't send their best chaps. They sent officers on contract to the RMN. We were never on contract, we were on loan. I think we had a tremendous effect on their procedures, and in instilling in their officers an idea of professionalism which had hitherto been lacking.[105]

The RAN loan personnel might well feel that they did a good job in the development and support of the RMN, but the real test of the benefits of their contributions properly belongs to Malaysians.

Of course, we were all brought up on naval traditions which were common in the RN and RAN, but definitely I think the Australians tried hard to influence the way we conducted affairs in the RAN way, and I think today we still follow a lot of the standing orders and manuals that the Australians had given us.[106]

I think that the Australian Government was very wise to provide a spectrum of very good officers for loan service with the RMN. It was a win-win situation. The RMN benefited from the RAN officers filling the various vacancies until we were ready to take over or until there were sufficient numbers of us, not just to fill vacant posts but to upgrade ourselves in overseas professional and staff courses. In return the RAN benefited by having three of its senior officers command the RMN for nearly eight years, and in having meaningful and challenging appointments for its officers, especially command of seagoing ships during the stressful *Konfrontasi* period. On the social side, both the RMN and RAN personnel involved got to know each other's culture intimately.[107]

Indeed, the shaping of the RMN along RAN lines and the forging of the relationship between the two navies were to be the most important legacies of this interesting interaction. They were strong enough to survive a prolonged period of political animus between the two countries and are still firm to this day.

5 Indonesian Confrontation

Although the initial stages of Confrontation took the form of cross-border raids by Indonesian forces into British territories in Borneo — from September 1963 East Malaysia — by the latter half of 1964 the conflict had spread to the Malay Peninsula and Singapore, West Malaysia. The military topography of the battlefield shaped both the Indonesian threat and the Commonwealth response. In East Malaysia, the internal transport network was poorly developed, with the sea and major rivers serving as the principal arteries of access, travel and trade. Consequently, the helicopter became the tactical weapon able to be employed with unanswered effect upon the Indonesian border-crossers by the Commonwealth forces. The 1600 km long North Borneo–Kalimantan border area was generally thick jungle and contained rugged mountain ranges with few settlements of any size. The coastline is generally flat, with numerous beaches useable for minor amphibious landings. The only inhabited border area accessible by sea is near Tawau, in the extreme east of East Malaysia, where the boundary runs to the coast and divides the island of Sebatik

Opposite Singapore lies the Riau Archipelago, a collection of islands large and small, and only a few miles to the south and east of the city and the main international shipping channel. With a long history as the base for piracy, this dense complex of islands was ideal for the launching of raids by fast native craft across Singapore Strait into Singapore itself, or neighbouring Johore State. The volume of cross-Strait commercial traffic, added to the endless stream of international shipping, the large number of ships in Singapore Roads, and the presence of numerous fishing boats and fishing traps, favoured the concealment of raiding vessels.

In the Riaus, and in Sumatra, the Indonesians maintained around 10,000 men of the SIAGA command, charged with the conduct of Confrontation operations. To these regular service units were added so-called Special Forces, comprising Indonesian volunteers, Malaysian citizens who had been trained to infiltrate their country either to stir up political and ethnic trouble or to conduct sabotage operations, and a leavening of regular soldiers and sailors seconded to provide a structure and leadership for the force.

The Riaus and southern Sumatran ports were also the centre for the barter trade, in which small craft would cross, principally to Singapore, with cargoes of primary produce to be exchanged for money, food or manufactured goods. This was such an important source of revenue to Singapore that the Indonesian Government attempted to prevent it, temporarily bringing the trade to a halt. The trade was supposed to be overseen by armed Indonesian customs launches — known to the Commonwealth forces as BT (barter trade) boats. These BT boats were quite unscrupulous in raiding returning barter traders and seizing money and goods for their own use, and often constituted the most aggressive Indonesian vessels involved in Confrontation. Local craft engaged in the barter trade were obvious vehicles for the conveyance of weapons, explosives and infiltrators and in 1964 the Malaysian Government attempted to ban the trade for this reason. Singapore was less enthusiastic about cessation of the trade and, as will be seen later, a compromise was eventually reached.

To some extent, these issues continued north along the long Malacca Strait separating the Malay Peninsula from Indonesian Sumatra. The southern reaches of the Strait are complicated by extensive banks and shoals, narrowing the passage for safe navigation, which runs for some distance on the Indonesian side of the maritime boundary line.[1] There were major Indonesian naval and air bases in Sumatra, and smaller Indonesian warships actively patrolled their side of the Strait.

Both East and West Malaysian waters were susceptible to mining, and British intelligence reported that the Indonesian Navy (*Angkatan Laut Republik Indonesia* — ALRI) had a stock of moored mines kept in Pontianak on the western edge of Kalimantan, about 320 nm from Singapore.[2] Both ALRI and the Air Force (*Angkatan Udara Republik Indonesia* — AURI) had been recent recipients of considerable volumes of Soviet ships, aircraft and weaponry, although the state of readiness for operations of these sophisticated weapons systems was thought to be low.[3] More concern was felt for the light naval forces, which included over sixty patrol boats, including those equipped with Styx surface-to-surface missiles.

At the same time, the operational capability of the Soviet submarines acquired by ALRI (and thought by British intelligence to still be Soviet-crewed) was considered inadequate for attacks in the vicinity of Singapore. The ostensible reason was the shallowness of the waters around Singapore and the Borneo coasts. This conclusion apparently ignored the exploits of British and Dutch submarines in the same region during World War II, and overlooked the fact that British submarines could, apparently, conduct successful intelligence collection operations against Indonesian military targets throughout Confrontation without detection. Set against this, the Indonesian armed forces had gained valuable experience in the course of their campaigns against separatist movements and religious extremists in the years since Independence. They had planned an amphibious assault on West New Guinea in January 1962 which, apparently detected by Dutch Sigint, had been comprehensively defeated at sea. In addition, AURI attempts to land paratroopers in West New Guinea in the weeks afterwards were disastrous, with twenty-two troops killed, 119 captured and nearly 300 missing believed dead.[4]

And to some extent the Indonesians had given the

Commonwealth forces a head start by telegraphing their intentions in Borneo by tacit support for the Brunei insurrection. Using the lessons of the Emergency, the British had reacted swiftly by establishing a joint headquarters at Labuan, and by bringing police and military resources into the one command chain in the Borneo colonies. Although the position of Director of Borneo Operations (DOBOPS) was not formally established until 1964, the structure and relationships created in response to Brunei served as the framework for the rapid development and expansion of Commonwealth operational and intelligence capacities to resist Confrontation in Sabah and Sarawak.[5] A diagram of the command and control organisation in East Malaysia is at Figure 5-1.

The Commonwealth command structure elsewhere was also in place. As Malaysia was now an independent sovereign nation, the key decision-making body in resisting the Indonesians was the National Defence Council in Kuala Lumpur. This worked through a National Operations Committee — OPSCO — comprising the

Command and Control in East Malaysia

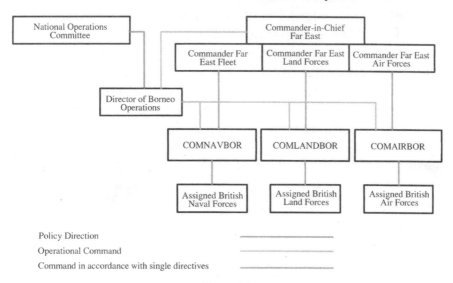

Figure 5-1

British CinCFE, the Malaysian Chief of Armed Forces Staff and the head of the Malaysian Police.

Conduct of operations was delegated by OPSCO to CinCFE, whose joint service staff was headquartered in Singapore. In the planning wing, a succession of RAN officers held the position of leaders of Team A. These officers were apparently totally integrated within the British organisation. When asked whether he had encountered any difficulties through restrictions of access to highly classified British information, Commodore Alan Robertson, one of the Australian officers to have served in this position, replied:

> No. In fact, as an Australian I wasn't meant to see UK EYES ONLY information and my colleagues said: 'Well, you can't do your job if you don't have the information', and they gave it to me ... Nothing was held back from me. [6]

Reporting to and responsible to CinCFE, and by extension to OPSCO, were the individual service commanders and their headquarters. Operationally, by the time the RAN became involved in 1964 forces assigned to Borneo came under the operational control of DOBOPS, specifically through the naval component commander, an RN captain in the joint headquarters in Labuan.[7] In other parts of the command, ships were assigned their duties through the Captain Inshore Flotilla on the staff of the Commander Far East Fleet (COMFEF) in Singapore. The overall command arrangements are shown at Figure 5-2.

Command intelligence was the responsibility of the JIC (Far East), which exchanged collated intelligence between Malaysian and other Commonwealth agencies. Single service representatives of the joint intelligence staff also held responsibilities to their own service headquarters. The JIC directed the work of the Joint Air Reconnaissance Intelligence Centre (Far East), operated on the Committee's behalf by the RAF and staffed by Army and Air Force.[8] The major part of this Centre's work was both photographic interpretation of the Borneo border areas to spot Indonesian units

Confrontation Command and Control

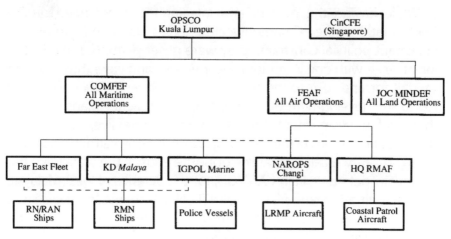

Figure 5-2

and activities, and the mapping of the areas over which operations had to take place. Intelligence provided to ships of the Far East Fleet, to which the RAN units were attached, was the responsibility of COMFEF. At one stage during Confrontation this fleet comprised more than eighty ships of the British, Australian, Malaysian and New Zealand navies, including three aircraft carriers. The RN 7th Submarine Squadron carried out intelligence collection patrols as well as operational tasks.

The Australian Government was kept well informed of the Confrontation situation and command responses to developments, as the Australian Commissioner (from 1965 the High Commissioner) in Singapore attended bi-weekly CinCFE meetings. This continued the tradition that had been established in during the Emergency. CinCFE meetings covered a broad range of political and operational topics. For example, the sixteenth meeting of 1964 on 17 December discussed clearances for the employment of Commonwealth forces, while the fourth meeting of 1965 (9 April) was concerned with anti-infiltration operations around Singapore. Two weeks later, the meeting discussed the possibility of Indonesian amphibious operations against Malaysia. CinCFE meeting minutes were cabled back to Canberra.[9]

While having the military and intelligence upper hand during Confrontation, the Commonwealth forces laboured under an important political constraint: they were never permitted to take the initiative — with one important exception — and were thus required to wait for and to respond to Indonesian moves.[10] This uncertainty led to the development of a number of contingency plans, many of them defensive in intent, but others very aggressive, designed to demonstrate to Jakarta the resolve of the Commonwealth should there be any military escalation. At the opposite ends of the scale were the essentially defensive Plan CANNON, for the defence of West Malaysia against infiltration, and Plan ADDINGTON, which would have seen a major air assault on Indonesian military targets from bases around the archipelago's periphery, including Darwin. Fortunately, this was never required.[11] The exception to the rule was the authorisation of Operation CLARET, permitting British special forces to cross the border into Indonesia to carry out pre-emptive attacks on Indonesian units preparing for intrusions into Malaysian territory.

As intelligence was to prove the key factor in the Commonwealth response to Confrontation, the Australian contribution to this should be recorded. In the first instance, Australia had accepted responsibility for providing intelligence on a very large slice of Asia — from China through Southeast Asia to Burma. This had an immediate impact on the size and structure of the Australian Joint Intelligence Bureau (JIB). A similar path was being followed by the signals intelligence agency — the Defence Signals Bureau (DSB) — where extended responsibilities accrued under the 1947 UK–USA Sigint agreement were stretching both the intercept and analysis capabilities of the organisation. In the early 1950s both agencies were in difficulties, caused by manpower ceilings and the shortage of trained personnel.[12] Language training was another bottleneck, and strenuous efforts were required to match the output of service linguists to the tasks accepted.[13] However, these issues appear to have been overcome by April 1955, when there were 773 military and civilian personnel working in JIB and DSB, and both agencies were working towards a combined strength of 1106.[14]

By the mid-1950s Australian service personnel were being dispatched overseas to assist in the manning of British intercept stations in Hong Kong and Singapore: in fact, the planned overseas strength was 265 service personnel.[15] The service of RAN Sigint operators during the Malayan Emergency has already described in Chapter 2. As well, Australian capacity to cover targets of Sigint interest also expanded, with stations at Darwin and Perth providing better coverage of Indonesian targets. To an extent, the intelligence used by the British Commander in Chief Far East (CinCFE) and his staff to direct the operations during Confrontation was sourced in Australia from JIB or produced in Australian Sigint stations or those part-manned by Australians in Asia.

There were sources of intelligence on Indonesia other than Sigint. Commodore Robertson recorded that the Australian Naval Attaché in Jakarta was a ready source of background information, gathered by himself and his staff by observation or from conversations with Indonesian naval officers. Commander Bob Nicholls, a former member of the CinCFE Intelligence Staff, recalled that if an intelligence question exceeded the capability of the staff to respond, 'We'd get onto London or some of our friendly agencies'.[16] But Commonwealth Sigint on the Indonesian military and diplomatic communications was apparently excellent.

> I can't remember the specifics, but we used to be briefed on the way the local Indonesian commanders would report back to Jakarta that they had done this or that or they were planning to do that or the other — Sigint. And we would know bloody well that they hadn't done it. So we knew there were great rifts between the outlying commands and Jakarta.[17]

The result of this intelligence cooperation was impressive. The high command had an extremely good idea, not only of the Indonesian order of battle, but also of its state of preparedness and the difficulties that the Indonesian Army and sister services were having in operating and maintaining their equipment.[18] This situation was kept under constant review, as was the likely thrust of Indonesian attacks on Malaysia. In November 1964 the Australian JIC concluded that the Indonesians would concentrate on stirring up racial tensions in Malaysia rather than direct military intervention, one of the reasons being that:

> Although the size of the armed forces in Indonesia is formidable, her logistic capability to support such forces is severely restricted by economic problems and administrative inefficiency. It is unlikely that Indonesia, unaided, could sustain operations in a limited war in defence of her own territory for more than a few months at the most. In the event of limited war situation involving air and sea attacks against target throughout Indonesia it is unlikely she could maintain effective operations for more than a few weeks.[19]

As this assessment of likely Indonesian actions proved very accurate, it can be appreciated that intelligence often made up for any apparent numerical disadvantage that Commonwealth forces had during the campaign.

As Indonesian incursions in to Malaysian territory in Borneo increased in number and scale, in January 1964 the Malaysian Government asked that the Australian battalion of the 28th Commonwealth Brigade be released for anti-CT duties on the border with Thailand, to relieve Malay Regiment troops for operations against the Indonesians in East Malaysia, and this was approved. Shortly afterwards a military mission was sent to Malaysia to discuss how Australia might best help and in April 1964, in answer to a further Malaysian request for engineer, maritime and air transport assistance in Borneo, the Australian Cabinet finally agreed to the dispatch of two minesweepers and other direct military assistance.

The Government has decided that two RAN coastal minesweepers will be made available at once for patrols off the coast of the Malaysian Borneo States, supplementing the patrol work already being undertaken by two ships in the Strategic Reserve, and that provision of two further vessels of the same type will be considered in early June. The converted carrier HMAS *Sydney* will be used for the movement of personnel and equipment from Australia.[20]

The minesweepers *Hawk* and *Gull* arrived on station in late May 1964, the first direct Australian naval commitment to Confrontation.[21] In July 1964 the FESR Directive was modified to permit the employment of RAN units against Indonesia.[22]

We were getting ready for a visit to Urungan in Queensland when the word came we were going to sail to Borneo instead. Well! We had about two weeks to get ready and all sort of amazing things happened. Piles of new charts arrived and they had to be corrected, and a man came from Newington Armament Depot and said, 'Where do you want the guns?' 'What guns are they?' 'Well, you're going to put some more guns on aren't you?' I said, 'OK. What shall we have?' 'What about another Bofors?' Perhaps that had been designed into the ship, but we had another Bofors installed aft of the funnel, and in no time the ship was bristling with weapons. We had light machine-guns, grenades, mortars, pistols, sub-machine guns! 'How much ammunition do you want?' I was a properly brought up young officer: 'The regulations state ... ' 'Do you want some more stuff?' 'Alright', so we embarked additional ammunition. People came by from other ships: 'Do you want some more .303 ball?' 'OK.' We had 20,000 rounds of .303 ammunition that nobody knew about, because it had already been written off.[23]

The two minesweepers were followed closely into Malaysian waters by HMAS *Sydney* and her frigate escorts *Parramatta* and *Yarra*, on the former aircraft carrier's first voyage as a troop transport. Her conversion had barely met the assigned dates, and she was able to spend only three days on a shakedown at sea before returning to Sydney for runs over the degaussing range, to check her protection systems against magnetic mines. Then she moved to an ammunition buoy in the harbour and embarked her own outfit of ammunition as well as a cargo of explosive stores and ammunition for Malaysia. From 18 to 23 May she was berthed alongside at Garden Island where the major part of the embarkation of stores, equipment and men took place. When she sailed shortly after midnight on 24 May she had 1245 personnel embarked, including the engineers of the Australian Army's 7th Field Squadron, bound for construction tasks in Sabah, the gunners of the 111th Light Anti-aircraft Battery of the Royal Australian Artillery and four Iroquois helicopters of 5 Squadron RAAF on their way to Butterworth near Penang.

No chances were taken on any hostile reaction to this reinforcement. On entering New Guinea waters *Sydney* imposed radio and radar silence, the Army's anti-aircraft guns were sited on the flight deck to back up the ship's armament, and the ship's company went into defence watches. The frigates joined on 30 May and, on approaching the Basilan Channel south of the Philippines on 3 June, the force commenced a zigzag, and radar and sonar restrictions were relaxed to put the ships in the best state of defence preparedness. However, no opposition was encountered, and by the afternoon of 4 June unloading of the 7th Field Squadron and its equipment was under way at Kota Kinabalu, with the assistance of the pre-positioned Army landing ships *Vernon Sturdee* and *Harry Chauvel*. The task was completed within twenty-four hours, with the frigates maintaining surveillance of the anchorage and its approaches throughout this period.

During *Sydney*'s off-loading program the following security measures were in force. Bottom searches carried out at first light and before sunset; ships remained in the third degree of anti-aircraft readiness, navigation radar was operated continuously and boat patrols were carried out in the vicinity of *Sydney* between sunset and sunrise.[24]

One frigate patrolled to seaward of the harbour entrance on each night, until the big ship sailed at midnight on 5 June. After fuelling, *Sydney* made a fast passage to Singapore, where 250 tonnes of ammunition was unloaded on 8 June before the ship went alongside in the naval base. By 16 June the ship, escorted by *Parramatta*, was anchored off Penang, where bombs, ammunition, defence stores and the Battery were offloaded onto lighters, and the helicopters flew off to Butterworth. Two days later the ships were on the return voyage to Australia, passing round the northern tip of Sumatra. A high speed of advance and an enhanced degree of anti-aircraft and submarine readiness were maintained until 21 June, but on the morning of the 23rd the force received intelligence of the possible presence of an Indonesian submarine. Readiness states were increased, the course altered and high speed resumed for eighteen hours until they were well clear of the danger area, when conditions were relaxed and the passage to Fremantle resumed.

Thus, by May 1964 the RAN had four ships on patrol in Malaysian waters and more were on their way. As the Indonesians commenced their campaign of incursions into Singapore and West Malaya, these ships were in the thick of the action. By the end of 1964 Australian ships in Malaysian waters were intercepting and — occasionally — killing Indonesian servicemen and irregular infiltrators in Singapore Strait, but the Australian component of 28th Commonwealth Brigade in Malaysia was not permitted to be deployed in East Malaysia on a similar task. This puzzled the Malaysians and frustrated the British.[25] But the intelligence the Australian Cabinet continued to receive must have given it much food for thought, and encouraged its reluctance to make any hasty decisions. For example, in late 1964 it was being advised that possible developments in Confrontation could include a military escalation by Jakarta, attempts by the Indonesians to provoke a powerful Commonwealth retaliation against them so as to gain non-aligned and Communist Bloc support in the UN, and a 'major military move in South East Asia' by the Communist Bloc. Such a move would be used by Sukarno as an opportunity to invade Malaysia.[26] Fortunately this did not occur, but Cabinet's caution in committing Australian ground forces to almost inevitable clashes with the Indonesian Army (*Tentera Nasional Indonesia* — TNI) is, perhaps, understandable.

The Confrontation operations that ensued in which the RAN participated are discussed under four headings, because they took place in very different operational settings. However, it needs to be borne in mind that, with the exception of the minesweepers, Australian warships remained committed to the FESR and undertook tasks outside the Malaysian area throughout Confrontation. A significant and growing concurrent commitment was to Vietnam, and FESR destroyers and frigates, as well as the carrier *Melbourne*, performed escort duty for the troop transport HMAS *Sydney* on all of her voyages to and from Vung Tau. It was nothing unusual for a ship's company to find itself at defence watches and at a heightened state of alert for air and submarine attack off Vung Tau one day, and a few days later be patrolling for Indonesian infiltration craft in the Malacca Strait.

East Malaysia — East Brigade

Naval patrols in East Malaysia were established as a precaution in early 1963, but there were no challenges posed by ALRI until the following year. A map of the region is at Figure 5-3. The maritime areas of East Brigade presented a set of unique patrol challenges to Commonwealth warships. These arose from the topography, from the Philippines claim to Sabah based on historical precedent, and the vigorous activities of the pirates and smugglers of the Sulu Sea islands.

The principal focus of naval patrols was around Tawau. In this

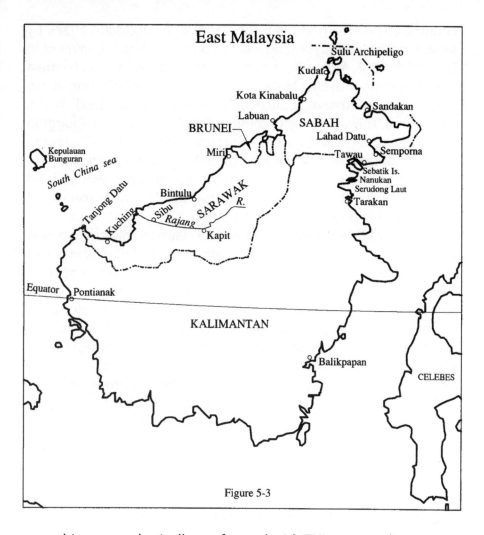

Figure 5-3

area ships were physically confronted with TNI gun emplacements on Nunukan Island, positioned to contest the use of the waters separating the divided island of Sebatik from the mainland. From early 1964, ALRI units were frequently seen in the vicinity of Sebatik and Nunukan, and in June 1965 the submarine chaser *Todak* was involved in efforts over two days to harass Commonwealth patrol craft and to force them back from the median line between the two countries. The area had been the scene of a successful attack by an Indonesian raiding unit on a battalion of the Malay Regiment in December 1963, forty miles northwest of Tawau. As well, in contrast to the remainder of East Malaysia, Sabah had an ethnic Indonesian population estimated at 30,000, of whom 20,000 lived in the Tawau area. They had mostly come to Sabah to work in the logging operations and tea and rubber plantations of the area.[27] The region was marshy and mostly covered in primary jungle, and the road system was undeveloped: both attack and defence would need to be supported by sea.[28] Charts of the coastline were somewhat suspect; the river deltas were not charted.

The Philippines Government had laid claim to areas of Sabah in the discussions leading up to the formation of Malaysia, and had declined to renounce this claim once the new state was a political reality. While there had been no evident attempts by the Philippines to take advantage of the uncertainties created by Indonesian Confrontation, the possibility of infiltration and agitation had to be considered.[29] Philippines naval forces did conduct patrols in the disputed areas and were, on occasion, detected and intercepted by Commonwealth forces. On 18 June 1965 HMAS *Yarra* on passage to Tawau detected a darkened ship on a converging course and illuminated it with flares. It proved to be the Philippines Navy ship *Negro Occidental*, but the Filipino captain refused to confirm his identity and asserted that *Yarra* was in Philippines-claimed waters. This was refuted by the Australian ship and after an amicable exchange of messages, during which the unwisdom of closing a warship darkened in disputed waters was stressed, the ships proceeded on their separate ways.[30]

A similar incident occurred on 13 April 1966, when HMAS *Hawk* was patrolling between the western end of the Sulu Archipelago and East Malaysia. Again, the approaching vessel was detected by radar, darkened and on a converging course. In case it proved to be Indonesian, *Hawk* went to Action Stations and illuminated the contact.

As the rocket flares activated, we saw immediately it was indeed a warship, a patrol boat type unknown to us but not Indonesian. He had a gun trained on us and thankfully nobody was trigger-happy. I ordered our guns trained fore and aft as soon as I realised the vessel was not Indonesian … One of our signalmen requested the vessel to identify itself but the patrol boat refused to answer and it was not wearing a national flag … As both of us were in international waters and both a bit shaken up by the contact, I did not pursue any conversations but reversed course. [31]

Piracy was historically rife in the area. Operating from bases in the Sulu Archipelago, heavily armed bands of Filipino pirates would raid the Sabah coast from Sandakan to Tawau and attack shipping and small craft in the offshore waters. They used native craft equipped with multiple, powerful outboard motors and achieved speeds well in excess of Commonwealth patrol craft. One report gave this at 40 knots, while a pirate boat detected by the frigate *Yarra* had a crossing speed too fast for the gunnery fire control system to track it, this having been designed to engage ships capable of up to 50 knots only.[32] Difficult to intercept or take under fire, and dangerous to approach, the pirates could be deterred by the Commonwealth naval effort but were far from eliminated. To complicate the security problem, there was traditional smuggling and peaceful barter trading between the Philippines and Sabah which continued throughout Confrontation. These activities could easily be exploited by the Indonesians to infiltrate into Sabah. This all made for stressful conditions in the patrolling warships.

The time in sweepers was very hard, as I know now, although I thought it was great at the time. You did a heck of a lot more than you would have done on any bigger ships but sweepers were meant to do no more than about a week away from a base port and we were doing up to six weeks out in Borneo. The food was never very good and the conditions were never great: we could search up to twenty-four boats a day so you were fairly short on sleep most of the time. I ended up coming back with quite a few funny diseases out of my time in sweepers in Borneo, but it was fun at the time and we were doing a real job. Searching *kumpits* full of copra or dried fish is not something I'd wish on my worst enemy — the smell that it gets after being at sea for about a month![33]

While the regional military command was in Sandakan, the centre for naval activity was Tawau. To contest any Indonesian attempt to interdict the free use of waters on the Malaysian side of the border, and to provide NGS as required by ground forces, the role of Tawau Guardship was created and filled by a destroyer or frigate. [34] This had the necessary firepower and the command, control and communications capabilities to command the 'Tawau Assault Force' — something of a misnomer, comprising up to a dozen assorted patrol boats and minesweepers, which kept the border and infiltration routes from Indonesia under surveillance.[35]

The Guardship's command team had a number of intelligence sources to enable them to plan and conduct their missions. As Confrontation proceeded, there was a great deal of information on local patterns of water traffic built up and incorporated in handover notes.[36] Intelligence gathered by army posts ashore was reported to and collated by East Brigade Headquarters in Sandakan, and signalled in intelligence and operations summaries as required. Intelligence was also provided by civilians, particularly the staff of the Wallace Bay Timber Company, whose resource holding occupied a major part of the Malaysian half of Sebatik Island. The ships of the Assault Force also generated and reported information in the course of their patrols. A map of this area is at Figure 5-4.

As in other areas, a major source was police intelligence, derived from the interrogation of captured raiders, and from reports from local people living close to the border. There was apparently no noticeable inclination of the Indonesians living in Tawau to find common cause with their compatriots on the other side of the border. Furthermore, guardships quickly established close links

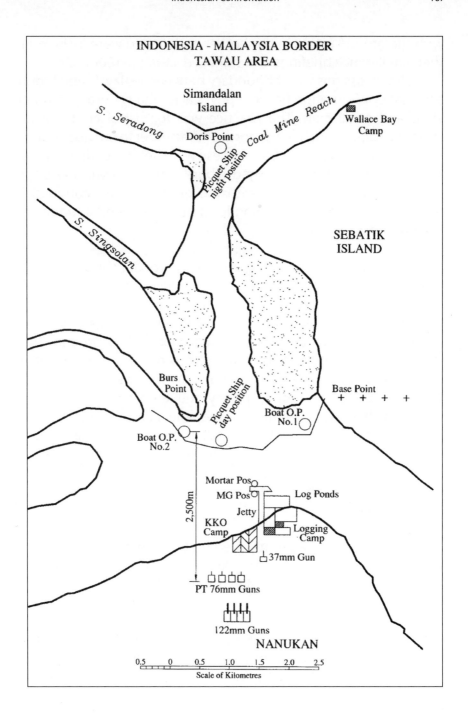

INDONESIA - MALAYSIA BORDER
TAWAU AREA

with the ground forces in the border region, and were included in their intelligence briefings and signalled situation reports.[37]

It was across this water boundary between Malaysia and Indonesia that Confrontation became physical for many Commonwealth ships and small craft. The practice was for patrol craft like the minesweepers to anchor just north of the border to provide support for Army-manned assault boats. These were held in readiness for an Indonesian incursion or engaged in border observation, or resupply and communication duties with the ground forces stationed in the vicinity, as well as searching local boats engaged in trade and fishing across the border.

> At 1200 it's off on patrol again. This is probably at anchor with the anchor buoyed for a quick getaway if necessary. During the afternoon some six *kumpits* or *jalampas* [local boats] come alongside to be checked. Sometimes up to 40 passengers are carried. All have their documents checked. At around 1600 the fishermen go out. They are checked out and their details recorded, and these are compared when they return in the early hours of the morning. They queue up astern normally to be searched. We know most of them now and the search teams have learned enough Malay to talk to them. They're all races — Chinese, Kadazans, Bougis and Indonesians resident in Tawau. In the course of a 24 hour period, up to 60 boats have been searched. As no chances are taken, this process keeps just about everyone busy.[38]

The Indonesians frequently fired on Commonwealth ships with mortars and light anti-aircraft guns to disrupt these proceedings and on the nights of 6 and 7 March 1966 HMAS *Hawk* provided the target.

> At 1940 the Indonesian Commandos fired mortar illumination shells directly to our front and 37 mm gunfire over our heads and well on the Malaysian side of the median line. We were well

and truly lit up, which was not a good feeling. Further I was concerned that the Indonesians might fire their heavier 76 mm Soviet PT55 tank guns or even their 122 mm field guns. After urgently consulting SOTAG [Senior Officer Tawau Assault Group] by radio, we agreed to return fire on Nanukan, while making every endeavour to land shells clear of civilians, which was part of our Rules of Engagement. I ordered our Bofors to engage the KKO [Indonesian Marine Corps] camp. Salvos of four were fired, decreasing the elevation each salvo to obtain accurate ranging. At the same time, the Malaysian 105 mm batteries engaged the camp with direction being given from *Hawk*.[39]

'Friendly fire' was another hazard on the border at Tawau. On at least two occasions RAN ships were surprised to observe shell splashes in close vicinity to their positions which had clearly not originated from the Indonesian side. The culprits were Commonwealth artillery batteries 'registering' the border for indirect fire should there be an Indonesian incursion across it. For *Gull* in August 1964, it was the Royal Artillery, and for *Hawk* in March 1966 it was a Malaysian battery. There were apologies all round, of course, but shells don't discriminate and these were close calls, revealing a breakdown in the system advising Commonwealth positions of the location of friendly ships.

But not all contact with the artillery was so unfriendly, and in 1964 *Teal* offered assistance to the Royal Artillery in clearing trees which were complicating the gunners' range clearance problem.

On reaching the base we marched off into the jungle and picked the largest tree we could find. We used our small hatchet to cut into the trunk (which was as hard as rock) at the base, and wedged about 1 kg of plastic explosive into the small V shape cut we had made. We set up the detonator and fuse and retreated the appropriate distance to wait for the tree to fall over. After the smoke and dust cleared the tree was still standing and the only result of our efforts was a piece of bark about the size of a handkerchief missing around the cut. Not too good for our first try.

After discussion we decided to climb the tree and plant explosives in the first limb fork, about 3 m up the tree. This time we spent a lot more time and effort making a cut and setting the charge but with little more result. The day was spent repeating the effort, and we eventually managed to blow a dent in the tree about 45 cm deep. After expending 15 kg of explosives and many expletives on one tree with zero effective results, the intrepid *Teal* demolition team returned to the ship in severe depression.[40]

Communications associated with Indonesian military movements were often intercepted, and these assisted DOBOPS in ordering ground force retaliation and harassment shoots by the Guardship into Sebatik Island to disrupt them. Occasionally, as in the case of *Hawk*'s engagements at the border in March 1966 with Indonesian gun positions on Nunukan to protect British observation posts, the intelligence was immediate and direct, and called for an immediate and direct response under the Rules of Engagement.[41] When available, Commonwealth patrol aircraft were able to exchange surface contact information with the Tawau Guardship to widen the area under surveillance. Intelligence on a broader scale was available from daily and weekly reports originated by COMFEF, and from the quarterly Far East Fleet Intelligence Reports, which contained current intelligence, political and economic items. DOBOPS signalled a weekly situation report to all units under his command.

More close and personal contact with other units of the security forces was encouraged, and in November 1965 two parties from *Vendetta* spent a week ashore at Serudong Ulu (Company Base 26) and Serudong Laut (Company Base 27) as guests of the British Army, while seven members of the 1st Battalion Scots Guards took their places on board.[42] It turned out to be a working holiday! Following briefings and weapons instruction, the parties went on patrol with the troops, loaded with packs, spare ammunition and weapons. One of the lucky sailors told the story:

> We stood to and watched the jungle change shape at night; it got dark pretty quickly. It looked a bit disconcerting to inexperienced sailors. Little shrubs took on the shape of heads, and that sort of thing. Then we settled down for the night and I got up in the middle of the night and did my sentry trick for, I think, half an hour or an hour, I don't remember now, back-to-back with another bloke so they couldn't sneak up behind you and cut your throat. When I finished the sentry trick I got my head down again and then we then stood to in the middle of the night with all these guttural sounds in the jungle; it turned out to be a feral pig that charged right through the middle of the camp and set everybody's heart pumping, I suppose.[43]

They made no contact with the enemy but learned the hard way about the life and work of an infantry soldier. A point made very strongly was the relative comfort of shipboard life and the better quality of food they enjoyed. After seven days on Army rations, the sailors gratefully rejoined their ship, and enjoyed second servings of both the meals that the rest of their fellows were casting aspersions about.[44] But on a more serious note, the visits also brought home to the naval personnel the importance of their work of surveillance and patrol of the waterways, which provided the only feasible means of communication between bases and for the delivery of men, food, equipment and ammunition. The *Vendetta* sailor continued the saga.

> The following day we took troops up the river in 16 foot aluminium dinghies. The things were so overloaded that I was a bit surprised, as a leading hand with about five year's experience, that the freeboard was only about two inches with the troops with their kit and about five days supplies for their patrol embarked. We headed up the river making hardly any headway at all — we were

doing about three or four knots, I suppose. It felt as if we had a big target stitched to our backs as if you can imagine sitting out in the middle of the Brisbane River off Kangaroo Point, it was about that width I think, and you just felt that everybody was looking at you.[45]

Unfortunately, the use by the British Army of the water routes between their Sabah bases, and apparent disregard for overloading of their craft, was not always cost-free, as members of HMAS *Derwent*'s ships diving team found in 1966.

We got a shake one morning; 'Get up and get yourself loaded with bottles'! Two or three British Army chaps had drowned in a river up in the middle of Borneo somewhere near Kalabakan, and we had to go up and dive for these blokes. We got them and then they had to bring them back in our helicopter, a RAF aircraft flown by a little pimply faced 19-year-old, and we weren't very happy![46]

After the initial raid in December 1963, and the Commonwealth response to it, there were no further seaborne incursions into the Tawau district. Indonesian attempts to apply military pressure to the maritime activities on the Malaysian side of the border were sporadic and effectively dealt with by the Guardship and the Assault Force. The results of the harassment firings by RAN guardships into Sebatik Island are unknown: since the Indonesian forces were unable to deny or to limit Malaysian use of the island they must be considered successful. But this expenditure of ammunition was questioned by at least one Guardship commanding officer, who was told by the British Army that, 'The Indonesians are particularly frightened of bombardment in the jungle. Apparently it is an unusually nerve-racking experience.'[47]

Besides this element of psychological warfare, the strong and continuous naval presence at Tawau also played its role in ensuring the loyalty of the local community, regardless of its ethnic origins.

As Confrontation waned in 1966, this presence was backed up by the deployment of parties from the ships into isolated coastal communities to render medical and other services to the populace. This 'showing the flag' was not a principal role of the Guardship, the patrol boats or the Assault Force, but was a collateral benefit from this typical and effective application of maritime power in an insurgency situation.

The outcomes for the security forces repaid the effort exerted in Sabah generally. DOBOPS commented after Confrontation had wound down that:

> There is no positive evidence of any successful infiltration after January 1964. There is evidence that an incursion party which did set out for Tawau in June 1966 turned back as a result of Naval patrol activity. Naval gunfire support was constantly available, occasionally called for and demonstrated actively on the border in the Sebatik/Wallace Bay area ... The effectiveness of each CMS [coastal minesweeper] and Patrol Craft deployed off Tawau was enhanced by the capability of the frigate or destroyer which was widely known to be deployed there as Guardship[48] ... There was a marked reduction in piracy and pillage.

East Malaysia — West Brigade

The former British colony of Sarawak, now forming the West Brigade area of operations for the Commonwealth, had two characteristics to challenge the security forces. The first was that within Sarawak dwelt some 24,000 ethnic Chinese, from amongst whom around 2000 members of the Clandestine Communist Organisation (CCO) had been recruited.[49] The CCO was hostile to the concept of Malaysia, on both ethnic and ideological grounds. The Chinese of Sarawak, like their ethic cousins in Singapore, saw the imposition of rule by a Malay majority government in Kuala

Lumpur as the end of their hopes for political advancement, and a continuation of their inferior status as citizens. The CCO was thus at least sympathetic to the Indonesian cause. Like the CTs of Emergency days, CCO cadres could move within and expect (or extort) the support of the extensive Chinese community in the state. The second challenge to the security forces was that the border between Kalimantan and East Malaysia ran a scant 50 km from the regional capital and largest town, Kuching, and the large Indonesian port of Pontianak was few hours away by sea from the Commonwealth area of operations.

Two factors favouring the security forces were, first, command of the sea, which allowed military force to be applied quickly from aircraft carriers, commando carriers and smaller warships, right down to the lightly-armed converted stores barges of Naval Force Kilo. The latter could penetrate well inland up the large rivers, which are a feature of western Sarawak, and were the conduits for transportation and commerce. Secondly, despite the concentration of Chinese in the towns, the majority of the inhabitants were Ibans and Dyaks, dwelling in the thickly forested hinterland and along the rivers. They took exception to both Chinese commercial pushiness and intrusions by Indonesia into their traditional lands, and became enthusiastic scouts for the Commonwealth and valuable sources of intelligence.[50]

The international boundary between Indonesian Kalimantan and Malaysian Sarawak reaches the sea at the prominent headland Tanjong Datu, at the western extremity of the island of Borneo. Infiltration of men and supplies around this border, using military or traditional trading craft, was always a possibility, as was the supply of arms and equipment to the CCO; landings had been made in 1963. There was also a faint possibility that the Indonesians could choose to interdict the Commonwealth supply routes from West Malaysia with missile or torpedo boats, or with submarines, — but at the risk of causing a major escalation of hostilities. ALRI could have attempted to mine the river mouths and contiguous waters to hamper Commonwealth operations, and the Indonesians could also have staged raids or minor landings on the beaches east from Tanjong Datu to take the security forces in the flank. However, these threats were not regarded as serious and the mainstays of the patrol force off the Sarawak coast were minesweepers. Here was the first application of intelligence: CinCFE and COMFEF were sufficiently confident in their knowledge of Indonesian intentions that they found it unnecessary to deploy more capable warships in West Brigade.

The Commonwealth warships patrolling off the coast of Sarawak were performing traditional naval missions — demanding, continuous and essential. Grey described these patrol operations as 'repetitious and uneventful', as they largely were.[51] But they were not unimportant, and they involved at least the possibility of close quarters action.

> The basic job on this patrol is to stop the infiltration of arms and illegal persons into the country from seaward. All vessels that are found on the Sarawak coast are stopped and searched. To assist with the searching and to act as the interpreter, each patrol ship has a Sarawak marine policeman on board. He could be Malay, Chinese, Dyak or a mixture ... Patrolling is both day and night. At all times a proportion of the armament is manned and the guns are always loaded. The pattern of life can be fairly regular, or with patrol changes or nights when a lot of searching takes place it is far from routine.[52]

To the numerous fishing boats plying their lawful trade, whose work was disrupted by the peremptory order to stop for searching, the warships were undoubtedly a profound nuisance. But the searches demonstrated Commonwealth resolve to defeat Indonesian incursions and gun-running in an area where the concept of Malaysia was still very new, and Kuala Lumpur was far away. They also enforced the government policy on registration and licensing of boats as part of the nation-building process. A Chinese Malaysian watching in Kuching as a minesweeper berthed and disembarked a company of Ghurkhas can have been in little doubt that adventures involving Indonesian irregulars would be countered with effective force. Certainly, the word that the coast was regularly patrolled did filter back to Indonesia. It was a situation to which could be applied the observation by Sydney Waters: 'Thus was exemplified the truth of the old saying that nine-tenths of naval warfare is made up of the continuous drudgery and monotony of patrols and the search for enemy ships, which are not there but would be if the patrols were not'.[53]

The minesweepers proved effective in their patrol role, remaining on station for ten days, fuelling and replenishing once from a Royal Fleet Auxiliary tanker during this time. Lacking suitable boats, they could be manoeuvred alongside most of the craft stopped for search. Generally, one of two 40 mm guns was manned for every boarding and remaining armament kept at a high state of readiness. However, experience proved that the principal dangers were large semi-submerged logs, which could, and did, damage the hull, screws and underwater fittings of wooden minesweepers. As well, a surprising number of false targets, which showed no lights and did not stop when ordered to heave to, were created by clumps of vegetation scoured from the banks of rivers and washed to seaward. Each had to be investigated.

Initially, there had been some concern about the state of charting in both East and West Brigade areas. The sea bottom off the Sarawak coast is sandy and gently shoaling — not a problem for the Ton Class or smaller craft. The rivers are another issue altogether. Carrying heavy loads of silt from the interior, they are prone to the creation of shoals, especially after heavy rains. Navigation of the rivers by Ton Class was reasonably safe, and the more serious obstacles, such as rock shelves, were marked. But it was never easy, especially in the lower reaches, where local knowledge, and briefings conducted in Singapore and via Handover Notes, became as important as printed charts, as the navigator of one minesweeper recalled.

We had many memorable trips up to Kuching, which was one of

the best cities in the Far East with some of the best food. We did run aground once in the river, but that was the Captain's fault. We had the Squadron Commander in company and he asked whether anything was wrong. The Captain signalled back 'No'. When we got out of the river and the Squadron Commander disappeared on his way, we quickly sent a diver over to have a look, but it was nice soft mud in the river so nobody learned about that one.[54]

Occasionally the patrol routine was interrupted by other tasks. In October 1964 HMAS *Ibis* spent two days salvaging what it could from a beach on which two Malaysian Army assault boats, an RAF pinnace and an RN naval stores lighter had successively stranded themselves. The shallows along the beach compelled recovery attempts to be launched at a distance of 550 m offshore, and this necessitated the exhausting work of manually dragging a heavy sweep wire to the stricken craft, a task that took three hours. Refloating of the pinnace was successful at the first attempt, but a falling tide and the parting of the wire meant that the ship had to return the following day to salvage the lighter. The assault boats had been swamped and were located by the ship's diving team, but only one outboard motor was recovered despite twenty hours of effort. It was a very weary ship's company that resumed its patrolling that evening.[55]

In April 1966 HMAS *Hawk* was positioned to blockade the mouths of rivers in the Matong area northeast of Kuching, in an attempt to intercept survivors of an Indonesian incursion group which had been ambushed and defeated by the border security forces. At regular intervals, Captain Inshore Flotilla would organise mine countermeasures exercises, so that the ships' primary skills were not lost, and would be available if the latent ALRI mine threat ever eventuated. But, as recalled by one officer, the lot of most RAN ships operating in West Brigade was coastal patrolling.

Patrolling was tedious and hot — we were right on the Equator. The cockroaches lived in the freezers; they knew a cool place to go, but the rest of us lived in pretty uncomfortable circumstances. But it was work that was, again, professional and challenging. We had to make sure we inspected all the boats and we went up the rivers occasionally. Runs ashore in Kuching were not much fun but they were better than nothing. I remember going ashore on a beautiful beach to carry out my monthly destruction of classified material and building a bonfire, with sailors positioned around with sub-machine guns.[56]

The intelligence provided in support of West Brigade maritime patrolling was not extensive. Fishing boats were not restricted to established areas as in Singapore, nor was there any effective track kept of Indonesian traditional craft. Maritime patrol aircraft occasionally overflew the area, and there was a daily fighter sweep from Singapore. However, there were daily summaries of military activities compiled from individual unit patrol and incident reports, and a weekly appreciation of the Borneo situation distributed by DOBOPS.[57] There was also a joint intelligence organisation in Kuching, which provided verbal briefs during breaks between patrols. At the operational level, watch was kept on the West Brigade Command Net, which provided a voice reporting network for units engaged in operations in the vicinity of Kuching. This was a useful channel for instant reporting of incidents or for the seeking of information of the whereabouts of friendly forces. It was the means of avoiding the consequences of misidentification between Commonwealth forces by eliminating the element of surprise in unscheduled encounters.

Did all these tiresome patrols achieve their objectives? A definitive answer is probably unlikely, but in a post-Confrontation report, DOBOPS made the following observations:

Rather than using the sea for infiltration Indonesian military units, special forces and communist groups continually crossed the border by land. This, although disappointing to naval units, was clearly a direct result of successful interceptions at sea, together with the effect created by conscientious patrolling and boarding night after night throughout confrontation. Coupled with this must have been the knowledge of our success in West Malaysia, where the only approach for Indonesian infiltrators was sea or air. The very low radar coverage provided by only one CMS off Kuching could never have been appreciated by the enemy.[58]

West Malaysia — Singapore Strait and East Coast

The Singapore Strait was by far the busiest stretch of water in Malaysia. Singapore itself was (and is) an entrepot port, serving the whole region and, therefore, a major destination and port of departure for local, domestic and international shipping. These maritime routes intersected with one of the crucial sea lanes of the world, carrying cargoes to and from the nations of East Asia from Europe, South Asia and the Middle East. A map of the Singapore area is at Figure 5-5. At that time, Singapore had a less developed wharf infrastructure, and in those pre-containerisation days, most of the cargoes being handled were breakbulk. Loading and unloading took place at anchor in Singapore Roads, with hundreds of lighters, tugs, bunker lighters and communication boats crisscrossing the busy harbour, and ships and smaller craft constantly leaving and arriving.

The demanding task of monitoring all this traffic was eased to some extent by the imposition of controls on the movements of the thousands of fishing boats which also ply these waters. A number of permitted night fishing areas were established, with the remainder of the southern coast designated a night curfew zone. Any craft moving in these at night was liable to interception and search. As well, remote areas of the Singapore coastline were rigged with nets to prevent landings and backed up with 'vigilante patrols' using immigration and customs launches, and floating boom defences impenetrable to outboard-powered sampans were laid off focal

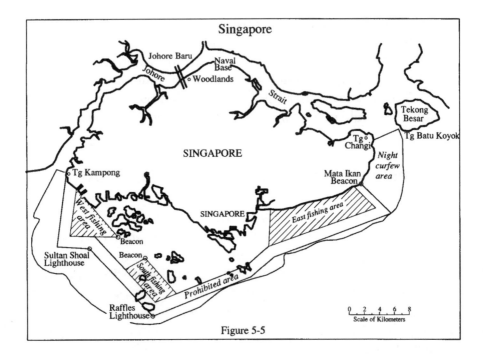

Figure 5-5

points. Four naval shore radar stations were set up to improve the radar coverage of the area, and Army and RAF radar stations, although primarily concerned with air defence, were encouraged to report in surface contacts.[59]

Primary responsibility for the security of the Singapore area was assigned to the Singapore Marine Police, and coordination of all units operating in a maritime surveillance role was done through a maritime operations room at police headquarters, known by its radio callsign Coastguard. Naval units remained under COMFEF, but they reported to and coordinated their movements through Coastguard, where naval liaison officers kept watches for this purpose. Understandably, there were a number of successful infiltrations by the Indonesians into Singapore, particularly before controls on boat movement had been imposed, Coastguard had been established and its procedures refined, and the patrol network had been sufficiently established from mid-1964.[60]

But as forces available to COMFEF built up, a relatively dense network of patrols was established in the Singapore Strait, built largely around minesweepers. Despite their limitations being exploitable by infiltrating craft, this class of ship accounted for 64 per cent of all interceptions, well ahead of any other method [61] Involved were the Australian 16th, the Malaysian 25th, and the RN 6th and 11th Squadrons, the RN squadrons manned with some assistance from the Royal New Zealand Navy (RNZN). New Zealand provided the RN with a number of officers and sailors to man the ships of this squadron, which had been largely mothballed prior to Confrontation. The inshore and coastal minesweepers and Vosper patrol boats of the RMN were also involved, as described in Chapter 4.

As the major RAN contribution to this effort was the Ton Class minesweeper, a brief consideration of the capabilities and weaknesses of this class, matched to the intelligence and operations background in which they were employed, is appropriate at this point. The Ton Class was not totally suited to this task, because of its low top speed and the vulnerability to small-arms fire of its wooden hull and aluminium alloy superstructure.[62] The first RAN ships deployed in 1964 had no ballistic protection against small-arms fire, nor was body armour apart from steel helmets available for exposed members of the crew. By 1966 this had changed, with flak 'blankets' fitted around the bridge area and bullet-proof vests issued to bridge personnel and weapons crews.

But the minesweeper possessed some advantages in this kind of close work.[63] The ship was highly manoeuvrable, had long endurance, a rudimentary capability for command and control of cooperating smaller units, good high-definition surface radar, and a height of eye superior to smaller, faster units. As one officer described, techniques to take advantage of this were soon developed for patrols. 'I used to sit in the charthouse [where the radar display was located] with the cursor up the middle, and watch for anything crossing the cursor. As soon as you found something crossing the cursor you'd go and investigate it.'[64]

A Ton Class minesweeper was typically armed with two 40

mm Bofors guns and small arms, including .303 Bren guns. For illumination it had its 10-inch signal projectors — which unfortunately made excellent aiming points for the infiltrators — and carried 2-inch mortars. These proved a mixed blessing: when chasing a target upwind, mortar flares tended to illuminate the ship rather than the target. The mortar was also particularly dangerous, as it had to be hand carried to the bow, held on a shot mat to take the recoil, muzzle loaded and fired by one or two sailors. Some RN ships were fitted with rocket flare launchers on the foredeck, which had a greater range than the mortars and were much less hazardous, and the RAN later followed suit. Thus equipped, the minesweeper was more than a match for the small traditional craft favoured by the Indonesians, and its weapons could be fired in the confined waters of the Singapore Strait with less risk of inflicting damage on non-targets or shore installations than the larger guns of bigger warships. The greatest potential drawback of the class was that its diesel engines were relatively noisy, which could have alerted infiltrating boats to its presence, although this seems not to have been an impediment to interceptions.

Infiltration boats — *kumpits* — were normally long, low and narrow, and equipped with high-powered outboard motors. Generally made of wood, they could absorb a lot of punishment and made extremely small and fleeting targets for radar operators to detect. A patrolling ship without serviceable radar was useless, and even when the radar was operating well, care had to be given to its tuning: satisfactory returns from the shore or large merchant ships were no guarantee of its efficacy in detecting the *kumpit*. The RAN attempted to reduce the difficulties experienced in radar plotting the enormous numbers of surface contacts in the Singapore Strait, and eliminating the innocent from the suspect, by experimenting with a special (Fanwise) sonar, designed to detect the noise of high-speed propellers. The system was developed and deployed in HMAS *Hawk* in 1966, but does not seem to have significantly reduced the complexity of the ship's operational problems, mainly because of the high ambient underwater noise levels in the areas in which it was used.[65]

When a vessel had been intercepted, the warship generally put a boarding party on board it. The small arms supplied for RAN boarding parties were sometimes a problem. The 9 mm Owen automatic sub-machine guns provided had a very loose safety catch, and the possibility of accidental discharge was high. In one incident in *Teal*, a sailor was climbing up the main ladder from the main to foredeck behind the bridge with an Owen gun slung over his shoulder, barrel pointed down. The weapon discharged when the trigger caught on an obstacle, spraying the main deck area below. Luckily no one was hit and after that incident the procedure was changed so that magazines were carried separately until weapons were ordered readied when approaching targets.[66]

The operating environment was a challenge. As described by the commanding officer HMAS *Teal*, the Singapore Strait was

by far the most interesting and demanding patrol area in Malaysia. The attention required to keep the darkened ship clear of the very heavy mercantile traffic is both challenging and tiring. The area abounds with unlit contacts, most of which are innocent fishermen or floating bamboo stakes (which give a surprisingly solid radar echo). Median line navigation, patrolling Indonesian ships, and infiltrators add to the general requirement of unremitting attention to the job.[67]

Teal was the first RAN ship to clash with the enemy during Confrontation operations. On 5 December 1964 she was vectored onto a sampan southeast of St John's light by Singapore Marine Police, only to discover the vessel was unmanned. The following night, she intercepted an unlit vessel just south of Raffles Light and fired to stop it. The sampan had two outboard motors which, if they had both worked, would have allowed the boat to escape, but one of the motors failed. The sampan could not manoeuvre well and was easily caught: an Indonesian officer and two soldiers were captured. Following the interception of the darkened vessel and a short pursuit, which was brought to and end with the aid of a burst of Bren gun fire across the intruder's bows, *Teal* and her capture drifted over the median line into Indonesian-claimed waters, which brought a diplomatic note from Jakarta.[68] But the incident illustrated the fine margin for error that existed in the Strait.

Back on patrol on 13 December, *Teal* intercepted two boats off Raffles Light. The boats separated and refused to stop, one firing at *Teal* when illuminated. Fire was returned and one stopped, and when the boat was boarded, one Indonesian was found dead, two were wounded and two uninjured; another two had fallen overboard during the action, but their bodies were not recovered. An Indonesian Marine officer was amongst those arrested, and a quantity of arms and explosives was captured.[69] The second boat escaped during the firing. The incident was recalled by the officer of the watch:

Teal was on a 5 mile patrol line from Raffles to St Johns at about 10 knots when I sighted two contacts on radar transiting from South to North at the south westerly end of the line. As we came to investigate this first one we switched on the searchlight and the bastard had a go at us with a sub-machine gun. By this time I'd got the Captain on the Bridge we were chasing the firing boat at 16 knots. We had three two-inch mortars on a shot mat right up in the bows and you'd rev the ship up to 15 or 16 knots and you'd throw a couple of mortar illumination rounds up in the air. By the time they burst you were almost directly under the star — illuminating yourself perfectly so the bastard could shoot you! It wasn't quite as bad as that but if you were going into the breeze, that's pretty much what would happen.

Anyway, this guy shot at us. We had Bren guns either side of the Bridge and I jumped out onto this Bren and shot the prick in the boat. There were two of them and we think one of them fell over the side, and I shot the other in the neck. By the time we got him alongside and they tried to lift him inboard his head fell across and he pumped blood all over the place and died. So we took him back ashore, dead along with the other two wounded and two unhurt.[70]

Teal's experience was not an isolated incident and infiltrators continued to shoot it out with patrol vessels, causing casualties on both sides but, fortunately, not to Australians. In one particularly serious incident, the occupants of a boat rigged for destruction if intercepted chose to detonate when it had been hauled alongside a British minesweeper and the ship's boarding party had climbed down into the boat.[71] The boarding party and the infiltrators were all lost in the explosion, but it says something for the rugged construction of the wooden Ton Class that the ship survived and managed to make harbour under its own power, although severely damaged. The patrol forces had no way of knowing whether the next interception was to result in a close quarters fire fight or a similar 'suicide boat' incident.

Thus even when the patrolling warship had made a successful intercept, the issue of the appropriate treatment of prisoners came into play. Some who surrendered were found to have brought weapons and grenades on board the patrol vessel, and there was the possibility that damage to the ship and injuries to its crew would result if these practices were not stamped out. The result was a rather robust prisoner-handling procedure, involving a strip search, blindfolding and binding or handcuffing. There is no suggestion that captured infiltrators were ill-treated on board RAN ships, but it was noted that the Singapore Marine Police were not gentle when the prisoners were handed over to them.

Singapore had such an array of tempting infiltration and sabotage targets for Indonesia, including airfields and aircraft, radars, the naval dockyard, warships, and other military facilities.[72] The attempts detected by *Teal* — amongst others — caused COMFEF to reduce the extent of Borneo patrolling temporarily in 1965, and to boost the number of ships available in the Singapore Strait.[73] Up to fifty vessels could be on patrol in the Singapore and Malacca Straits on a single night. It was not true, as the apocryphal story had it, that one could walk dry-shod from Raffles Light to Malacca Strait on the decks of Commonwealth warships, but the patrol line certainly was tightly packed at the time.

Commonwealth determination to resist and defeat incursions across the Straits was clearly effective, as the number of attempts and interceptions went into a steep decline in the early part of 1965. It was later estimated that the naval forces, together with those of the marine police, were successful in intercepting 80 per cent of the infiltration attempts.[74] Such a high success rate in an environment as challenging as the Singapore Strait points to the influence of superior operational intelligence.[75]

There were three principal sources of this. The first was Sigint. Indonesian tactical and strategic communications were easily intercepted from Commonwealth sites in Singapore and in East Malaysia. Indonesian signals security was lax, making the task of Commonwealth cryptanalysts very easy. Foreknowledge of Indonesian attacks enabled the Commonwealth high command to assemble and deploy its forces where they would have the highest likelihood of intercepting the raiders.[76]

A second, highly significant, source was the Singapore Marine Police. This force dispatched its officers to the Riau Archipelago to collect information on Indonesian forces assembled there, and to ascertain what actions were being planned. The Riaus remained a centre for smuggling and illegal barter trading with Singapore throughout the conflict, making it easy for the police to get in and out without attracting any special attention. This was clearly a very risky procedure, requiring courage of a very high order from the officers involved.[77] A considerable proportion of the security forces' success can be attributed to this fine contribution by a few highly professional Singaporean personnel.

Third, the Commonwealth forces had the benefit of intelligence derived from the interrogation of captured infiltrators and their supporters in Singapore, and from captured documents. Initially, the infiltrators were mostly disaffected Malay youths; later Indonesians were found amongst them. In mid-1964 a number of ethnic Chinese were implicated, and evidence of contact with the remnants of the MRLA in the Malaysian–Thai border area was detected. The survivors of an Indonesian airdrop in southern Johore later in 1964 turned out to be both Malaysian Chinese and Indonesian TNI regulars. Taken as a whole, the prisoners contributed significant intelligence on the purposes of and plans for Indonesian infiltration, and this was fed back into the arrangements for the deployment of Commonwealth units.[78]

Finally, to some extent Indonesian operational inexperience — often verging on ineptitude — assisted the maritime patrol force to maintain high levels of security. The courage and determination of those Indonesian personnel who chose to fight when called upon to stop by a Commonwealth warship was unquestioned. But flight would often have been a better option, and a more objective Indonesian analysis of the weaknesses of the patrol force could have led to the development of better tactics for concealment and evasion.

COMFEF ran an efficient patrol operation, backed by good training and intelligence support. Included in the Fleet's training repertoire was a captured Indonesian *kumpit* infiltration craft, manned by a determined and experienced crew of 'infiltrators' to train and test the capabilities of the patrol force. Distilled knowledge gained from operations in West Malaysia was contained in two documents. The first was *Orders for Ships Patrolling in Defence of Western Malaysia Seaboard* — known by its short title MALPOS.[79] The second edition of MALPOS, issued in March 1965, was a comprehensive set of instructions on how to prepare for and conduct patrols. Its Intelligence Annex had information on Indonesian infiltration bases and likely targets, as well as comprehensive details on friendly forces likely to be encountered. Officers of ships sailing on patrol were briefed at the Malaysian Joint Operations Centre before departing, and were also required to submit *pro forma* debriefs of their operations on return. Access to this accumulated knowledge on the practical problems of maintaining effective patrols, plus the comprehensive intelligence support provided, satisfied the majority of any command team's background intelligence needs.

Supporting MALPOS, but at a higher security classification, and issued only to RN, RAN and RNZN ships, was Far East Fleet Confidential Document 041, *Fleet Operational and Tactical Instructions* — FOTI. In this document, the section titled 'Indonesian Confrontation — Action to Counter Infiltration by Sea' gave guidance on the authorised occasions when force could be used, a checklist of actions to be taken on encountering Indonesian forces, and the reporting arrangements.[80]

But the Indonesians did not always behave in the expected manner. While encounters with infiltrators always held the possibility of an exchange of small-arms fire, the engagement of Commonwealth ships operating in Singapore Strait by shore batteries was distinctly out of the ordinary. This befell HMAS *Hawk* on 23 March 1966, while she was patrolling near Raffles Light. The ship had stopped and deployed her (Fanwise) passive sonar to detect any fast-revving propellers typical of infiltrator vessels in her vicinity. Around 1900 the quiet of the evening was disturbed by two salvoes of shells, thought to have come from batteries on a nearby Indonesian island. Although she was on the Singapore side of the median line, her rules of engagement did not permit her to return fire and *Hawk* decided that discretion was the best part of valour and withdrew northwards.[81]

Firing on an Australian ship was an incident worthy of a diplomatic protest to the Indonesian Government, but none was made. The Minister of Defence, Alan Fairhall, clearly piqued by the shelling, asked why not, and was assured by his Secretary that 'The incident was without consequence since HAWK was not hit, and it has not come to public notice', and that it was not out of character with 'various other recurrent hostile incidents'. It is reassuring to be able to report that, although the bureaucrats of the Department of Defence were not disturbed by the incident — which happened a long way from Russell Offices in Canberra — the Minister was grudging in his acceptance of this advice. He scrawled on the minute 'Suggestion accepted. But I hate being shot at!'[82]

Singapore was not the only tempting target for Indonesian

infiltration attempts. In a scenario reminiscent of the showing-the-flag visits of the Malayan Emergency, in April 1964 the frigate *Yarra* was ordered to Khota Baru close to the border with Thailand on the east coast of West Malaysia. The state of Kelantan was and is strongly Muslim in outlook, and intelligence suggested that this might be exploited by the Indonesians by landing infiltrators staged through the Anabas Islands in the South China Sea. Her stay was short, but the message was not lost on the locals; the Commonwealth maritime forces were alert to the possibility. During the following week surface forces, as well as aircraft from the carrier *Victorious*, carried out patrols in four search areas across the routes from the Riau Archipelago to the Anabas and thence to the Malaysian east coast.

These plans were interrupted by the detection of two Indonesian submarines operating in the area. One was shadowed clear into Indonesian waters by a British frigate, but the second proved more elusive. A search the same night proved negative, but the following night, while in company with *Victorious*, *Yarra* made a radar detection of a small surface contact, and a target was shortly afterwards acquired on sonar. This was assessed as a possible submarine and *Yarra* continued to prosecute, assisted by ASW aircraft and helicopters from the carrier. Contact was eventually lost, but it left no doubt in the minds of the Commonwealth forces that ALRI could maintain submarines in patrol areas used by them, and that they must be taken seriously as a potential threat to ships.[83] More directly, Indonesian submarines were credited with the ability to land infiltrators using inflatable boats.

The Pengerang Peninsula in southeast Johore State was another attractive infiltration site for the Indonesians. This had been a favourite haunt of CTs during the Emergency because of the relative lack of population and infrastructure, and the maze of swamp and jungle in which an insurgent force could evade security forces. Two attacks were launched into this area in early 1965, and the second landing near Kota Tinggi on 25 and 26 February 1965 led to a major engagement in which thirty-seven infiltrators were killed and thirty-three captured, at the cost of eight men of the 3rd Singapore Regiment killed and five wounded. As General Walker noted: 'It brings home to everyone that no matter where they are, danger is lurking in every area of Malaysia'. Moreover, these infiltration teams were specially trained Indonesian Police units, who proved very skilful and determined foes. When intercepted by patrolling vessels they stood and fought, using mortars and high-powered Armalite rifles against the minesweepers. Fortunately no serious casualties were sustained by the ships.

This incident almost involved personnel from HMAS *Vampire*. More than twenty engineering apprentices from the ship had been sent on a weekend cross-country expedition from the Johore River to a point on the Kota Tinggi–Kuala Lumpur highway, which they were due to reach and be transported back to the ship on the Sunday afternoon. The paratroop drop into the same area on the Saturday night certainly complicated the issue, and the apprentices did not keep the appointed rendezvous. On Monday morning, a search party from the ship set out to locate the missing men, found their trail and then got lost. They were lucky not to have become victims of the personnel mobilised to round up the Indonesians, as one of the search party recalled:

> We could hear helicopters [searching for the infiltrators] but couldn't see through the canopy. Everything was wet and I could hear a motor. So I got out my machete and carved my way through about ten yards of bush towards the sound, and there's a road! Coming up the road was a jeep full of plantation workers and they saw us falling out of the bush in uniform carrying side arms and were out in a flash with *parangs* ready to take our heads off. One of us spoke Malay and put them at ease — sort of — and got them to point out where the main road was, and we stumbled down to it.[84]

The party of apprentices arrived at their rendezvous a day late and in high spirits, and very surprised to find they had been sharing the jungle with Indonesians.

Commonwealth operations in the Singapore Strait and South China Sea coast were very successful. The majority of infiltration attempts were intercepted or deterred and the police quickly dealt with the few craft that did get through the security cordon ashore. It was an impressive display of a marriage of accurate intelligence, sufficient appropriate resources and operational competence.

The comparative ease with which Indonesian infiltrators could, potentially, enter Singapore, together with the existence of active anti-British and anti-Malaysian elements in the city, meant that the threat of attack on ships in the Naval Base and those moored in Johore Strait was commensurately high. While the landward approaches were secured and the water boundaries patrolled, assault by underwater swimmer was always possible. Under these circumstances, Commonwealth ships took precautionary measures — Operation AWKWARD — and the RAN deployed for the first time its newly formed Mobile Clearance Diving Team to Singapore.

There were two categories of divers in the RAN. The first were ship's divers, who were members of a ship's company who had undergone some preliminary diving training. Their tasks were relatively simple — bottom searches to detect ordnance attached the ship's hull by enemy swimmers but not their removal, the clearance of a ship's underwater engineering intakes, removing cables and nets which had become entangled in a ship's underwater fittings, and the recovery of items dropped over the side. Ship's divers performed their normal duties until called upon to perform diving duties. They were qualified to dive to sixty feet (eighteen m), but only in company with another diver, using surface supply breathing apparatus — that is, their air supply was delivered by a hose tended on the surface from a compressor on a diving tender or from their ship.

Clearance divers formed the other category. Qualified first as ship's divers, they undertook additional training in more complex diving operations and ordnance disposal, and in delivering attacks on enemy ships. Some were posted to ships, while others were formed into an independent team based at HMAS *Rushcutter* in Sydney, where they were employed on demanding general diving tasks. Their call to battle came abruptly. On 23 February 1965 the team was ordered to HMAS *Melbourne,* which sailed for Southeast Asia two days later. It was only then that the divers were informed that they were bound for Singapore to join up with the RN's Far East Diving Team.

The integration of the RAN team with the British was accomplished quickly and with little difficulty. There were no differences in tactics of techniques used by the two navies and, although the British had more advanced diving equipment, the Australians were fitter and seemed to have more endurance; it was a happy mix. Located in the Naval Base, the combined group formed two teams to operate as directed by COMFEF. Principally, they maintained the capability of responding to underwater incidents in the vicinity of the base which were beyond the capabilities and experience of ship's divers, such as the discovery of ordnance attached to hulls. One of the RAN divers described one such incident.

> There were a couple of occasions when we went into a two-watch system, Red and Blue, with Red on watch and Blue on standby. That was just after one occasion there, when a leading hand, Bill Burrows, and I and some of the RN-ers were called out to one of the RN ships. We don't really know, but it looked like a home-made bomb made out of a coconut held on by magnets. It was obviously not something natural, and whether it was a joke or not we didn't know, but we treated it as live. We put a metal shim underneath it, tied it off, and towed it out on a long rope and put 1 pound charges on it and blew it up down in the Straits.[85]

The team was also called out to investigate sightings of bubbles alongside a ship, but these were almost always assessed as frivolous attempts by the ships' companies to dodge work. When the presence of a diver was suspected the standard drill was for the ship to be secured at the highest state of watertight integrity and for the ship's company to muster on the wharf. Only when the CD team had given the all clear could they return on board to resume work. But it was unpleasant work for the divers, as one of them described.

> Ships alongside there used wooden fenders, about six metres long and two metres wide, as buffers between the ships and the wharves, with about six metres between them. To get in the water you dug a hole, literally, like digging in ice: it was twelve to eighteen inches thick, with rubbish, scum, slime, and that was your entry and exit out of the water if you had to get in the water between the ships and the wharf.[86]

There was, however, a more serious incident in HMAS *Yarra* on the night of 4 June 1965 — 'the extraordinary affair of the missing diver', as the Report of Proceedings termed it. Briefly, bubbles were seen alongside the ship, which was berthed in the Stores Basin at the Naval Base. Underwater lights were switched on and hand grenades and one pound (454 g) scare charges dropped as the ship went to the highest state of watertight integrity. The diving guard ship was informed and a harbour patrol craft summoned. Twenty-five minutes after the alert, *Yarra*'s divers were in the water on a bottom search, but nothing was discovered. The following morning the ship's divers conducted a follow-up search and a sweep of the sea bed under the ship.

> At 0720 they surfaced and reported sighting the body of a diver dressed conventionally in a diving suit, face mask and underwater breathing apparatus. The body was resting on the bottom in a crouched-over position. No sign of life was evident. Divers then re-entered the water in an effort to re-locate the body.[87]

One of the divers thought there might have been a large charge in the vicinity of the body, which caused preparation for moving the ship, but on re-examination, nothing was found. The Fleet Diving Team then took over the task but their efforts were unsuccessful, despite three hours of searching. One reason might have been the actions of a tug sent to stand-by *Yarra*, whose use of a 'large amount of engine power' would have flushed anything under the ship out of the basin into the Johore Strait.

Meanwhile, both *Yarra* divers who had seen the body were closely questioned to confirm their report. As the ship's report noted, the less experienced diver 'was extremely frightened by this experience and his evidence is clouded by this fright'. However, his buddy 'after initial fright investigated to the fullest extent with due regard to caution', even though he had lost his diving knife and was completely unarmed — a testament to the quality of the training he had received. His observations over ninety seconds at about a metre from the body included a full description of the foreign diver's dress and equipment, and he concluded with the statement that:

> I am sure I saw a person with diving gear on; whether he was lying doggo or dead I'm not certain, but it was definitely a human being. I came to the conclusion that he was dead because there was absolutely no movement and no bubbles.[88]

Intelligence in October 1964 stated that 'It is known that an underwater sabotage frogman threat exists and that the Indonesians may demonstrate their capability shortly'.[89] Subsequent consideration of the incident concluded that there had been a diver under *Yarra*, although the identity of the body was never established.

The RN/RAN diving team was engaged on other tasks as well. One of the strangest was the recovery and disposal of World War II ammunition dumped by both the British and Japanese in Johore Strait. Both nations had picked the same dumping ground, and this readily accessible cache of high explosive proved irresistible to those who had a use for it. The divers were told that the people who were diving down and retrieving the bombs and shells, and then 'sweating' the explosive contents out, were Communists. The description is plausible but not confirmed, and this dangerous ordnance disposal task was described by one of the RAN divers.

> One of the roles we had there with the RN-ers was diving down, picking up some of this stuff and walking into deeper water with it, and others were brought to the surface, put on the boat and examined, and then some were taken away to be destroyed. Others were just dumped into deeper water. They stopped bringing a lot of it up, because on a couple of occasions when we got it onto the deck it started bubbling. I don't know if it was just air escaping from the rusty casings of the bombs, or the ordnance; I don't know, but it deterred some of the chiefs [team leaders] from bringing too much of it up onto the deck.[90]

The chiefs were right. It was a hazardous practice, even if no attempt was made to disturb the explosives. But that is what the alleged Communists were doing, and it had tragic consequences, as recalled by one of the RAN team members.

> There was an explosion in the Straits, and we drove out there at first light. I can remember there were over a dozen dead bodies caught in the trees — blown to bits. It was explained by the chief that what they had been doing was cutting ordnance open and getting explosives. There must have been a group of them there; they had tripods made up for the bombs, and they were cutting them with hacksaws and one must have gone off. I remember there were at least twelve dead there.
> I didn't go out for the second one, but about two weeks afterwards there was another explosion and there were a couple dead, I think they said. But what they'd done was moved away from where they were, although not far away, set up and they had buckets of water in the trees with wicks out of them dripping water. They must have thought it was the heat of the hacksaw blades that had set the bomb off, not realising that it was just old ordnance and friction which had set it off. After that there were

no more incidents.[91]

One of the teams was dispatched to Borneo in April where it was engaged in attempts to recover two Royal Navy Wessex helicopters which had crashed in the water. The Wessex was designed to operate over the sea and had flotation arrangements to keep it afloat long enough for the crew to escape, but it usually toppled over shortly after. Salvage attempts were unsuccessful, as was the attempt to raise another Wessex which had crashed from an aircraft carrier off Penang in March.

Other team duties included exercise underwater attacks on the ships of the Far East Fleet, recovery of exercise mines laid by submarines, the surveying of a submarine bottoming area off the east coast of West Malaysia, training the Ghurkha engineers in explosives demolition, and diving on the wrecks of HMS *Prince of Wales* and *Repulse* north of Pulau Tioman, which involved training and practice in deep diving. But by 23 June, the Australian team was back in *Rushcutter*, following its passage home in *Melbourne*. It had had an interesting four months, and one which confirmed the training and equipment readiness of the RAN divers to undertake deployed operations.

While the Mobile Clearance Diving Team had been engaged in its specialised duties, the procedures for defence of their ships against underwater swimmers kept the other divers of the fleet busy, particularly at berths in Johore Strait. Outside the ambit of the naval base boat patrols and with pristine jungle to the north — which might conceal underwater saboteurs armed with those explosives salvaged from the Strait — diving bottom lines and underwater lights were rigged, upper deck sentries were armed and placed and boat patrols started. The aircraft carrier *Melbourne* experienced two incidents of possible underwater attack while in a Johore Strait berth.

Shortly before 10 pm on 27 April 1965 underwater lights were reported off the port beam of the ship. A higher damage control status was ordered and within fifteen minutes the ship's diving team was in the water searching the hull. The search continued until 2 am, without result, although the boat patrols were continued. Then at 0040 on the morning of 30 April, knocking on the hull was reported under the starboard side forward. Shortly afterwards bubbles were sighted emanating from the same section of the hull. Again, divers were sent to investigate, and one described his reactions:

> I was ordered into the water to follow a line of bubbles towards the source where the knocking came from. On my way down in pitch black darkness underneath a 20,000 ton aircraft carrier looking out for maybe an underwater saboteur armed to the teeth with an unexploded limpet mine or spear gun or whatever, was an extremely scary situation, for all I was armed with was the standard issue anti-magnetic knife. Fortunately, all I found was trapped air bubbles under the bilge keel seeping their way to the surface.[92]

On a similar dive, also in *Melbourne*, one young ship's diver nearly lost his life. He had been sent over the side to carry out a bottom search with a buddy diver, making his way down the ship's underwater hull on a swim line rigged for the purpose. A strong current was running and, during his descent, his air hose became entangled in the swim line. He was trapped in black turbid water, alone and nine metres below the surface. His tugs on the line to free himself were interpreted on the surface as demands for more hose, so he shortly found himself trapped and at the end of fifty-five metres of air hose. He tried to coil the excess hose around his arms while panic rose, but his training took over and he continued with his efforts. Shortly afterward his buddy diver arrived and, after he had cut the swim line, both divers went to the surface and were recovered by the diving boat. Then, as a tribute to of the high quality of training of both men, despite the close shave, they both then re-entered the water and completed their search.[93] Ironically, this naval virtue — carrying on with the job — later became a compensation 'sin'. According to the Veterans' Review Board, the diver had been stressed by his close shave, but not stressed enough because he had had the courage to return to duty.[94]

Diving in the Johore Strait was dirty work, but at least the water was flushed by the tides. A team of ship's divers in HMAS *Ibis* had the experience of being required to dive in the Kuching River in response to the sighting of bubbles coming from under the ship. Like all the Borneo rivers, the Kuching could best be described as liquid mud, because of the heavy load of silt it carries from the interior to the sea. The ship was secured at the oil terminal at Biawak at the time, so swimmer attack was arguably possible, but the divers were working against the flow of the river, at night and in complete and muddy obscurity, using their 'ten eyes — five on each hand' as they had been taught. They found no divers or devices attached to the hull, but as they groped around they did encounter plenty of sea snakes![95]

The success of the deployment of the Mobile Clearance Diving Team in 1965 led to the deployment of a second team, titled Clearance Diving Team 1, in March 1966. Taking passage in HMAS *Melbourne*, the six-man team arrived in Singapore on 12 April. Once again, the Australian sailors were integrated with the RN's Far East diving organisation and shared its duties. These included a survey of the *Prince of Wales* and *Repulse* wrecks at fifty-five metres, and the recovery of the wreckage of an RAF fighter which had crashed off Changi. The recovery of exercise mines, general diving duties around the naval base and underwater maintenance and survey occupied the rest of the team's time.

Unconnected with Confrontation, but reinforcing the point about the growing involvement in Vietnam, half of the team joined HMAS *Sydney* at sea in late April and disembarked when that ship departed Vung Tau on 6 May, for discussions with the staff of US Naval Forces Vietnam and a short visit to the Navy Explosive Ordnance Disposal team based in Saigon. This was in preparation for a short attachment in early June, which laid the foundations for the permanent deployment of Clearance Diving team 3 to Vietnam in September 1967.

One more group of RAN personnel was deployed to Malaysia in

May 1964, when twelve sailors were posted to Singapore to back up the staff in the minesweeper depot ship HMS *Mull of Kintyre* and to form a posting pool for the RAN minesweepers. They were accommodated in the naval barracks at HMS *Terror* but wore *Mull of Kintyre* cap tallies — which surprised more than a few Australian ships' companies when the wearers turned up begging meals to relieve the tedium of RN rations.[96] Their work involved maintenance of the weapons and sensor systems in the RN, RAN and RMN minesweepers which were beyond the capacities of their ships' companies, including engine and gearbox replacements and other than routine servicing of weapons and sweeps. One of the RAN maintainers recalled:

> Yes, engines as well: they had teams to do the engine changes and anything else required, whether it was British, Australian or Kiwi sweepers, or Malaysian, for that matter. Everything that we were required to do within the dockyard and the sweeper squadrons, and anything else, we did it. So it wasn't just on sweepers. I recall going over to a Malaysian Loch Class frigate — the same Class as *Gascoyne* and *Barcoo*. The Malaysians had a bit of strife, and they wanted to know whether anybody had served on these things. I said I'd done twelve months on *Barcoo*, so I went over and did a little bit of work for them.[97]

A collateral duty was to serve as spare numbers for RAN minesweeper crews, and almost all did at least one operational patrol during their deployment. While in Singapore they also participated in patrolling activity in the dockyard, boat patrols around the ships moored off the base, and foot patrols along the naval base foreshore. The foot patrols, designed to detect any infiltration, seem to have shown a degree of complacency on the part of the British, as the patrols were not equipped to respond to one. An Australian sailor recounted his experience of this duty:

> There were two of you, and you were armed but had no

ammunition. If you found anything you had to run back to the main gate to get the ammunition for the rifle. They used to drop you off in what they called a 'tilly', which was like a van, and it was a local driver and he would stay well in the background. He'd drop you off at one point and you'd walk and he'd pick you up at another point somewhere else and you'd walk that patrol. But they never patrolled the same area at the same time; it was always different. They did an area every day, or every night, but at a different time and you were dropped off at different places.[98]

On occasion, only one sailor was rostered for these patrols, which was particularly nerve-racking for the individual concerned, and irresponsible of his superiors.

In 1965 as civil disturbances grew in Singapore the Australian sailors were assigned for training to form riot squads to protect the naval base. This was drawn to the attention of the RAN liaison officer attached to *Mull*, who promptly acted to have this order withdrawn. The RAN had not been deployed for internal security duties in either Singapore or Malaysia, as was expressly made clear in the FESR Directive. However, the RAN sailors did go to sea in RN minesweepers, and even in the former fast minelayer HMS *Manxman*, which was used by the Captain Inshore Flotilla as a command ship. They also formed teams and were flown, with their equipment, to Hong Kong to undertake major maintenance on RAN minesweepers sent for refit to the naval dockyard there.

This admirably flexible employment and posting policy was not matched by the quality of the regulating effort to keep track of Australian personnel serving in *Mull*, as Kevin Pickett found out in a dramatic way.

My last patrol was on board *Teal*, and when we returned to HMS *Mull of Kintyre* for fuel and water one Sunday morning I was met by the Redcaps [British Military Police] and escorted to my mess in HMS *Terror*, where I found my kit had been packed, and I was told to be at the Guardhouse at 0600 on Monday morning. When

I asked what this was all about I was told I was booked on the Air India flight to Perth that day. The reason for the Redcaps was that I was supposed to join HMAS *Sydney* when it berthed in Singapore to return to Australia, but nobody told me and at the time nobody of any authority knew I was on patrol in HMAS *Teal.*[99]

While the presumption that the sailor had gone absent without leave, while he was actually on operational duties at sea, was bad enough, but the major outcome for many veterans of this type of sloppy book-keeping was that their postings and attachments were never recorded, making it difficult for them to demonstrate the extent and nature of their service in the years to come.

West Malaysia — Malacca Strait

While the problems confronting the security forces in the Malacca Strait were similar to those in the Singapore Strait with regard to transiting vessels and cross-strait traditional traffic, there were some significant differences and additional challenges. The first of these was the rather less concentrated nature of targets for sabotage, making it much more difficult to defend them and considerably easier for Indonesian infiltrators to carry out attacks on the infrastructure along the coast. The second was the length of the common sea boundary, which required security forces to be spread more thinly. A map of the area is at Figure 5-6.

The third factor was the rather more aggressive nature of Indonesian naval patrolling, and the array of bases from which raids and infiltrations could be launched into West Malaysia. Major launching sites for infiltration attempts were at Sinaboi, Makroh, Kembong and Selat Panjang, all opposite Malacca. As early as October 1963 Malaysian patrol craft had intercepted Indonesian warships in Malaysian waters, but the ALRI ships turned away

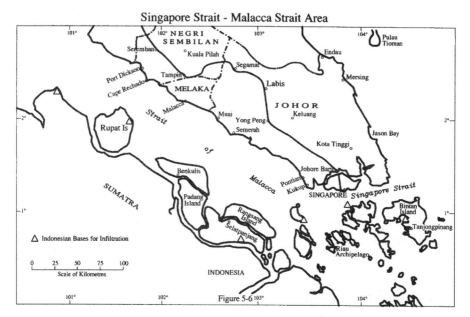

Figure 5-6

without engaging. There was a minor piracy problem for traditional traders and Malaysian fishing boats in the Strait, in which ALRI and Indonesian Police craft were sometimes involved.[100] There were also strong ethnic links between the populace on either side of the southern reaches of the Strait: a significant proportion of Malays living in the modern states of Malacca and Johore are ethnic Indonesians, and retain family ties across the strait. Accordingly, the Indonesian High Command believed the inhabitants of this part of Malaysia were ready to rise up against their government, once activated by Indonesian military cadres. In fact, these same Malaysians proved their loyalty by quickly turning Indonesian infiltrators over to the security forces, rather than welcoming them.[101]

Set against these challenges, the security forces had in place a most efficient police intelligence network, which had been developed during the Emergency. This could, and did, give early indications of Indonesian attempts at infiltration. A second advantage was that the Malacca Strait did allow the employment of Commonwealth maritime patrol aircraft, particularly in the northern reaches, which could be used to surveil traffic and to report unusual activity for closer investigation by naval patrols.[102] They were also able to monitor any build-up of Indonesian military strength in ports along the Sumatra coast.[103] Third, while there may have been fewer Commonwealth naval ships to respond to Indonesian aggression, there was a radar warning net of sorts in Johore.[104] Finally, a rather higher level of attack aircraft resources was available from bases in Singapore and Penang, should this type of response be required to deter or defeat an Indonesian attempt at air or sea insertion. Despite these defences, not all Indonesian attempts at air insertion were detected, let alone intercepted. One hundred infiltrators were parachuted into northern Johore near Labis from two AURI C-130 aircraft in August 1964. This gap in radar coverage, dramatically revealed, was temporarily filled by the assignment of a guided missile destroyer to an anti-aircraft patrol in the Malacca Strait.[105]

The Labis raid had two important consequences. First, the Malaysian Government sought and got assurances from its Commonwealth allies that they would support attacks on Indonesian facilities if that kind of aggression recurred. Envisaged were air attacks on AURI bases, especially those in Sumatra, and additional RAAF fighters were sent to both Darwin and Butterworth in case these plans were activated.[106] Confrontation had moved decisively towards war, and the tension was heightened when it appeared that the British would insist on exercising their right to route the carrier *Victorious* and her escort through Sunda Strait on passage to Fremantle. The Indonesians made it clear that they would oppose this with force. Frantic diplomatic manoeuvring resulted in a British decision to use the Lombok Strait instead, and the Indonesians accepted this decision. It had been a close call.[107] In talks with an Australian Foreign Affairs delegation in October 1964, CinCFE noted that the crisis had been recognised by the Indonesians as serious enough to disperse AURI assets widely in expectation of Commonwealth retaliatory action, but he was not at all sure that 'the Indonesians properly appreciated that their own actions over

Malaysia could bring military action' and the possibility of action through 'mistaken calculation' remained.[108]

Second, the Malaysians appealed to the UN Security Council to condemn the Indonesian attack on their country. A resolution 'deploring' rather than condemning the Indonesian landings was adopted nine votes to two on 17 September, and although vetoed by the Soviet Union, it was a victory of sorts for Malaysia and a blow to Indonesia. This was, eventually, to result in Indonesia's withdrawal from the UN in January 1965.

Because of the higher level of overt Indonesian presence, the Malacca Strait patrol comprised at least one frigate or destroyer, with cooperation from patrol craft, usually RMN and Marine Police but, on occasion, an international cast was involved.

> H.M.A.S. DUCHESS arrived on the patrol area [off Cape Rechado] at 1740GH and as OTC [Officer in Tactical Command] allocated patrols to H.M.A.S. TEAL, H.M.S. PUNCHESTON, K.D. SRI PAHANG and K.D. MELAKLA. No incidents occurred during the night of 21st/22nd February.[109]

It was the following night that *Teal* made her fourth successful interception of the deployment when she captured nine Indonesians, late during the first watch on a dark moonless night about thirty miles north of Malacca. As her officer of the watch recalled, the ship was patrolling a line parallel to the Malaysian coast at about 10 knots, with numerous fishing boats cluttering the radar.

> [B]ut one stood out as crossing the line from west to east at about five knots so we went to 'approach stations' and slowed to intercept the target on our port bow. At about 100 yards we illuminated the target with our signal lamp and saw a *kumpit* with nine Indonesians, fully armed but with all their weapons wrapped in plastic. Our approach had been silent so they had no time to prepare their weapons and the capture proceeded in a straightforward manner.[110]

"IT'S another undersize invasion — should we throw it back, sir . . .?"

Jeff cartoon HMAS *Teal*

This, plus the three prior interceptions earned *Teal's* commanding officer, Lieutenant Ken Murray RAN, the Distinguished Service Cross for meritorious service in the presence of the enemy.[111] It was the only naval decoration awarded to the RAN during Confrontation.

The frigates and destroyers had the facilities for constructing and maintaining a plot of shipping in the patrol area, and for commanding and controlling cooperating maritime forces.[112] A Malaysian Police interpreter was embarked for interrogating intercepted vessels, and for manning the regional police radio net.[113] It was anticipated that infiltration attempts would be made by night, so a heightened state of alertness was required during the hours of darkness. This carried some risks for the warships patrolling one of the busiest shipping lanes in the world, while fully darkened.[114] There were three patrol lines established from Singapore to Port Dickson and beyond: the more capable ships patrolled the outer line, followed by inshore and coastal patrol vessels closer in. A coastwatching network was set up to report any infiltrators successfully breaching these lines.[115] By 1965, intelligence gained from infiltrators and analysis of incidents had enabled COMFEF to devise a mathematical model to assist in the calculation of the size of patrol zones to be assigned to particular ship classes in areas of infiltration threat to optimise detection probabilities.[116]

The patrolling destroyer or frigate command team had access to a variety of intelligence to assist it in its task. A good surface picture was obtained using the ship's own radars, and this was plotted in the Operations Room. A watch was kept on the local air command net to monitor the presence of friendly aircraft, or of air activity on the Indonesian side of the boundary. The ship's own air warning radars could contribute information to this net. The frigate or destroyer was in radio communication with cooperating Commonwealth ships in its patrol area, and the activities of Marine Police vessels could also be tracked via the embarked marine policeman. Command teams had the information in MALPOS II and FOTI, as well as the benefit of pre-departure briefings and signalled updates.

While the ship's command team may not have been aware of it, the patrol area had been assigned based on intelligence derived from Sigint, aerial observation and marine police intelligence sources, which enabled the operations staff in Singapore to station resources where there was most likely to be activity.[117] The same sources provided the frigate or destroyer with an update of known or suspected Indonesian maritime activity. To this, the ship would also contribute as, after a few days on patrol, the identity and operating schedule of the corresponding Indonesian vessels in its area would become known. The ALRI vessels encountered tended to patrol to the edge of claimed territorial waters, making them prime subjects for photographic and electronic intelligence collection by Commonwealth units. If interceptions did take place, intelligence might be gained from the prisoners captured, although these were not always reliable sources.[118]

These defensive arrangements were strained when intelligence indicated that simultaneous infiltration attempts would be launched from two bases. The solution adopted was the traditional naval blockading response of trailing one's coat. The frigate or destroyer would be authorised to patrol by day ostentatiously off the second launching base up to the three mile limit, demonstrating its presence and, hopefully, deterring the infiltration attempt. The ship would then withdraw after nightfall to its patrol line off the first base to be in a position to control the interception of the infiltration craft leaving from there. [119] On three occasions British submarines were deployed off infiltration bases to give warning of the departure of infiltration craft as part of general surveillance duties carried out under Plan HEDGEHOG, which had developed against the contingency that offensive operations against these bases might be undertaken.

Despite the failure of the airdrops near Labis, the Indonesians pressed on with their infiltration, successfully landing them near Malacca, at Panchor in Perak and again at Pontian. On 29 October 1964, fifty-two infiltrators landed at the Kesang River in Malacca, but they were seen and reported to the police by local fishermen and rounded up by troops from the 28th Commonwealth Brigade. The naval patrols were picking up many more attempts. On 24 December, perhaps relying on the Commonwealth forces to be at less than maximum readiness, the Indonesians made an attempt to land sixty-one infiltrators northwest of Kuala Lumpur. The force was conveyed in ten pirated Malaysian fishing vessels from an island close to the middle of the Malacca Straits, escorted by an armed customs vessel, but it was intercepted by the RN frigate *Ajax*. Seven boats, their passengers, explosives and stores were captured. Two weeks later it was the turn of the RMN, when the patrol boat KD *Sri Perak* on 9 and 10 January intercepted two separate infiltration attempts off Negri Sembilan, capturing thirty men with others being drowned.

Despite the success of these patrols, groups were still getting through the cordon, and discussion took place in the OPSCO on the concept of making offensive raids against the bases from which raids were launched. The RMN went so far as to begin training a commando force to undertake these raids, using British Royal Marine instructors. The idea of raids was discouraged by the British (and the Australians) who wished to avoid any escalation of the level of hostilities. According to Grey, raids had been launched the previous year, but there is little collateral confirmation of this.[120] But after March 1965, the large-scale infiltration attempts petered out, as a tribute to the success of the maritime defences along the strait, and any raiding suggestions were shelved.

The Malacca Strait patrols were remarkably successful in limiting the number of seaborne infiltration attempts the Indonesians successfully concluded. While the percentage intercepted is unlikely ever to be known, the incidence of landings and sabotage was remarkably low, considering the relatively easy target which the southern states of West Malaysia presented to a determined aggressor. Clearly, accurate intelligence thoughtfully applied had much bearing on the result. RAN warships participating gained a great deal of experience in the factors leading to the successful outcome of such a sea denial effort.

As action at sea and on land to contain Confrontation continued, ANZAM planners examined and projected forward likely Indonesian courses of action. When it became apparent that its reverses in military operations and even in the United Nations had not blunted Sukarno's taste for adventure, the planners thought that the only way forward for Indonesian was escalation.

> We consider that Indonesia will step up her confrontation against Malaysia throughout the period under review [August 1965–March 1967]. Nevertheless, she will try to avoid escalation into open war ... she will keep up a war of nerves, while continuing to exploit subversive and dissident movements within Malaysia.[121]

The Australian Government, however, urged caution in responding to Indonesian provocations. In response to British Government requests to approve the use of Australian forces and bases in possible retaliatory strikes, it demurred. Australian strategists were concerned that tit-for-tat attacks would only lead to full-scale hostilities which, they assessed, the Indonesian military did not want, but would have to move to in response to any Commonwealth military attacks on their country.[122] By March 1965, however, the ANZAM appreciation of Indonesia's likely course of action had shifted. The situation had become increasingly uncertain, largely because of evident tension between the Indonesian armed forces and the PKI, apparently fostered by Sukarno himself. The Indonesian President had announced that 1965 was to be 'The Year of Living Dangerously' and had set a personal example of doing so. However, even nearer to CinCFE's headquarters than Jakarta, event were about to take an interesting turn.

The integration of Singapore into Malaysia had been a marriage of convenience. Whatever steps Singapore wished to take to demonstrate its 'Malaysian-ness' — including having its national anthem in *Bahasa* — it would never be seen as other than a Chinese enclave to the politicians in Kuala Lumpur. There remained in the city significant pockets of sympathy towards the Communist cause, which made it a particular target for Indonesia's wishful thinking on the disintegration of Malaysia, and Premier Lee Kuan Yew retained political power by a thin majority.

On 21 July 1964 there was a serious outbreak of racial violence in Singapore lasting four days. Twenty-two were killed, over 500 injured and 200 arrests were made. It was claimed at the time that the riots had been instigated by Indonesian infiltrators, although the activities of Malaysian *agents provocateurs* were given rather more weight by external observers. The Australian High Commission in Kuala Lumpur viewed the situation without optimism.

> Its [Singapore's] long term place (if one exists) in the federal structure will need a great deal of care and patient work. At this point I see no ready solution to the problem posed by Lee's vigour, talents and ambition, however this is assessed, on the one hand and the unpreparedness of the present [Malaysian political] alliance to give Lee a role.[123]

Then the Indonesian airdrop of nearly one hundred infiltrators

at Labis on 2 September coincided with a second outbreak of racial
riots in Singapore. This time the casualties were fewer, but over 700
were arrested. Senior Malaysian ministers were alarmed as most of
the victims had been fellow Malays; ANZAM planners were alarmed
because Singapore was the platform on which all their military
policies and plans in the region were based.

It was clear to all in the first half of 1965 that relations between
Kuala Lumpur and Singapore were deteriorating. Despite attempts
by their Commonwealth partners to urge caution — especially with
the question of the continued use of British bases high on their list
of concerns — Premier Lee and Tunku Abdul Rahman embarked on
a series of secret meetings at which they planned the detachment
of Singapore from Malaysia. In fact, Lee wrote to Australian Prime
Minister Menzies in April asking for his intercession with the British
and the Malaysians to stave off this decision, but it seems probable
that this was a mere smokescreen. On 9 August 1965, Singapore's
separation from the Federation of Malaysia was announced
simultaneously in Kula Lumpur and Singapore. Lee Kuan Yew
communicated the decision personally to Prime Minister Menzies:

> By the time you have decoded this message you will know that
> the Tunku has proclaimed, and I have agreed and simultaneously
> also proclaimed Singapore as a separate and sovereign nation …
> Because of your moral support we were spared [extermination]
> and given the choice either to leave Malaysia while remaining
> under the umbrella of the Anglo Malaysian Defence Treaty or
> facing the consequences which in the Tunku's words is communal
> trouble and 'bloodshed'.[124]

While not totally unexpected, the decision came at a very bad
time for the British. A Labour government had been elected in
October 1964, and it had commenced a review of measures which
could lead to a solution of a chronic balance of payments problem.
A key target area was defence, on which the country was spending
more than 8 per cent of its GDP, and the distribution of its defence

capabilities was wildly out of kilter with its international obligations; there were more British defence resources in the Far East than in NATO, facing the principal threat of the Soviet Union. When Singapore was detached from Malaysia, some Whitehall planners decided that it was probably time for Britain to cut its losses and withdraw from Malaysia. At a meeting of officials from Britain, the United States, Australia and New Zealand in September 1965 the British expressed their position thus:

> The result of separation [of Malaysia] was that the security of tenure in the [Singapore] bases had been significantly weakened. A number of influences had been released which had accelerated the situation they had expected would develop in 1970 or later. They expected pressures to grow which would limit their freedom to use the bases for their own purposes, including SEATO. In short, Singapore could no longer be regarded as the key to the presence of a significant British defence effort in the Far East. [125]

The response from the other three nations was swift and unanimous; the British were being too pessimistic by far. Both Malaysia and Singapore had explicitly agreed that the bases should remain and that they should jointly pursue the defence of their countries against Indonesian Confrontation. Furthermore, it was too soon to declare Confrontation a lost — and too expensive — cause. Even Lee Kuan Yew weighed in, talking of the bases staying for as long as twenty years and certainly not less than ten. Lee had no illusions about what would happen to the new nation's economy if the British closed their bases. It did not take long for the British to back away from the threat to negotiate a way out of Confrontation, but the price was a commitment of more contributions from other partners in the region to ease the burden it was shouldering.

Meanwhile, events in Jakarta had taken an even more unexpected turn. On 30 September 1965, an officer of Sukarno's palace guard with PKI sympathies had led an attempt to eliminate the senior echelons of the TNI as part of a coup. Although six leading generals were murdered the coup failed, and it led to a horrific bloodbath throughout the country, as anti-Communist elements settled scores with the PKI. The question now was what would the new leadership — still nominally Sukarno but with General Suharto calling the shots — do about Confrontation? There was a perceptible slackening in Indonesian offensive operations against peninsular Malaysia, but cross border incursions in Borneo continued. The ANZAM planners made two observations in their review of the situation in September — before the coup attempt — which proved unusually accurate.

> There are a number of imponderables, however, which cause us to be less sure that, should Sukarno die, a successor regime would continue in its present form ... Indonesia appears as yet uncertain how to exploit fully the separation of Singapore from Malaysia.[126]

On the battlefront, events could not wait for these events to reach their outcomes. With the barter trade so important to the Singaporean economy, a way needed to be found to safeguard the island nation's security from infiltration with the resumption of the trade. Malaysia was vehemently opposed to allowing the trade to resume; there was even talk of a blockade by Malaysia of Singapore should the latter resume any kind of relations with Indonesia, a proposal which excited grave concern in Commonwealth political and defence circles. However, diplomacy won the day and in January 1966 it was agreed that the Indonesian barter boats should trade through a merchant ship moored offshore from Singapore, thus obviating the need for them to approach the island. This idea was so successful that eventually ten ships were engaged in this activity in four declared areas off the Singapore and Malaysian coasts.[127]

Sukarno did not die — for the moment — but his powers were steadily assumed by General Suharto. The country was in an economic, political and diplomatic mess and reeling from the ethnic and political bloodletting that had followed the failure of the coup.

The Indonesians were unaware of the weakening of British resolve over fighting Confrontation and, although Singapore had left the Federation, it was still resolutely standing alongside Malaysia in combating Indonesian incursions. Suharto instructed his foreign minister to quietly open a dialogue with Kuala Lumpur to bring an end to the hostilities, and on 11 August 1966 at a ceremony in Jakarta the foreign ministers of Malaysia and Indonesia signed a document ending Confrontation between the two countries. The Australian Foreign Minister cabled his congratulations to the Tunku:

> The achievement of an honourable settlement owes much to the spirit which you and your colleagues have engendered in Malaysia since its formation since 1963, and the example you have set in combining resolution with flexibility, and forbearance with strong leadership. In standing with you during these three troubled years we have never ceased to look forward to a time when peaceful conditions would obtain in the region. I am confident that the associations between Malaysia and Australia, already fortified by their closeness in the recent past, will be further strengthened in the years of peaceful co-operation now in prospect.[128]

What had it all meant for Australia in general and for the RAN in particular? Confrontation was a serious issue, but one unfolding in the shadow of the war in Vietnam. While it was huge for the British, the Australian Government had attempted to limit Australian involvement out of concerns for potential commitments in Vietnam, and a disinclination to offend Indonesia. The military contest was clearly a victory for the security forces. In the Borneo jungles, on the busy waterways of Malaysia, and even on land in Western Malaysia, the Indonesian and Indonesian-controlled forces were repulsed, often bloodily, in almost every engagement. At sea, if not deterred, captured, or eliminated, Indonesian survivors were quickly rounded up by the security forces waiting for them onshore. Given the dispersed nature of the battlefield, this result would not have been possible without the contribution of superior operational intelligence support and the application of seapower, in which the RAN had played a full part.

> Sea power, usually taken for granted by those who have it, was equally vital. Its loss would have made land and air operations pointless as well as largely impracticable. The need for minor naval units to operate inshore was well illustrated, as it has been on a larger scale in Vietnam.[129]

Confrontation did provide the RAN with new understanding and new skills. A great deal of knowledge was accumulated by the command teams of the eleven ships that served in Malaysian waters, knowledge which could have been (but was not) applied in the Vietnam War. It is arguable that the RAN in its most recent campaigns in the Persian Gulf has been using similar skills. Perhaps recognisable only in hindsight, Confrontation was the future shape of operations for the RAN.

The RAN had demonstrated its capacity for sustained patrol and surveillance operations, its ability to command Allied forces in operations, and its grasp of concepts developed and applied by the RN. Its clearance divers and maintenance personnel had worked with their counterparts from other navies with complete success. RAN ships and their companies had performed well in comparison with the British. In ways that neither Korea nor Vietnam could be, Confrontation was a coming-of-age experience for the Australian navy.

What of the Australian naval personnel who had fought it? The operating conditions in Malaysia and off its coasts were enervating for the men involved. The new destroyers and frigates had a relatively comfortable time of it, but the same was not true in the carrier *Melbourne*, whose design made life difficult for most on board, and especially those in machinery spaces. In commenting on the state of the ship's company's health in April 1966, the Fleet Medical Officer made the following observations:

The second cause of the spread of this [upper respiratory tract] infection is the confined living space in hot, poorly ventilated Mess Decks ... Normal, healthy individuals may have their resistance to disease lowered by bad living conditions. That this is the case in *Melbourne* there is no doubt. In the period between Singapore and Hong Kong, long hours were worked in hot, humid conditions with poor facilities for adequate rest and sleep, particularly in the case of Machinery Space watchkeepers who have the worst working conditions in the ship.

Investigation of the working conditions of Machinery Space watchkeepers, especially in the after machinery space, disclosed an ambient temperature of 120° F [49°] in the control position. Keeping a four hour watch in this position, provided the individual doesn't have to do heavy work, is dependent on the forced draft ventilation system. On the night in question [a collapse], the ambient air temperature was 130° F [54°], and the forced draft ventilation was picking up hot air exhausted into the plenum, making it impossible for watchkeepers to stand in the vicinity of the ventilation outlets upon which they are dependent for working in these conditions.[130]

It was even more difficult for *Sydney*, reconfigured as a troop transport, in which spaces like the former air direction room and the sheet metal workshop were pressed into service as accommodation for the troops. As well, eighty men had to sleep in camp stretchers in 'A' Hangar, and almost 140 had no accommodation other than the ship's company cafeterias. Most of these spaces had poor ventilation, and the heat and overcrowding provided an ideal breeding ground for respiratory illness. There was an influenza epidemic on board, with five cases of pneumonia developing. The sick quarters were stretched to overflowing with seventy-one admissions, and part of the ship's forecastle had to be rigged as a ward.

In writing on problems in *Vendetta* during the Vietnam War the official historian of the medical aspect of Australian service in the campaign made the following remarks:

The British-built [*sic*] *Vendetta* did not escape these problems either, as its air-conditioning system did not function properly for a good part of the ship's deployment. From a medical viewpoint, the crowding and lack of ventilation in living areas contributed to the rapid spread of upper respiratory tract infections, most of the ships' MOs reporting outbreaks and recurrences of these illnesses. The effect of the inadequate supply of fresh air was also evident in the showers and heads, which were both stuffy and smelly.[131]

Nothing had changed in the ship from her time serving in the FESR during Confrontation.

In the minesweepers the living conditions were better — provided the air-conditioning was functioning — but the cumulative effect of long patrols with frequent stand-to's for investigating contacts had much the same effect. Many commanding officers took to sleeping on a camp stretcher on the wing of the bridge to be available at short notice, and the watchkeeping and boarding routine in the generally hot and unpleasant conditions made all on board tired, and there were health consequences later on, as one officer described:

It was all good fun at the time, but again I came out of that second tour with malaria and various other odd diseases. In fact, I was in Melbourne when, after a third attempt, the malaria was diagnosed by a local GP, who had never seen it before in her life. I had regular visits to the Tropical Diseases Unit for a while. But nine months in a sweeper in Borneo was too much for anyone, I think. Several captains volunteered to carry on for a second tour, but in every case after about another month they requested to get out; it was just too much, just the stress of doing the same thing all the time.

There were only two watchkeepers in harbour and three at sea, with the XO and navigator taking alternate days as boarding officer. So if you didn't have the middle watch you would certainly be up for several boardings during the watch. We all carried loaded Owen guns at sea all the time as there was never any time between boardings to put them away, and every boarding involved all officers. They did top us up with some midshipmen, but untrained officers only added to the workload. When we did let them keep a day watch I often found I was sitting on the wing of the bridge just to make sure they were actually keeping out of other ships' way. [132]

Thing were as bad for the sailors, many of whom were being asked to man their weapons while potentially exposed to small-arms and heavier calibre weapons fire on the upper deck. Recreation opportunities were few and of short duration. The wonder is that most coped with the stress of these operations as well as they did. The one significant breakdown occurred in HMAS *Hawk* during a recreational visit to the Sabah port of Semporna on 29 March 1966. A junior sailor was noted by his shipmates to be drinking heavily ashore and was brought back on board, where he took the opportunity of seizing small arms readied for a possible raid on the port by Filipino pirates. In the ensuing forty-minute melee, he fired over 300 rounds into various spaces in the ship, wounding several of the ship's company but, by some miracle, causing no serious injury, until return fire from a posse of volunteers incapacitated him. The subsequent Board of Inquiry blamed alcohol, but it seems likely that the grind of patrol operations was a more substantial cause of the sailor's aberrant behaviour.[133]

It is impolitic and unnecessary to select one group of men out for special mention, and I do not wish to do that, so let the following example stand for all the naval veterans of the Confrontation. In a message marking the unveiling of a plaque at the Australian War Memorial dedicated to the 16th Minesweeping Squadron on 31 March 2006, the Prime Minister of Australia, John Howard, acknowledged the contribution made by its ships and men to the defeat of Indonesian aggression.

Members of this squadron served a country which, due to the sensitive nature of the Confrontation, was largely unaware of their efforts. It is time to remember and show gratitude for their service. The Squadron played a vital role in this conflict. The unit patrolled water surrounding Malaysia interrogating suspicious vessels and making arrests. On several occasions, Australian ships came under fire. The members of the Squadron served in difficult conditions; they served bravely and valiantly.

The 'butcher's bill' for Confrontation was, mercifully, relatively light but more than 750 people were dead at the end of it, none of them RAN. It had claimed the lives of 114 Commonwealth servicemen, and a further 182 had been wounded. Thirty-five Malaysian civilians had died and fifty-five had been wounded. Indonesian fatalities were estimated at 602 — keeping score in remote jungle and at sea was difficult — and 886 had been captured, twenty-two of these wounded. It may have been of some consolation to the grieving relatives and colleagues of the Commonwealth dead that their cause had been just and had prevailed, and this was recognised by Tunku Abdul Rahman in an official expression of appreciation made in August 1966:

I have expressed on behalf of the Government and the people of Malaysia our gratitude to Britain, Australia and New Zealand for assisting in our defence for the last three years. Their soldiers [*sic*] fought side by side with ours and some sacrificed their lives. We are very gratful.[134]

PRIME MINISTER

CANBERRA

MESSAGE: 16TH MINESWEEPER SQUADRON REUNION SOCIAL CLUB UNVEILING OF A COMMEMORATION PLAQUE AT THE AUSTRALIAN WAR MEMORIAL

I am delighted to send this message to mark the unveiling of a plaque commemorating the service of the 16th Minesweeper Squadron during the Indonesian Confrontation from 1964 - 1966. Members of this squadron served a country which, due to the sensitive nature of the Confrontation, was largely unaware of their efforts. This is a time to remember and show gratitude for their service.

The Squadron played a vital role in this conflict. The unit patrolled waters surrounding Malaysia interrogating suspicious vessels and making arrests. On several occasions, Australian ships came under enemy fire. The members of the Squadron served in difficult conditions; they served bravely and valiantly.

As we remember the contribution of the Squadron during the Confrontation, we think of our service men and women overseas, in particular in Solomon Islands. They are contributing to the same important task of ensuring ongoing stability and security in our region.

The Indonesian Confrontation posed a real threat to the peace and stability of our immediate region yet it received very little coverage in the Australian press. We are grateful for the contribution of the members of the 16th Minesweeper Squadron. Today, we remember and honour their service to this country.

John Howard

(John Howard)

6 The British Withdraw

The end of Confrontation brought a halt to the fighting, but it opened a new chapter of anxiety for Australian strategists and military planners. The doctrine of forward defence had proved itself in sustaining Australia's interests in the region and, hopefully, in ensuring that the nation's value as a partner to each of the three Asian nations involved had been strengthened. A nasty regional dispute had been settled amicably without the application of aggressive military force, and 'face' on all sides had been preserved. There were, however, three new problems which Australia had to consider once cordial relations had been restored.

The first was the stability of Indonesia, now increasingly under the control of General Suharto. Sukarno remained President, although he was effectively detained under house arrest in his palace in Jakarta. The country remained weak economically, and the bloodletting in the wake of the failed September coup had reawakened suppressed ethnic and regional tensions. The question for strategists was; 'How stable is the new regime?' For military planners, it was, 'How much control does Suharto have over his armed forces?' There had been isolated incidents of cross-border incursions by Indonesian forces in East Malaysia since the agreement ending Confrontation.[1] Was this mere opportunistic banditry, or did it mean that military commanders in Kalimantan had decided not to heed instructions from Jakarta?

The second problem was the increasingly icy relations between Malaysia and Singapore, particularly between the two prime ministers. While Confrontation had kept the city state and the rump of Malaysia working cooperatively in defence and foreign affairs after Singapore's separation from Malaysia in August 1965, the end of the conflict allowed both to consider and to proclaim quite different views and policies. Strategists might have hoped that the example of what cooperation between the two could achieve in frustrating Confrontation would have served as an object lesson for both sides, but the language being used to exploit differences grew increasingly strident, especially from Singapore. For Australia and for Britain, success in defeating the Indonesian designs to crush Malaysia would have been for naught if the governments of their two Asian partner states continued to develop their mutual animosity to possibly destructive levels.

But the third and largest problem facing all parties was the declared intention of the British to withdraw their forces East of Suez. This was nothing new. As the relationships between the British and Malayans on one side and the Indonesians on the other began a spiral towards confrontation in early 1963, the Australian Government was even then having doubts about the commitment of the British to stay the distance in militarily defending the proposed Malaysian Federation. Accordingly, Australia had raised with the US Government the question of the invocation of the ANZUS Treaty should Australian forces come under Indonesian attack while defending Malaysia. Fortunately Australian, New Zealand and American pressure had convinced the British Government to continue to resist Confrontation, but with hostilities apparently at an end, the British wasted no time in dusting off the plans for a military withdrawal. By October 1966 responsibility for the defence of East Malaysia had been handed over to the Malaysian Army and the majority of British troops had been withdrawn.[2]

At the strategic level, a British withdrawal raised questions about the sustainability of AMDA, the future of ANZAM, the commitment of the British to SEATO and the composition of the FESR. At an operational level, in naval terms it raised questions about of what commitment in ships Australia should continue to make to the region in support of forward defence, and how this might be supported logistically. With the war in Vietnam escalating, in May 1966 the RAN had deployed twelve of its ships and nearly 3600 personnel on operations in Southeast Asia, a heavy load on a small navy. Diplomatically, there needed to be a decision on whether Australia should try to negotiate some kind of regional successor to the FESR and on the degree to which it might want to make a commitment to assist Malaysia and Singapore — and Indonesia — in defence matters. These considerations inevitably generated a considerable volume of discussion in official circles.

As early as June 1966 the Australian Defence Committee was examining the implications of the proposed rundown of British forces as proposed by CinCFE. The Australians thought the drawdown of forces somewhat precipitate in view of the uncertainty of developments in Indonesia. This thought was expressed by the Australian Intelligence community to the ANZAM Defence Committee thus:

> We assess that Indonesia, preoccupied as she is with her internal security and serious economic problems, will not initiate any overt military action against Malaysia, Borneo [*sic*] and Singapore during the next 12 months. While it is most improbable that any senior Indonesian army commander would deliberately attempt to embarrass Suharto's government by carrying out independent military activities, we cannot rule out, however, that an activity on a very small scale might occur, particularly in East Malaysia, due to the irresponsibility of junior commanders.[3]

ANZAM consideration was not far behind, and a planning meeting on 3 February 1967 was presented with a revised British withdrawal plan in three stages: the intention was that, apart from a garrison maintained in Hong Kong, British troops would be withdrawn from the Far East, leaving only air and naval forces.

Amongst measures taken under the first stage, ANZAM plans for action against Indonesia were either cancelled or put into abeyance, based on acceptance of intelligence assessments which estimated that Indonesia was unlikely to threaten Malaysia and Singapore in the foreseeable future. As well, CinCFE relinquished operational control of Australian forces in their Confrontation roles; this decision was implemented a few days afterwards and marked the official end of Confrontation duty for RAN ships. In fact, the last of the minesweepers — *Snipe* — had departed the region in December 1966. The FESR was to continue pending further decisions.

An ANZAM Defence Committee minute in March 1967 included the transcript of a paper presented by the UK Chief of Defence Staff which reviewed British defence commitments globally, but which also contained a statement on the defence of Malaysia and Singapore which was to become the guiding principle for all that came afterwards:

> Relations between Malaysia and Singapore continue to give some concern to the United Kingdom. There would appear to be no desire on the part of their political leaders to establish cooperation in the field of defence. The United Kingdom considers the defence of Malaysia and Singapore to be inseparable.[4]

Turning to relations with Malaysia and Singapore, as described in Chapter 4, the RAN had made a commitment to the development of the RMN, and continued to support this into the next decade. But what of assistance to Singapore? The situation was complicated. The major RMN base at KD *Malaya* was now in the independent country of Singapore, as was Singapore Naval Base and its supporting infrastructure. To the astonishment of many, Lee Kuan Yew had first reacted to the news of the impending British withdrawal with an attempt to forestall it. When this failed, he resorted to threats based on expelling the British forthwith. Wiser counsels prevailed, but Singaporean interest in building its defence force up from its post-separation levels in August 1965 was quite clear. However, emphasis had been concentrated on land forces, a curious choice for a nation dependent on maritime trade. In the case of Singapore in 1966, however, this reflected fear of a somewhat unlikely invasion threat from Malaysia, and the imperative to 'de-Malayanise' the Singapore infantry and artillery regiments and the police.[5]

As a 1967 Department of External Affairs paper identified, all these issues were interrelated and — for Australia, at least — there was also a growing diplomatic and military problem in Vietnam. There were finite limits on what Australia could provide, but it had to stretch those limits to the utmost to meet its commitments for the reasons outlined by the Secretary DEA to his opposite number in Defence:

I appreciate that with the Defence vote under considerable pressure as a result of the Australian commitment to Viet Nam, the present may not be a particularly propitious time to propose further military aid to Malaysia and Singapore. However, it is the considered view of this Department that the case for a continued programme in these countries is a sound one. Indeed, it is difficult to see how, unless we were willing to incur considerable embarrassment, the Government could avoid continuing some aspects of the present scheme. This applies particularly to the training and secondment arrangements which the Malaysians and Singaporeans have probably come by now to regard as long-term.[6]

The Secretary DEA supported this contention with a paper which argued his case in some detail, in the process of which it revealed that Malaysia in particular was in financial difficulties in attempting to meet its defence goals along with other national development programs of its 1966–70 five year plan. Confrontation might be over, but the potential threat of internal dissent, especially from the CCO in Sarawak, would continue to place a heavy burden on the Malaysian armed forces 'especially since the British can be expected to go to any lengths to avoid becoming involved again in the defence of Borneo'. The defence budget absorbed 5.5 per cent of the GDP — high for a developing country — and Malaysians were taxed to the point deemed prudent by the International Bank.

Australian interests were also involved. The development of efficient and effective armed forces in Malaysia and Singapore might 'in an emergency prove to be a saving in terms of Australian lives and money'. Continued Australian support for the defence plans of both countries could be regarded as 'an integral component and expression of Australia's concept of forward defence'.

> Looking ahead to the day when Britain might no longer be in force in Malaysia, the part we had played and the links we had established in helping to create the Malaysian armed forces would be of immense value to us in discharging our security role in South-East Asia.[7]

The case advanced for supporting Singapore harked back to the strategic importance of Singapore and the debacle of 1942, and the practicalities of maintaining forces in Southeast Asia without access to the bases there. As well, there was concern about the ability of Lee Kuan Yew and his People's Action Party to control 'the growth of Chinese influence, Chinese chauvinism and anti-Western feeling'. The DEA thought that 'Whether they can do so, and whether they have the will to do so, could depend on the extent of Western backing they receive'.

The DEA viewpoint did receive Defence support and a program of assistance was approved in April 1967. In June 1967 the Australian Government despatched a combined Defence and Treasury mission to both Singapore and Malaysia 'to make a factual assessment of the two countries' defence and internal security needs'. As a result of the Mission's report, in September Cabinet approved $A16 million in defence and internal security aid for Malaysia and $A4 million for Singapore for the period 1968–70.[8] The same month, the ANZAM partners agreed to the extension of the FESR Directive to include Singapore. On the subject of aid, in October 1970 a Defence submission to Cabinet reported that in the period 1964 to 1970 Malaysia had received $A38.9 million and Singapore $A6.3 million in Australian aid, mostly in the form of equipment.

In July 1967, the British Government had issued a Supplementary Statement on its defence policy which quantified, for the first time, its withdrawal plans. The first reduction of 20,000 had been achieved in the wake of the ending of Confrontation; a further 30,000 were to go by 1970 and that would leave around 20,000 servicemen and women and an equivalent number of Defence civilians in the Far East.

> The reductions will be so phased that, by the early 1970s, the British forces still stationed in Singapore and Malaysia will consist largely of naval forces (including an amphibious element) and air forces; there will still be some Ghurkhas in Malaysia. Corresponding cuts will be made to our base facilities.[9]

However, Britain's economic circumstances deteriorated further that year, culminating in a devaluation of the pound in November. The Wilson Government decided that 'our security lies fundamentally in Europe and must be based on the North Atlantic alliance'. In January 1968 it announced cuts to the defence vote, and revealed an accelerated, and more stringent, withdrawal plan.

> We have accordingly decided to accelerate the withdrawal of our forces from their stations in the Far East ... and to withdraw them by the end of 1971 ... Again, by that date, we shall have withdrawn our forces from Malaysia and Singapore. We have told both Governments that we do not thereafter plan to retain a special military capability for use in the area. We have assured them both, and out other Commonwealth partners and allies concerned, that we shall retain a general capability based in Europe — including the United Kingdom — which can be deployed overseas as, in our judgement, circumstances demand.[10]

As alluded to in the statement above, there was one other player in the discussions over the future of Commonwealth forces in the region, namely the United States. Fully engaged in Vietnam and with the Cold War with the Soviet Bloc ongoing, the major US interest was to ensure that there were no more security problems in Southeast Asia into which it might be drawn. The Americans expected, and made clear that they expected, the Commonwealth partners to resolve the situation in favour of the West, and to ensure the security of the strategically important international straits passing through the region. The US was, itself, developing a policy of withdrawal from the Asian mainland, and twelve months after the British announcement, the US President was to make his own announcement at Guam of the Nixon Doctrine, which put primary responsibility for their defence upon regional nations.

The planned departure of the British also meant that the legal basis for Australia's military presence in Malaysia and Singapore was in need of review. Their status was based on the 1957 AMDA negotiations between Britain and Malaya, to which Australia had 'attached' herself in 1959. AMDA had been extended to Malaysia in September 1963, and to Singapore when that country became independent in August 1965. It was clear that AMDA was reaching the end of its effectiveness and an alternative — or alternatives — was required.

The British decision also heralded the end of ANZAM. At a meeting in October 1968 the ANZAM Defence Committee was informed that:

> After 1971 Britain will have no forces committed to SEATO plans … Only in the event of a major military attack against Malaysia or against Thailand posing a significant threat to Malaysia, might Britain contribute air and sea, and possibly land, forces.[11]

The committee commissioned two studies, one on the modifications — if any — required to the ANZAM machinery in the period up to 1971, and the second on what might take its place after 1971. These studies were considered at its next meeting in February 1969. The first suggested that the inherent flexibility of the ANZAM machinery required no change to take the organisation through the period of transition. The second proposed the formation of a reduced version of ANZAM, similarly based on the Australian Defence organisation, but without the formal planning machinery of ANZAM. It would be consultative in nature and would be concerned with the interests of the three partner nations in the Indian-Pacific area generally.[12] However, with the dissolution of the CinCFE command and the departure of permanently stationed British forces in the region, there would be a need for either Australia or new Zealand to provide the commander and headquarters organisation for the new force structure.[13]

While the strategic and diplomatic conferring and consideration ramped up in intensity, the RAN continued to perform its FESR duties, with each of the four River Class frigates deploying, as well as the destroyers *Vampire* and *Duchess*. On 1 July 1967 the RAN itself made an important statement of its own independence from Britain when the white ensign it had shared with the Royal Navy ever since 1911 was hauled down and the new Australian white ensign, on which the red cross of St George was replaced by the Southern Cross in blue, was hoisted in its place. There was more than mere symbolism in this change as it marked the end of a long process of disengagement of the RAN from its parent service.

The post-confrontation duties of RAN ships were related to the primary role of the FESR — preparation to defend the region against Communist aggression. With ANZAM in decline, their principal focus was SEATO, but they fulfilled a number of tasks, including exercising with Malaysian and Singaporean armed forces, acting as escorts for HMAS *Sydney* during her voyages to and from Vietnam, showing the flag in Southeast Asian ports and participation in SEATO exercises. It was during one of these in July 1969 that HMAS *Melbourne* collided with USS *Frank E. Evans* in the South China Sea and seventy-two US personnel were lost.

Thus British, Australian and New Zealand defence cooperation in Southeast Asia continued strongly. However, the development of cooperative defence relationships between Malaysia and Singapore was to take somewhat longer, with a great deal of posturing before sensible planning could take place. The British use of the word 'inseparable' to describe the defence of both countries made strategic sense — in 1942 Singapore had only capitulated because Malaya had been lost — but it also struck a resonant chord with Australian planners. Sometimes this generated odd policy decisions. With the RMN paying rent to the Singaporean Government for maintaining its main naval base in Singapore, an important step forward for national self-respect was the disentanglement of this arrangement. As the former RAN commanding officer of the base, Commander James Hume, observed:

> KD *Malaya* was not only on Singapore territory but also within the Royal Navy's dockyard. So I had two landlords to cope with, and that would create difficulties from time to time. Most of the problems I had were things you wouldn't expect — they were landlord problems as much as anything else. Of course I also had a Singapore prison in my establishment. They had lifers — I think some thirty — and the Singapore gaolers were on my establishment as well. They did the gardens for me, and kept the grounds nice and clean for us. There was no memorandum of understanding about that at all; it just went on.[14]

In 1958 Tunku Abdul Rahman had declared his intention of building a base for the RMN at Port Klang, but circumstances and financial reality had intervened. Now, in September 1967, the Malaysians approached the Australian Government for financial support in constructing the new base. The request was turned down as the Defence Committee considered that to support it would be 'tantamount to subsidising the disengagement of Malaysia and Singapore in the defence field'.[15] This was curious thinking indeed, in the light of rising animosity between Singapore and Malaysia, but it does demonstrate how wedded the Australians were to the 'indivisible' principle.

As far as Singapore was concerned the main issue for Australia was the preservation of access to and rights to use the workshop and accommodation facilities of the naval base. One option was to make a takeover bid for the base. This was ambitious, considering that it was a bigger installation than Australia's own Garden Island dockyard, and therefore considerably larger than necessary to support the modest naval contribution Australia was making to the FESR, even if a frigate from New Zealand was added. However, the thought process was sound.

> [I]t should be borne in mind that if we fail to take advantage of the availability of the real estate, bases and facilities thrown up by the British withdrawal we shall never have the same opportunity again.[16]

However, with the British plans to withdraw apparently slimming its Far East Fleet down to a few frigates, there was not much prospect of any belated realisation of the Harwood Working Party's recommendations that the RAN should take over the base. Long before the British announcement, Defence had discussed the alternatives which Australia might face if the British did withdraw. In a Cabinet submission on this issue in January 1966 Defence had taken the worst case scenario approach and assumed that Singapore would not be available. The ramifications for the RAN were huge, including the necessity for the development of the RAN as a 'two coast' navy with a base in the west and forces permanently stationed there, much expanded afloat support to allow two task groups to operate simultaneously and a consequent increase in the infrastructure required by the RAN.[17] It is interesting that all of these developments were to come to pass, but not for almost thirty years. In 1966, negotiation of access was seen to be the less costly and more achievable option, as it proved to be. As Commander Hume recalled:

Well, first of all, we were going to take over part of Singapore Naval Dockyard. Then that went by the board for political reasons, I gather. Then someone thought perhaps we ought to look at KD *Malaya*, which we knew the Malaysians were giving up. I said; 'It's a huge establishment, just like Flinders Naval Depot. If we're keeping one frigate on the Far East Station, that's ridiculous'. So that was thrown out the window. Then I got moved on again before any decision was finally made.[18]

Some effort was expended on the idea that the US Navy might be interested in the use of Singapore as a refitting and operational port, but this prospect proved illusory. The major issue was sharing the cost of keeping the dockyard facilities operating and a feasibility study suggested that the Americans might be prepared to contribute by having ships up to destroyer size refitted and repaired there. The US Navy was interested in having access to Singapore, but not as a refitting port for its warships: it had its own advanced facilities developed to support US equipment under national control at Subic Bay in the Philippines.[19] Rather, the US was considering only refitting US Army vessels used as troop and equipment transports — merchant ships, which did not require the technical specialisation of a naval dockyard. In the end control of the dockyard was transferred to the Singapore Government in December 1968.[20]

As for the nature and size of the continuing naval commitment to the region, the Australian Government was receiving plenty of advice. One set of arguments was advanced by the Joint Planning Committee in a 1968 report, in which it suggested that an Australian naval presence would 'contribute to the security of a focal area which is important for allied military operations in South East Asia generally'. What those military operations might be was not explained, but this was an argument directly descended from of Australia's 1948 acceptance of responsibility for sea lines of communication into and out of Southeast Asia under ANZAM. The second argument was interesting: 'Without a Naval presence there is a danger that Malaysia and Singapore navies would develop along separate lines'.[21] Here, again, was the 'inseparable' nature of regional defence appearing, this time in an Australian document. Again, the Committee failed to elaborate on the separate ways in which the two navies might develop, or what the resultant 'danger' might be in this.

Not that there was a great deal of leeway open to the Australian Government in the matter of the naval resources it could commit to the Malaysia–Singapore region, but the residual force levels needed to be such that any likely regional task force that could be assembled was appropriate to the need and credible in deterrent terms. The Joint Planning Committee thought that one destroyer was the minimum but that 'two ships would be preferable and would provide a better contribution in terms of mutual support and effectiveness'. In December 1968 Cabinet decided that 'Australia would maintain until the end of 1971 a naval presence of two ships, including a New Zealand contribution'.[22]

Of course, the impact of any Australian naval involvement in the region not only depended on guaranteed access to basing facilities but upon the existence of regional navies with whom to operate. By 1968, the RMN was making impressive progress towards establishing itself as a competent naval force capable of undertaking the main burden of providing for its own maritime defence. In May 1969 it hosted a minesweeping exercise off Pulau Tioman in which its own ships, as well as those from Australia, Britain and Thailand participated — a significant demonstration of the RMN's growing confidence, and a boost to its regional credibility.

This was far from the case in Singapore. In 1966 the Singapore Government appeared content to rely on the Singapore Marine Police for its offshore defence needs, possibly because it did not fully appreciate the extent of the support being provided by British, Australian, New Zealand and Malaysian naval vessels to the maritime defence of the island and its approaches. There followed some intense lobbying by the Australian Defence Adviser (a Captain RAN) to lift the level of interest in development of a naval patrol boat force — possibly based on the new Australian *Attack* Class, but it was not until changes were made in the Marine Police hierarchy that progress was made. In May 1968 the Defence Adviser notified Canberra that: 'The new officer in charge Marine Police is now quite firm about the requirement for higher speed [for patrol boats] and has decided that 21 knots is not sufficient. The Singaporeans aim at a speed higher than 30 knots.'[23] The Singapore Government acted on these views, and within two years it had begun to take delivery of a class of six fast patrol boats from Britain. More ambitious plans for a new class of Israeli missile boats were under development.

The future of Anglo–Australian intelligence facilities was another issue requiring resolution. Singapore bases were important parts of the British and Australian intelligence collection organisations in the Far East, performing a number of functions in accordance with their UKUSA responsibilities. RAN personnel were very much part of this; up to a dozen were posted to work alongside other Australian and British personnel. Two of them commented on their duties.

I went into the Special side of it and learned how to be a traffic analyst. From there I worked mainly at DSD, although I did twelve months in Darwin as a traffic analyst. So when I did go to Singapore that was the work I did. There were Indonesian linguists — one air force and one navy linguist, and there was also an Army linguist in the same room as we were. We were detached from the people who were actually listening to the radios and doing the intercepting, although they were in the same building.[24]

While intelligence on Indonesia was of value, the stations were also intercepting information from other Asian targets, especially from Chinese and Vietnamese sites, the latter of particular interest to the Australians, who had troops on the ground there.

I worked with the linguists, because some of the stuff we were intercepting from Vietnam was pretty hot, and once we received it and decoded it, the linguists got hold of it and sent it straight to the Yanks, because it was pretty hot. It was mostly about ambushes.[25]

However, the Singapore Government was not comfortable having activities directed against its neighbours and, from 1967, partners in the Association of South East Asian Nations (ASEAN) conducted from its territory.[26] By 1970 the signals intelligence stations in Singapore were winding down and their duties transferred elsewhere.

Attention was diverted temporarily from these complex defence and diplomatic issues by the dramatic reassertion by the Philippines Congress of that country's claim to sovereignty over Sabah. No overt military moves were initiated to enforce this claim, but the Malaysians were taking no risks. They sought the support of their AMDA partners in making a demonstration of military preparedness, to reassure the citizens of East Malaysia as much as to deter the Filipinos. The British agreed, somewhat reluctantly, but the Australian and New Zealand governments were averse to becoming involved in this dispute between neighbours.[27] They had an alliance with the Philippines, and the forces of all three countries were engaged in Vietnam, a conflict that the British had refused to support. With Malaysia they had only an agreement, and that in the process of a long and frustrating renegotiation process. This prolonged uncertainty caused the RMN some operational anguish, as one of their staff officers recalled:

The only worry that year, 1968 or around that period, was I was Staff Officer Grade 3 (Ops) in MINDEF when the Philippines annexed Sabah. We had to reinforce our people there and the Australians refused to be part of that do. I was sent to Tawau for the second time to set up the joint headquarters. The Brits were willing to take part but the Australians and New Zealanders were not. I also had to be prepared to take over one of the ships; I'd never had command experience but I had to be prepared in case the Brits pulled out too.[28]

The matter blew over, with plenty of alarms but no Filipino military action. However, the episode only deepened concern and some frustration over the apparent inability of Malaysia and Singapore to see things in the same light as their Commonwealth partners. As the Secretary of the Australian Department of Defence remarked, with some impatience, in a minute in July 1969, 'The key to our interest in Malaysia/Singapore rests in both countries not only talking about the indivisibility of their defence, but doing something about it. At the moment I see no signs of this.'[29]

His sentiments were echoed by the US Secretary of State in 1970 when he remarked to the Australian ambassador to Washington that Australian efforts to 'bump Singapore's and Malaysia's heads together was very important and a step which he clearly applauded'. Not quite so forthcoming but just as frustrated was the British Government, which distrusted Prime Minister Lee not only for his threat to kick them out of Singapore but for his efforts to negotiate separately with the British in defence and security matters without any prior consultation with Malaysia.[30]

Perhaps the two Asian neighbours recognised this frustration because they themselves began to discuss issues that reflected the indivisibility issue of their defence. An Integrated Air Defence System (IADS) was one such issue, where cooperation was essential and agreed, and the system established linked Australian, Malaysian and Singaporean fighter aircraft through a common command and control system using radars in both of the Asian partners' territory.[31] The RMN agreed to continue to operate the Woodlands armament depot in Singapore on behalf of both countries and to provide training for the RSN.[32]

Of course, it was not only upon Australia that the British withdrawal compelled deep thought. The modern Malay state had evolved under the overall protection of British military power. This had failed it once in 1942, but since then it had successfully underwritten the defeat of first the CT menace and then the Indonesian threat to Malaysia; now that protection was to be dismantled and returned to a distant United Kingdom, preoccupied with Europe. Singapore was no less fundamentally affected. There the British had not only provided similar protection but, through the financial contributions made by the operation of its bases and the service people living in the island, had been a major factor in the local economy and industrial development.[33] The departure of the British would have a serious impact on the island, not least because their presence had been regarded by the Singaporean Government as an insurance policy against any Malaysian military adventurism directed towards the island state. So, for essentially the same reasons, although expressed quite differently, both nations needed to explore an alternative to AMDA, and a way of retaining some semblance of a British military presence.

This need was recognised by all interested parties, not least the Malaysians, and the first steps seem to have been taken by Tunku Abdul Rahman. In early 1968 the Malaysian Government proposed a defence agreement linking Malaysia, Singapore, Britain, Australia and New Zealand and a conference to discuss what were at that stage called Five Power Talks was held in Kuala Lumpur in June 1968. There were conflicting opinions about the outcomes of this conference, with the British Minister of Defence claiming in the Commons on 17 June that 'the responsibility for defence in South East Asia Area in future has largely been accepted by the other four participants'.[34] This was not how the 'other four participants' saw the situation, and a great deal of negotiation took place behind the scenes before the next conference, held in Canberra in June 1969.

The Malaysian Government was concerned that it was about to lose the shelter of AMDA without anything substantial to replace it; its situation was not unlike that of Australia after the end of World War II. The Five Power discussions seemed not to be making much progress, and in August 1969 the Malaysian Defence Minister, Tun Abdul Razak, called in the Australian High Commissioner to discuss their concerns. He described the significance of the Five Power arrangement as 'uncertain' and indicated that Malaysia had no clear idea of where it might stand in relation to its former allies and their commitments to his country after the British withdrew in 1971. In all probability, all the partner countries were in the same situation. If the Malaysian Defence Minister hoped that this might precipitate Australian interest in a regional defence treaty he was mistaken; Australia was content with ANZUS and SEATO, and would negotiate a new functional arrangement with Britain and New Zealand covering its forces in Malaysia and Singapore. It might develop individual understandings with regional nations, but it needed no more treaties. Moreover, there was an element of naïveté and special pleading in the Malaysian request. This was a country which, at independence, had opted for a 'non-aligned' position with regard to SEATO, and had maintained that stance. Now it wanted three SEATO member nations to enter into a separate defence pact to guarantee its security. Three years later, Malaysia would be espousing the cause of 'neutrality'.

In fact, the Australian Government's position had been established as long ago as December 1967, one that changed very little over the next four years, and whose aims were largely achieved. It was

> to confine ourselves at this stage to the steps necessary to enable us to stay in Malaysia/Singapore while keeping our options for the future entirely open ... We should not enter into bilateral arrangements with Malaysia and Singapore which would lead the United States or the United Kingdom to believe we had taken over the burden of security in that area and thus relieve them of future responsibility. Finally, we should work to bring Malaysia and Singapore together in future defence matters.[35]

For its part, the British Government wanted to demonstrate its continuing commitment to its Far East defence responsibilities and its ability to support that with military power. At the June 1968 Five Power Conference, it announced its intention to do so in the form of a major force deployment exercise.

In the context of a discussion on the ability of the United Kingdom Government to deploy forces in the area after 1971, the Conference agreed that there should be a major exercise in 1970 in which all five countries would participate. They noted that British participation would include a major reinforcement exercise from the United Kingdom.[36]

The exercise gained the codename *Bersatu Padu*, Malay for Firmly United (or Complete Unity), and was a large undertaking, with the participating nations contributed a total of twenty-seven planning staff who took eighteen months to complete their work. A Malaysian member of the staff recalled the experience.

After the British left ... I was attached to this *Bersatu Padu* group ... We planned that Five Nation exercise, which was not only Navy but also Army and Air Force. The focus of the exercise was to show that, even though the British had pulled out East of Suez, countries like Malaysia and Singapore can get any security assistance they required. That was quite successful and I was involved in the planning of it.[37]

In its final form, the naval segment of the tri-service exercise was designed to test the Five Power forces in coastal patrol operations, amphibious operations, mine countermeasures, task force operations and protection and anti-submarine operations, an ambitious program of work. The 'enemy' forces were from the Southeast Asian nation of 'Ganasia', represented for the most part by elements of the British armed forces, and the maritime play of the exercise scenario took place in the South China Sea. According to the Australian Minister for Defence, *Bersatu Padu* 'is designed to train and exercise combined forces of Australia ... under the conditions that would prevail after the United Kingdom withdrawal ... The setting of the exercise envisages overt military action against Malaysia by a fictitious country.'[38]

Australia contributed a large task force to the main naval part of the exercise — Crack Shot — which ran for ten days from 25 May. It was formed on the carrier *Melbourne*, with three frigates as escorts and the tanker *Supply* in support. *Melbourne* was operating her new air group, comprising Seahawk fighter/bombers, Tracker patrol aircraft and Wessex anti-submarine helicopters. Three RAN minesweepers were also involved, as was the submarine *Oxley* and the escort maintenance ship *Stalwart*. All told, about 4500 RAN personnel were involved, not including the shore headquarters Naval Component Commander's staff, led by Commodore Clarke RAN. In all, fifty warships from the five countries took part.

The naval element of *Bersatu Padu* was judged a success, and the navies of the five nations operated together more harmoniously than the army formations taking part. One unexpected outcome for the RAN was a renewed interest in amphibious operations, which had not been part of its capabilities since World War II. Amongst the conclusions of the report by the Australian observers at the exercise was the statement:

> a helicopter mobile amphibious force supported by a heavy lift logistic ship provides a very potent and flexible system for the application of military power from the security and mobility of the open sea. An RAN LPH ... would be the most useful contribution that the RAN could make to the tactical mobility and offensive capability of the services.[39]

Despite this most impressive demonstration of the principles of a potential new defence arrangement for Malaysia and Singapore, it was clearly an artificial construct so far as Britain was concerned. One effect of the British decisions on withdrawal was to scale down the British preponderance of power in the relationships with its Southeast Asian and pacific partnerships, and to 'scale up' the contributions made by Australia and New Zealand, Malaysia and Singapore. In a sense, it introduced an atmosphere of equality in the power equation and this was to bring a dramatic change in all four countries.[40] It made possible an agreement between the five countries as equals, which was the basis upon which a replacement for AMDA was ultimately negotiated.

In a ministerial statement in March 1970, the Australian Minister for Defence (and future Prime Minister), Malcolm Fraser, outlined the government's post-Guam Doctrine views on Indonesia, and its policy on a continued defence commitment in the region. He noted that Indonesia had been 'not so long ago a cause of concern to us', and acknowledged that remarkable changes had taken place under the new generation of Indonesian leaders. After remarking that the government saw 'no security in isolation', he summed up the future directions for regional defence engagement:

> This being the case, within our resources our military capability must be geared for deployment in the region of which Australia is part when in our judgement we conclude that this is demanded by our concept of regional security, as well as for the obvious purpose of meeting possible threats to Australian territory. This is the only proper conclusion, to which an analysis of our basic situation should lead us.[41]

While not committing Australia to a major defence presence in Southeast Asia, the Government clearly indicated its willingness to continue to work in conjunction with regional nations for the common security cause. This had the effect of calming some regional fears that perceived Australian ambivalence over the negotiation of agreements with Malaysia and Singapore indicated a propensity to 'cut and run' after the British withdrawal. There appears to be no evidence that the Australian Government ever seriously considered such a policy.

For the ANZAM partners it was also time for the details of the future relationships to be thrashed out. At a meeting on 11 June 1970, Cabinet considered a British proposal for the replacement of AMDA. The British agreed only to 'consult' on matters of overt attack and to have no responsibility for involvement in matters of insurgencies. This was not welcomed, and Australia pressed for the continuation of the policies which had underwritten AMDA. But progress was being made in detailed arrangements. The concept of

IADS, which would cover both Malaysian and Singaporean airspace, be commanded by an Australian air vice marshal, and employ resources from all five nations, had already been endorsed by the Australian Cabinet in March 1970.

Then, also in June 1970, the Labour Government in the UK was replaced by the Conservatives. One outcome was a reconsideration of the 'total withdrawal by 1971' policy, which their predecessors had modified slightly by an agreement to send a significant naval presence to the region in 1971 for an extended period. But the new government decided that Britain would retain a representative force level in Southeast Asia after 1971. This breathed life into what had been a lacklustre series of meetings on a successor to AMDA, which took on more purpose. In July ANZAM chiefs agreed on a series of changes to the organisation, including a widening of the area of interest beyond Malaysia to 'those Pacific and Indian Ocean areas with which the three countries are concerned, particularly in the maritime sphere'.[42]

For Australia, outside the seeming preoccupation with Malaysia and Singapore and the increasing attention being demanded by Vietnam, there remained the most important issue of its relationship with Indonesia. Under Suharto, Indonesia's attitude towards its near neighbours had changed to one of cooperation, and that country had been a motive force in the development of regional cooperation, the most tangible evidence of which was the formation of ASEAN in August 1967.[43] However, Australian strategists and policy makers had a particular problem in making progress in this vital work because of extremely hostile public perceptions of Australia's nearest neighbours. The suspicion with which the Indonesian military had been regarded a decade earlier — before Confrontation — had not abated, and the Australian Government and its advisers had to move cautiously. The Defence Committee considered defence cooperation with Indonesia in 1968 and concluded that this should be limited to training. So sensitive was the issue that there was to be no line item in financial documents identifying this program; the funds should be drawn from general estimates so that no attention was drawn to the activity. In fact, throughout the Confrontation period, HMAS *Diamantina* had been actively involved in hydrographic and oceanographic work in the vicinity of Indonesia with no demur from the Indonesians, and a joint program of charting Indonesian waters by the RAN resumed in 1970. Any residual resentments over Confrontation had been put aside in both countries.

The transition from AMDA, FESR and ANZAM produced two separate, but interrelated, structures. The first was the framework and organisation for the operation, control and support of the residual military contingents from Australia, New Zealand and the United Kingdom — ANZUK.[44] ANZUK was the direct successor to ANZAM and FESR, and the transition involved a number of steps. One of these was the adjustment of strategic communications in the Far East. With the imminent closure of British stations, it was agreed that joint service facilities would be set up in Singapore to serve the requirements of the service contingents of all three nations — something of novel experiment in those days. A contingent of RAN communications personnel continued to serve in Singapore until the final withdrawal in 1975, either manning the joint communications facilities, or in supervisory positions in the RMN communications network.

Australia's commitment to the new organisation comprised two squadrons of Mirage fighter aircraft, most at Butterworth but with a detachment in Singapore, an infantry battalion in Singapore, a frigate or destroyer permanently on station, and a submarine in rotation with one from the UK. In total, the Australian commitment was of around 3300 personnel, of 7000 from all three countries under the command of the ANZUK Commander, an Australian two star officer. A further group of ninety RAAF personnel were loaned to Malaysia as part of the transfer of ten Sabre aircraft to the Royal Malaysian Air Force. HMAS *Swan* became the first RAN ship to deploy under the new arrangements.

Under ANZUK, access to that part of the Singapore Naval Base necessary to support Commonwealth ships was successfully negotiated with the Singapore Government, with the remainder of the base becoming a government owned shipyard. The Stores Basin, as it was known, was placed under the control of the Commander of the Yard, who was an RAN officer from 14 April 1971. The title was changed to Port Manager in November that year and filled by a succession of RAN officers until 1976.[45] The Port Manager provided berthing services and made the logistic and engineering support arrangements for visiting Commonwealth and allied ships.

The second structure to emerge was the Five Power Defence Arrangements (FPDA), separate from ANZUK. It was a common failing of some observers to link the two, but they were set up and controlled quite separately, despite there being a commonality of three of the five partners in both. This distinction became important when the Whitlam Government withdrew Australia from ANZUK in 1975, but left its FPDA commitments in place.[46] These undertakings were based on the communiqué issued after a ministerial meeting held in London in April 1971 at which the five nations party to the talks agreed that:

> in the event of any form of armed attack externally organised or supported or the threat of such attack against Malaysia or Singapore, their governments would immediately consult together for the purpose of deciding what measures should be taken jointly or separately in relation to such attack or threat.[47]

FPDA was to be directed by a Joint Consultative Committee, a body comprising senior officials who would meet regularly to discuss and coordinate FPDA activities. As well, there was to be an Air Defence Council to oversee IADA. Thus FPDA was a pale shadow of AMDA, which had committed Britain and, by extension, Australia and New Zealand to the defence of Malaya/Malaysia, and later Singapore, against attack. Nor was it a defence pact. However, the wording closely resembled that of ANZUS, which also does not commit any of those three nations to the automatic defence of another.[48] This might have been a disappointment to some in

Singapore and Malaysia, but in a Britain in the process of slashing its non-Atlantic commitments, and an Australia in the process of disengaging its forces from Vietnam, it was probably the extent of the commitment they were willing to make. How well FPDA has served its purposes will be touched upon in the next chapter, but the fact that it still functions in 2007 says something for the wisdom of the framers of the 1971 communiqué.

What were the 'arrangements' designed to protect Malaysia and Singapore from? Not surprisingly, the Indonesians were somewhat puzzled and a little concerned that there was no 'threat' identified against which the five countries could direct their efforts. If it was against Communism, why didn't Malaysia and Singapore simply join SEATO? They could see that there was something to be said for Australia and New Zealand retaining forces in the region as a measure of stability while her two new neighbours built up their own defence capabilities. Neither Australia nor New Zealand was regarded as neo-colonialist, but could the FPDA be directed against Indonesia? Most pleasing to the Indonesians was that the British were withdrawing, which would remove the sole remaining colonial power from Southeast Asia, and Jakarta went to some trouble to ensure that the quite different approach of the Suharto Government to its neighbours, as opposed to the former Sukarno-ist policies, was clearly understood in all FPDA national capitals.[49]

Not that the Indonesian position was always enunciated clearly. In January 1971 the Indonesian Foreign Minister was quoted in the Singapore *Straits Times* as declaring that 'all foreign troops should be withdrawn from Singapore ... We stick to our principle that we cannot agree to foreign troops being stationed in any country.' This was contrary to the position that had been taken in diplomatic negotiations, but by May, when the Australian Foreign Minister visited Jakarta, the pronouncement had been subtly changed.

Indonesia did not support the presence of foreign bases which were established in the region by outside powers, nor of foreign troops. But Indonesia appreciated that some countries in the region accepted foreign bases of a temporary nature and that these were not directed towards Indonesia.[50]

The final acts in this long series of negotiations occurred at the end of 1971. On 31 October the British Far East Command was disestablished and on the following day ANZUK Force officially came into being. Its headquarters were in Singapore, and its first commander was Australian Rear Admiral D.C. Wells. In a most peculiar way, the recommendations of the 1948 Harwood Working Party had come to pass. Then on 1 December 1971, in execution of the FPDA, Australia signed separate agreements with Malaysia and Singapore which replaced its attachment to the 1957 AMDA and its subsequent extensions. Now Australia was directly committed to consult with these two nations in defence policy, and no longer through a British intermediary.[51]

With these agreements, both the nature and size of the RAN commitment in Southeast Asia changed, as had the environment in which its ships and personnel had discharged their duties. The conflicts had been won, two new nations had emerged from the colonial era, and their naval development had begun to produce sound results. The relationship between the Australians and their Malaysian and Singaporean counterparts had matured from teacher and student to a point not far short of equivalence.

As for the relationship with Indonesia, in 1971 the Australian flagship HMAS *Melbourne* conducted a visit to Tanjong Priok, the port of Jakarta, wearing the flag of none other than Rear Admiral W.J. Dovers. The admiral, his senior officers and staff participated in a non-stop exchange of calls and official entertainment, and during a one-on-one meeting with the Admiral's ALRI counterpart his flag lieutenant found himself with the Indonesian admiral's aide standing outside the meeting room. Noticing the few centimetres of solitary medal ribbon on the Australia's uniform, the aide asked; 'What was that for?' Thinking for a moment, and not wishing to give offence to his hosts, the Flag Lieutenant replied, 'For Confrontation'. The aide shrugged and fell silent and, to keep the exchange going, the flag lieutenant asked what the single medal ribbon on the Indonesian's uniform had been awarded for. He paused, not wishing to give offence to his guests, and replied '*Konfontasi*'. Both officers burst out laughing and shook hands.[52]

7 The Veterans' Struggle for Recognition

The often sketchy and sometimes almost non-existent reporting of events and activities by Australian naval authorities has caused a great deal of anguish to historians. But if ever there was an example of the grief that inadequate record-taking and keeping could lead to, this chapter will provide it. On learning that some naval veterans of the conflicts in Malaya, Malaysia and Singapore were still fighting for government recognition of their rights to repatriation and other benefits into the twenty-first century, one's first reaction might be incredulity. A second thought could be that they must be making claims that could neither be credible nor able to be substantiated. Historians have had to be careful in their writing to exclude stories contributed in good faith by veterans about incidents that did not happen, or which are not supported by any other records or accounts.

But on investigation, the reasons for non-recognition of the FESR naval veterans' claims were a series of refusals by both the Federal Government and its agencies — Defence and Veterans' Affairs — to consider claims justly brought, especially by veterans of the Malayan Emergency. There were, in fact, cases where the responsible officials and ministers refused to consider requests, actively obfuscated the issues involved or sought to deny veterans access to information material to their case, and even misquoted the facts to support their interpretation of the rules. At the bottom of it all is a strong suggestion of prime ministerial sleight-of-hand. Almost all of this has been clearly documented. What remains a mystery is why things ever came to that pass.

The seeds of the issue were planted at the very initiation of the FESR. The process necessary for RAN ships to be assigned, or more properly 'allotted' — remember that word — to the Reserve was a simple matter. There were few procedural differences between the RN and the RAN, which had operated in company as recently as 1953 in Korea, and arrangements were already in place for RAN ships to use the services of the British dockyards in Hong Kong and Singapore during their service in the FESR. The same was not true for the Australian Army or RAAF. The facilities for the former would have to be constructed; although RAAF squadrons had been operating in Malaya since 1950, new facilities were required for this new commitment of a wider variety and larger number of aircraft, and significant airfield construction work was also necessary at its new base at Butterworth near Penang. As the Australian Government decided that the term of service for Army and Air Force personnel in Malaya should be from two to two and a half years, married quarters and all that followed in their wake would also need to be provided. The result was a significant impost on the Defence budget. After a team of officials from the Treasury, Army and the RAAF had visited Malaya in May 1955 to inspect the situation at first hand, the cost estimates were presented to Cabinet in July 1955. In his budget submission, the Treasurer made plain what the decision on the FESR was going to cost the Australian taxpayer:

> The point to which I most wish to draw attention, however, is that while estimated revenue shows an increase of £42.5 millions over last year, estimated expenditure shows an increase of no less than £85 millions ... Estimates for increases in civil pensions, war pension and other repatriation benefits in 1955–56 is approximately £12 millions.[1]

So, whereas it was quite possible for the RAN to begin its

contribution with the dispatch of a few signals and the conclusion of negotiations on an appropriate Directive for the RN's Commander-in-Chief Far East Station and the ships' commanding officers, the same was not so for their brothers-in-arms. The tour of duty for RAN ships was set at just short of twelve months — that is, before the length of time away from Australia which would have triggered access to benefits such as family reunion visits. There is one other important difference, which appears to have given officials in later days a great deal of difficulty: the RAN ships attached to the Royal Navy were assigned as allowed by its Commander-in-Chief Far East Station.

> The Naval components will form part of the Far East Fleet. A force of at least four destroyers or frigates, drawn from all Naval forces in the Far East Fleet, will be stationed in the Malayan area. The Army and the Air Force components will be stationed in the federation of Malaya or Singapore. Apart from temporary moves for the purposes of exercises and training, for which prior approval would be sought from the appropriate National Authorities, these locations are not to be changed without prior approval of the ANZAM Defence Committee.[2]

In simple terms, for the period of their service with the FESR, Australian Army and Air Force units were located in Malaya or Singapore. RAN units, on the other hand, could be and were deployed on other duties as required by the British commander away from Malaya, but they continued to be allotted to the FESR. That this would occur was made explicit in the Naval Directive issued by the ANZAM Defence Committee, which required RAN ships to be rotated for service in Korean waters and requested 'as far as possible, HMA Ships be detailed for flag showing duties in South East Asia in order that their participation in the Strategic Reserve may be fully appreciated in the countries in this area'.[3]

RAN ships in the FESR were to be used as instruments of Australian foreign policy in a time-honoured naval exercise described as either 'showing the flag' or 'gunboat diplomacy', as explained in Chapter 2. Thus in this role of demonstrating preparedness to deter aggression, Australian ships visited ports in Thailand, the Philippines, South Vietnam, Taiwan, Korea and Japan during their FESR service. They also participated in many Commonwealth and multi-lateral exercises designed to improve combat readiness in all their roles, including the secondary role of 'anti-terrorist operations in Malayan waters, and to prevent infiltration by sea of communist agents or armed bands'. The extraterritorial excursions by Australian warships and the prevention of infiltration by sea were two other elements in the benefits debacle.

The final element was either legislative incompetence or a deliberate decision by Cabinet to exclude the RAN units serving in the Malayan Emergency from benefits being provided to Army and Air Force units in the FESR. It took the veterans' organisations some time to establish the facts although, having done so, the reasons for the denial of benefits did not become any clearer.

In June 1955 the Services/Treasury team which had visited Malaya recommended very generous conditions for the Australian Army and Air Force units serving in Malaya, and these were subsequently approved. The team's report, however, made it clear that:

> The foregoing recommendations apply to land-based forces and do not relate to Naval personnel serving in ships. Their conditions of service cannot be related to those of land-based forces and will have to be the subject of separate consideration.[4]

The Naval Board met to consider this and other issues associated with the conditions of service of naval personnel in the FESR. They reached two decisions. First, the RAN members should serve under the same allowance provisions as their RN counterparts — a supplement to their normal rates of pay to compensate for additional costs involved in service in the Far East. Second, 'It was decided to recommend that provision be made for RAN personnel afloat in any legislation designed to provide repatriation benefits for Service personnel of the Commonwealth Strategic Reserve'.[5]

This issue was taken up by the Minister for the Army and Navy in August 1955 when he wrote to the Prime Minister recommending that allotted RAN ships should enjoy equity of benefits with the Australian land-based forces in the FESR, but his recommendation made little headway. In October Prime Minister Menzies, who was also Acting Treasurer, responded that the conditions of service for the RAN contingent of the FESR had been considered by the Treasury Finance Committee and:

> I am now informed that the Second Naval Member was invited to attend at the meeting of the Committee at which the Navy proposals were considered and that, having regard to the requirements of Naval personnel afloat by comparison with land-based forces, the Committee concluded that requirements of Navy would be adequately met by payment to the personnel concerned of a sterling exchange supplement of 28% of pay and allowances less normal Australian commitments. This conclusion has my approval.[6]

No reasons were given for this decision to exclude naval personnel from the benefits extended to their landlocked brethren, and it is difficult to understand why the Prime Minister might have been moved to deny them to the Navy. One possible explanation can be found in a letter sent later that month by Menzies' department to the British High Commissioner in Canberra, which expressed the Australian Government's concern over the high cost of its commitment to the FESR at a time of balance of payments problems.[7]

What is even more difficult to explain is why the Naval Board apparently did almost nothing about this clear breach of faith to the men of the ships who were serving and would serve in the Malayan Emergency. There is nothing that can be found in official archives to illuminate the apparent decision to remain silent. Thus, from September 1955, as each and every member of the Australian

Army and Air Force who set foot on Malayan or Singaporean soil and spent just twenty-four hours there was entitled to a war service home loan, the 'Returned from Active Service badge, the General Service Medal and repatriation benefits, the crews of the ships that had been on station there since late June and had, in fact, escorted their troopships to port in Penang, were entitled to nothing.

Was this an anomaly? Certainly, but the Government was not quite finished. In November the following year the Repatriation (Far East Strategic Reserve) Bill 1956 was introduced into Parliament excluding RAN personnel of the Reserve from eligibility. There is nothing in the records to show that either the Department of the Navy or the Naval Board was consulted when this legislation was being drafted, and the Minister for the Navy voted in favour of its passage.

In November 1957, the commanding officer of HMAS *Voyager* wrote to the Australian Fleet Commander expressing surprise at advice he had received that that personnel serving in RAN ships in the FESR were not entitled to war service home loans. He considered this to be discriminatory because of the relative comfort of Army and RAAF personnel ashore compared with circumstances at sea. The Fleet Commander forwarded this letter to the Naval Board stating, 'I firmly support paragraph 4 of *Voyager's* letter'. The Naval Board responded that ships were not entitled, which prompted a more emphatic appeal by the Fleet Commander in January 1958. This produced a fuller response from the Secretary of the Navy, which stated that the issue 'was examined by Cabinet in the light of the role undertaken by RAN Ships as part of the British Commonwealth Strategic Reserve. Although the Naval Board made representations to the Prime Minister … it was decided that they were not to apply to RAN personnel in sea-going ships'.[8]

In August 1958 the RAN's Director of Personal Services circulated a minute in Navy Office discussing RAAF and Army non-operational casualties in Malaya who were entitled to repatriation benefits. The Deputy Chief of Naval Personnel, Captain R.I. Peek, who had commanded HMAS *Tobruk* in the FESR, and was to take the fight for recognition to the Government when he retired, noted on the minute: 'RAN casualties to date 3 fatal and 8 non-fatal. I have not the slightest doubt that the Navy's case for these benefits is at least as good as the RAAF (probably better) and that it is rather weaker than the fighting soldier's case'. This seems to have triggered an appeal to the Secretary of the Navy for the matter to be raised with the Cabinet, with the Chief of Naval Personnel stating that:

> It cannot be said that there is no risk of reprisal for naval personnel attached to ships on the Strategic Reserve. As well as taking part in bombardment and operational patrols [the Naval Board of 1958 knew what their ships were engaged in!] these personnel have landed on shore leave on Penang Island, Johore Bahru ('Black areas'), and travel on weekend leave between Port Swettenham and Kuala Lumpur, the road passing through a 'Black' area.[9]

The statement was based on actual experience in Malaya, but it was too late. The file shows that the Minister for the Navy saw the recommendation, but there is no evidence that he took it to Cabinet asking for reconsideration of the decisions enshrined in the Act. Mr Menzies was still the Prime Minister, and to change the rules retrospectively would have been admission of a mistake. But, apart from the Government's fears over the future cost of its liabilities to naval veterans, what reason could be advanced for this curious and inequitable decision — and the acquiescence of Parliament in its passage? There seem to have been three main arguments. Firstly, the CTs had no navy so RAN ships were not in 'danger': the officers and sailors were only doing the job for which they had enlisted, which was presumably as true for their Army and RAAF counterparts.[10] Secondly, the ships had never been 'allotted', and so their companies were not entitled to benefits. Thirdly, the ships spent a lot of their time doing things other than fighting the CTs. In a variety of forms and with subtle variations, these expressions of 'accepted wisdom' were to confront the veterans at every turn into the twenty-first century, so it is worthwhile examining their validity.

'Danger' has been through a few iterations since the 1950s, and has now been transmuted in repatriation-speak through 'operational service', 'active service', 'inferred' and 'objective danger' and 'warlike service', 'non-warlike service' and 'hazardous service'. The proponents of the view that NGS bombardments and patrolling and blockading operations by the ships of the Far East Fleet during the Malayan Emergency held no 'danger' for the personnel involved probably envisaged battles with the CTs in the jungle as the only source of danger which should count. In doing so they also demonstrated a profound ignorance of the nature of naval operations.

As the shipmates of Able Seaman Spooner learned in *Tobruk* in 1956 after he was killed by a spent starshell case, danger can come from friendly sources as well. And, as the collisions involving HMAS *Melbourne* in 1964 and 1969 most dramatically and tragically showed, naval operations and exercises are inherently dangerous. When the Australian Government committed the RAN to the FESR it was sent for operational service, with all its inherent dangers which could arrive from any quarter, over and above those of normal naval service. For example, who could know what reaction would be forthcoming from a coastal vessel stopped and boarded in the middle of a pitch black night off the Malayan east coast?

Supporters of the 'no danger' viewpoint should also have been asked to explain their attitude in the light of two other considerations. First, as the authorities had obviously foreseen sufficient danger to the troopships carrying the Army and Air Force contingents to Malaya to require them to have a naval escort, were not the escorts themselves exposed to the same danger? And second, how was it that the degree of danger faced by a lance corporal of the 111th Light Anti-Aircraft Battery Royal Australian Artillery or a leading aircraftsman at RAAF Base Butterworth was so much higher than that confronting an able seaman whose ship was undergoing self-maintenance for a period of weeks in Singapore Dockyard to warrant that benefits be accorded to the former two and not the latter? The answer is that they were in no more or less danger, but it was administratively more convenient to consider that the lance corporal, who may have been maintaining the weapons, and the leading aircraftsman cooking meals, faced the same risks as the infantryman crawling through the jungle on anti-CT patrol, or the aircrew of the Lincoln bombers attacking CT positions. One can only regard this administrative 'convenience' as sleight of hand.

Much later in the piece, in 1996, senior naval officers who should have known a lot better introduced the argument that service could only be considered 'active' while weapons were being discharged.

> Some time ago I received ... a letter which included the following incredible statement 'Indeed those vessels which participated in shore bombardments, and in the case of your own ship (Tobruk) were in fact on active service at the time of each bombardment' ... When asked by me he confirmed that he meant that active service ceased when the guns stopped firing. When challenged, he agreed that this was a stupid statement but that 'I had to sign the letter'.[11]

The writer went on to demand to know who had the authority to order a senior naval officer to 'sign such nonsense'. His suspicions fell on Defence, but rightly or wrongly, he was right in suggesting that the letter had the hallmarks of desperation. But Defence had picked the wrong opponent to try this on. Admiral Sir Richard Peek did not mince his words.

> I have the impression that Russell Hill [Department of Defence offices in Canberra] are hoping that the continuing delays, prevarications [strong language!], half truths and inaccuracies will silence us. Be assured that only parity of conditions to those granted the Army and RAAF in the Strategic Reserve, as far as is possible, will silence us. There are of course several items where parity is impossible e.g. freedom from income tax, accompanied service with servants provided and access to repatriation

benefits for up to 40 years or more but I want the remainder for my people.[12]

But Defence and DVA, the Repatriation Commission and even the courts became almost entranced by the various assessments of the degree of 'danger' a ship or a member of her company might have been in on Malayan service. In the report of his 1999 Review of Service Entitlement Anomalies in Respect of South-East Asian Service 1955-1975, General Mohr discussed 'danger' and how various authorities had sought to define it, and he cautioned that there were always likely to be grey areas which did not fit preconceptions of the nature of the service rendered and commented:

I believe that in making retrospective examinations of the nature of service many years after the event, as is now the case, the concepts and principles involved should be applied with an open mind to the interests of fairness and equity, especially if written historical material is unavailable for examination or is not clear on the facts.[13]

The issue of 'allotted' ships appeared out of nowhere in the debate over the entitlement of naval veterans of the Emergency to benefits. The concept of allotment of forces was originally developed to cover the case of the war in Korea for the Australian Army. The Australian Soldiers Repatriation Act 1950, designed to spell out the benefits to which returned soldiers would be entitled, deemed that if the Department of Defence 'allotted' personnel or units to the war it would be possible to clearly identify those who would be eligible to apply for repatriation benefits. The process was then applied in Malaya. Although the Act was not directed at naval personnel, the practice of 'allotting' was adopted in all three services and the RAN ships sent to the FESR were allotted.

The minutes of a Defence Committee meeting of 15 June 1955, which was attended by the Prime Minister, state that: 'It was confirmed that the two destroyers *Arunta* and *Warramunga* to be allotted to the Reserve are to remain in the area on the completion of their present ANZAM exercise'. That seems pretty clear — the two destroyers were indeed allotted. Then, in a minute to the Prime Minister in August 1955, the Minister for the Army and Navy discussed the costs of payments consequent on the allotment of ships to the FESR. Finally, in November 1955 the Department of Navy informed the Treasury that:'The date on which RAN Ships were allotted for duty as the RAN component of the Strategic reserve was 1 July 1955'. There was no demur from any part of the Defence bureaucracy at the time that RAN ships had been allotted.

Later in the fight, as the veterans and their supporters discovered these documents and made their point, Defence sought to reinterpret these unequivocal statements. It was alleged that 'allotted' actually only meant 'allocated'. That seems a bizarre *post facto* reinterpretation of some unexceptional facts, but it was seriously advanced by no less a personage than the Head of the Defence Personnel Executive. The importance of allotment was simply that repatriation benefits arguably depended upon it but, as General Mohr pointed out, ultimately it mattered naught as 1955–60 FESR naval veterans had been excluded from receiving those benefits by an Act of Parliament.

At some stage, the defenders of the status quo decided that although the RAN ships had served in the Malayan Emergency they hadn't done so with sufficient application. In support of this theory, they developed a defence based on a 1952 declaration by the Governor-General of Australia on an 'Active Service' area for Malaya which included the statement 'including the waters contiguous to the coast of Malaya for a distance of ten miles to seaward'.[14] This was seized upon to prove that if the active service undertaken by FESR personnel had not been conducted within ten miles of the Malayan coast then it was not active service at all. There followed a largely nugatory exercise, on both sides, of attempting to consult ship's deck logs and to plot positions on a chart of Malaya. What was lost in the excitement was the fact that the intent of the Governor-General's declaration was to resolve an issue affecting Army personnel only: it applied only to 'persons subject to Military

Law'. Although efforts were made to prove that this description included naval personnel, the provisions of the Naval Defence Act 1910 and the Naval Discipline Act were and are quite clear: naval personnel are required to serve wherever their duty requires and, if their superiors deemed that anti-CT patrols many miles to seaward of the Malayan coast were to be carried out, then they remained on active service.[15]

But whatever the arguments, as things stood after the passage of the FESR Repatriation Act in 1956, naval veterans of the Malayan Emergency were excluded from receiving any benefits from their service. Furthermore, because their service was not recognised as 'active' or 'warlike', this seriously downgraded their chances of receiving favourable consideration of claims for injuries suffered or illness contracted for their service. There were three other issues affected, the first of which was access to taxation benefits for FESR service.

Treasury's 1955 ruling on the tax-free nature of service in Malaya by Australian Army and Air Force personnel had no deliberate intent to exclude the RAN from the same benefits. As Treasury pointed out, these matters needed separate consideration before a determination could be made.

> It will be noted that although the Minister for the Navy's proposals were approved only to the extent of payment of a sterling exchange supplement on pay and allowances less normal Australian commitments, the way was left open for the Department of the Navy to state a further case for consideration that the tax concessions provided under Section 79B should extend to Naval personnel of the Strategic Reserve in HMA Ships.[16]

Cabinet did action this proposal, and in a letter to the Secretary of the Navy in September 1956 his Treasury counterpart stated, 'The approval which has now been given (in furtherance of Cabinet decision 256(DPC) of 6 June 1956) extends the above taxation concession to RAN personnel serving in ships in Malayan waters'. The concession had also been raised to £180.[17] So, after a considerable struggle with the bureaucracy, this meagre concession was gained for the naval men serving in the FESR. It is difficult to regard this as anything other than anomalous, considering the immeasurably better conditions under which Army and RAAF personnel lived, complete with living allowances and a special allowance for employing servants. In retrospect, it is remarkable that the companies of the RAN ships, struggling with the effects of their stifling and enervating surroundings on efficiency and health, had so few morale problems, given that they were frequently confronted with the hard evidence of government generosity to their companions-at–arms in the other two services on visits to their bases ashore in Malaya.

The second matter was the entitlement of RAN veterans to the Naval General Service Medal (NGSM) with clasp 'Malaya' for their service. This was not a matter of a few centimetres of coloured ribbon: award of the NGSM, in this case, would have conveyed entitlements to repatriation benefits. Once again, every member of the Army and Air Force contingents was entitled to wear the General Service Medal after one day in Malaya, but naval members of the FESR with the requisite twenty-eight days for the award were not eligible for the naval equivalent. Why not? Because Navy Office hadn't done the paperwork. Now, an argument that the proper role of Navy Office is (or was in those days) to administer the present RAN and to plan for and introduce into service the navy of the future has a great deal of merit. Very little time is available or allowed for dwelling on matters in the past, but it is immensely disappointing to have to record the poor performance of serving naval officers including a CNS in solving this issue left over from the Malayan Emergency.

The conditions attached to the award of the NGSM and Malaya clasp were promulgated by the Royal Navy in two Admiralty Fleet Orders, 612/58 and 2466/60. At that time these orders were deemed to apply to the RAN as well, so it was anticipated that the necessary awarding action would be taken in due course. This was not done.

As it later transpired after Admiralty clarification had been sought by Navy Office, qualifying service related to personnel not ships; an RN sailor who thought that he was eligible for the NGSM was expected to apply for it personally on a prescribed form. He would have to include with his application evidence that he had amassed twenty-eight days service in Malaya. The Navy Office comeback to RAN veterans was thus, 'You didn't get the medal because you didn't submit the forms'.

This position was undermined by two facts. First, for Indonesian Confrontation the RAN did promulgate its own Australian Navy Order spelling out the conditions for the award of the General Service Medal and associated clasps 'Borneo' and 'Malay Peninsula', and that qualifying service was associated with *ships*. The second was advice from the RN that, in the British view, it was and always had been up to the Naval Board to make its own determination of how qualifying service and eligibility for the NGSM was to be determined for the RAN. Unabashed, Navy Office went to the RN twice to extract data on the service of RAN *ships* in the Malayan Emergency, only to be told that there were insufficient records to support or dismiss RAN veterans' claims. The author can accept the truth of that statement. RN records returned to London after the British withdrawal were destroyed as a 'health hazard'.

This left Navy Office in a bind. Once again researchers pulled out deck logs, Reports of Proceedings, charts of Malaya and any other supporting evidence to demonstrate that the reason why the RN was unable to determine whether RAN ships had participated in the Emergency was because they hadn't. The Emergency, it was claimed, was virtually over by the time the RAN arrived — which is a difficult conclusion to reach, given how keen the British were to get hold of the RAN ships to supplement their forces, and the decisions by Prime Minister Menzies in April 1955 to commit the RAN to the FESR from June, and in November 1955 that they were allowed to attack CT positions with naval gunfire.

It is also evident … that the British Authorities researched every claim for the award post-1954 on a case by case basis [as the RN regulations required!]. This would indicate that few, if any, RN ships and personnel rendered qualifying service post this time ... the draft directive to COMFEF stated that although HMA Ships may be used to prevent infiltration of communist agents or armed bands by sea their role, as far as possible, was to be such that their participation in the Strategic Reserve may be fully appreciated in the countries of the region. Given the information extracted from the ROP's [monthly Reports of Proceedings] and Ship's Logs for the period this is exactly what occurred. [18]

What Navy Office researchers were unable to find were the detailed instructions issued to RAN ships by Flag Officer Malaya Area, including the operations orders concerning their duties in blockading the Malayan coast against infiltration. These, at a higher security classification than other than innocuous reference in Reports of Proceedings would permit, would have proved — or disproved — the case being made by the veterans. Unfortunately, the British were similarly handicapped in their assessments of RAN eligibility. Furthermore, Navy Office had not commissioned any search through relevant national archival records which, under the thirty-year rule, were all publicly available. Finally, evidence produced at the Mohr Review demonstrated that Navy Office had not even bothered to consult their own records withheld from the National Archives of Australia. Yet in 1995, the Navy claimed that it, and the Royal Navy, had carried out a 'comprehensive examination of the records' and that 'none of the HMA Ships deployed in the Far East Strategic Reserve' met the criteria for NGSM award. The poor research procedures adopted are even more surprising when it is recognised that the officers concerned felt themselves to be under some pressure to come up with the right answer as this had 'become a very contentious issue'.[19]

The third issue was the inadmissibility for the national Roll of Honour at the Australian War Memorial of the names of Able Seaman Spooner and Officers' Cook Cooper, an RAN sailor who had drowned during the Emergency. The argument circled the same points — the ship wasn't allotted for service; even if it was, the death of Spooner was a peacetime training accident, unconnected with the Emergency, as was Cooper's. In any case Spooner's death took place outside the Governor-General's ten mile limit; neither of the sailors had therefore been on 'active service'. The refusal to list the names of naval casualties rankled, especially as the terms for addition of the names of army and air force casualties of the campaign to the Roll of Honour had been applied differently.

[O]f the 27 members of the Australian Army whose deaths are listed on the Roll of Honour, seven were killed in action, four were killed by 'friendly fire', ten died in motor vehicle accidents, four died from illness, one fell to his death from the top of his barracks and one is thought to have been a suicide. There is no question about these dead being commemorated on the Roll of Honour ... Nine members of the RAAF are listed on the Roll of Honour. None was killed in action and all are understood to have been accidental deaths. Neither is there any question about those dead being on the Roll of Honour.[20]

Gaining no progress from appeals to Navy Office and rebuffed by the Department of Veterans' Affairs on repatriation issues, in 1990 two RAN Malayan Emergency veterans separately took the Commonwealth Government to the Federal Court to determine whether or not the ships in which they had served were 'allotted' for service in Malaya. The court found in the veterans' favour. That raised the spectre of the Commonwealth being liable for the payment of arrears of benefits to all RAN veterans of the campaign, and the Federal Labor Government, which had opposed the exclusion of the RAN from the 1956 FESR Repatriation Act, retrospectively amended the Veterans' Entitlement Act 1986 to ensure that it reflected the 'original intent' of the Liberal–Country Party government of that time — the effect was *post facto* non-allotment. But retrospective legislation was not to be allowed to plaster over the problem.

By 1994 the Department of Defence acquiesced to the demands of a large number of veterans' groups, including FESR veterans, and set up the Committee of Inquiry into Defence and Defence-Related Awards (CIDA), headed by a formed Chief of the Defence Force. CIDA's task was to examine the claims being made for the award of medals to defence and civilian personnel for a wide variety of service. Finding the existing guidance and its application complex, CIDA attempted to categorise and assess entitlements through a series of general principles it developed. For example, the committee suggested that the confusing ways in which the nature of a member's service was judged could be simplified by the use of 'warlike' and 'non-warlike hazardous' as descriptors. So far as the RAN veterans of the Malayan Emergency were concerned, CIDA ignored its own principles in rejecting their claims, but the stumbling block was that legislative non-allotment: Defence evidence was preferred to that produced by veterans, especially over this issue. If the ships had not been allotted then they failed the CIDA principles test. The Chairman, when he had the NGSM imbroglio explained to him expressed his opinion that it was just a matter of bureaucratic bungling and was easily fixed, but he had not counted on the tenacity of that bureaucracy in defending the indefensible. The 1955–60 naval veterans came away from CIDA with nothing.

Disquieted by the CIDA outcomes, and with the growing volume of veterans' complaints since CIDA, which had heightened their interest in their access to entitlements for their service, the Departments of Defence and Veterans' Affairs were prompted to conduct a further Review of Service Entitlement Anomalies in 1997. This was essentially an internal review, with input from veterans' groups not sought, nor was there an opportunity provided for them to comment on the arguments produced by the two departments. All the old arguments and misappreciations were rehashed.

It is also questionable whether this service could for the large part be considered operational service given that much of their time was spent conducting exercises with the Far East Fleet and on goodwill port visits. Certain activities such as bombardment of shore positions however, could be viewed as military activities where the application of force is authorised to pursue specific military objectives. This is balanced, however, by the fact that there was no real expectation of casualties. It is suggested therefore, that these activities could on the whole best be equated to hazardous service rather than operational service, given the degree of hazard, while not totally warlike in nature, would have been above and beyond that of normal peacetime duty.[21]

The Review Committee stopped short of agreeing that naval service in the Malayan Emergency was somewhat more dangerous than maintaining Bofors guns or cooking in an RAAF kitchen in Butterworth — which was regarded as operational service — but its suggestion completely demolished the argument put forward by the Government in 1956 about the nature of naval service in the FESR. It was a major shift of ground and led to a recommendation, eventually, that all service in the FESR between 1955 and 1963 be regarded as 'operational'. The recommendation was accepted by the Government, which meant that veterans could now claim compensation for injury or illness attributed to that service, but it did not mean that they had an entitlement to a service pension, as they still lacked the essential 'qualifying service' for that. The Government also agreed with the Review's recommendation that veterans of the FESR be awarded the Australian Service Medal, although the significance of that with respect to benefits was unclear. The naval veterans of the Malayan Emergency wanted their FESR time to count as qualifying service — if it counted for the Army and Air Force, why not for the Navy? — And they continued their campaign.

What caused the retreat from the position that Defence and the Navy had held as almost sacred for forty-one years? For one thing, the veterans were becoming more organised, and their research was turning up documents which were inconvenient for Defence and difficult to dismiss. As well, the veterans' organisations had begun to attract seriously competent and experienced personnel, including many former senior officers, to the campaign. Seeing more value in working towards a common cause, the Naval Association of Australia, the HMAS *Sydney* and Vietnam Logistical Support Veterans' Association (*Sydney* & VLSVA) and the FESR Association began to see wisdom in pooling resources against a common foe.

Critical to this development was the acceptance in 1996 of the position of national president of the Naval Association by Admiral Mike Hudson, former CNS from 1985 to 1991, very likely because of the advocacy of Admiral Sir Richard Peek. Although he had not had FESR service, Admiral Hudson quickly came to an appreciation of the justice of the veterans' case. But he also recognised that the earnest efforts of the veterans' organisations had created an atmosphere of mistrust and hostility towards them within Defence and DVA, even extending to the Minister for Defence Personnel and Industry.

In particular, the Navy had created a corner for itself to be backed into. Pursuing a definitive and authoritative response from the Royal Navy that would finally silence the Malayan Emergency veterans, in 1996 the CNS made a personal approach to the Second Sea Lord in the Admiralty seeking assurance that RAN ships had not qualified by their service for the NGSM. Instead the Second Sea Lord responded that, 'I very much regret that we will be unable to let you have the definitive advice you are asking'. This didn't prevent the CNS and the Minister for Defence Personnel, both possibly badly advised, from claiming that the RN advice had shut the door on the veterans' claims once and for all, but that they were unable to release the advice because it was 'personal'. When an application by the FESR Association through the Commonwealth Ombudsman's Office produced the release of the British response, the only door that had apparently shut was veterans' access to Navy and the Minister. But this was a pivotal point in the veterans' campaign. The Ombudsman had determined that the Minister could not withhold a document on private grounds if the content was used to make a ministerial decision, which elevated the dispute out of the bureaucratic 'noise' and into public and political view.

This situation needed to be defused, and a great deal more

cooperation was required to ensure that the case for all FESR veterans' — not just those from the RAN — was presented coolly and professionally, and in a coordinated process that drew on the organisational strengths and information sources resident in each association. In June 1998 the Naval Association convened a meeting of interested parties in Canberra, from which emerged the Joint Consultative Group, comprising representatives from the Returned Services League, the RAAF Association, the Australian Defence and Veterans' Association Council, the Defence Reserves' Association, the FESR Association. HMAS *Sydney* and Vietnam Logistical Support Veterans' Association (Vic. Inc.), the Regular Defence Forces Welfare Association, the Australian Defence Association and the Naval Association of Australia. This formidable assemblage of talent and enthusiasm identified a high degree of common ground in having the anomalies arising from FESR service resolved, particularly under the goad of the 'working party', an inner core of activists led by Admiral Hudson, and comprising the former NAA President, 'Nobby' Clarke and Secretary Peter Cooke-Russell, with Noel Payne from the FESR Association and Bob Gibbs from the *Sydney* & VLSVA.

There had also been some changes in Navy Office, and the new Chief of Navy (the title changed in February 1997), Vice Admiral Chalmers, expressed himself 'supportive' of the veterans' claims. In a January 1998 minute contesting the position adopted by the Head of the Defence Personnel Executive on the recognition of their Malayan Emergency service, he pointed out the inconsistency in the current principles applying to defence awards to personnel who had served in the Gulf War and those that Defence continued to want to apply to the earlier veterans. He dismissed the sophistry which had grown out of wrangling over the issue of 'danger' and made two other important observations.

It might be argued that there are individual awards which recognise the bravery of those who respond to significant danger in operations. I would suggest that, within the concept of determination of campaign awards, there is at least some recognition of the member's decision, taken in quieter and safer times, to embark for duty in circumstances which may well ultimately expose that member to incurred danger. We should ensure that we are able to encourage present and future ADF personnel to continue to make that decision in accordance with their duty, as we did in recognising service in the Gulf War. In that regard, any mean spiritedness in our dealing with earlier veterans has the potential to be noticed by presently serving personnel.

I have recently become aware of Ministerial correspondence which indicates that Departmental advice given to the Minister may not always have conveyed an accurate impression of the nature of RAN service during the Malaya Campaign ... The view expressed in this ministerial correspondence seems to be that the naval role in the campaign was simply to 'Show the Flag'. Such a view clearly does not appreciate the nature of naval operations, nor does it recognise the conditions under which RAN personnel operated at that time.[22]

With support like that of senior officers of the ADF, a concerted campaign to enlist the support of ministers and local members of parliament, and under the firm leadership of Admiral Hudson, the Consultative Group was successful in persuading the Minister for Veterans' Affairs, who was also the Minister Assisting the Minister for Defence, to commission a new review in 1999 to investigate the considerable volume of 'anomalies' which veterans continued to represent for all the Southeast Asian campaigns.

Titled the 'Review of Service Entitlement Anomalies in Respect of South-East Asian Service 1955–1975', it is better known by the name of its Chairman, Major General R.F. Mohr. Although General Mohr was an officer in the Army Reserve, he had served as a stoker and radio mechanic in the RAN during and after World War II, before pursuing a distinguished career as barrister and judge. He was assisted by retired Rear Admiral Phil Kennedy, an officer with extensive operational service in Korea, the FESR and Vietnam.

Consideration of the claims of the RAN veterans of the Malayan Emergency was one of the major issues raised in the review's terms of reference, and General Mohr discussed and decided the issue in a mere twenty-three pages of his report. He concluded that the exclusion of RAN personnel from repatriation benefits 'created an anomaly for which no satisfactory reasons were provided' and he recommended that this be removed to place them on the same basis as Army and RAAF veterans.

Turning to the NGSM, Mohr concluded that all the RAN Emergency veterans had qualified for the award by their service. He agreed with CIDA that a breakdown in communications (read 'bureaucratic bungle') had been the cause of the former denial of the award, and noted that the loss of most of the records of the British commanders in the Malayan Area had denied researchers the information they needed to confirm the RAN ships' qualifying service. A case against award could not be sustained by reference to the fraction of the information that had survived.

> Reports and logs were not kept with a view to setting out qualifying service for the NGSM. The need for such recording was not known in RAN ships. Furthermore there was, in all probability, a considerable overlap between the ship's movements in fulfilling their primary [presence] and their secondary [anti-CT] role. Showing the flag being one such overlap.[23]

He made another point which should have been the death blow for those officials who remained obsessed with what constituted the area of operations for the Emergency. He commissioned his own inquiries with the Royal Navy on this point and extracted the following response from the UK Ministry of Defence:

> I have searched through the various minutes of the Committee on the Grant of Honours Decorations and medals but have not found any reference to the boundaries of the qualifying area for the Naval General Service Medal (NGSM) with clasp Malaya

… I regret I am unable to confirm the distance from shore that ships had to be as the list that we hold of qualifying ships only state, alongside the qualifying periods, West Coast or East Coast patrols.[24]

Aside from making repatriation benefits available to RAN Malayan Emergency veterans, the consequence of these recommendations would be that the names of both Spooner and Cooper would be eligible for the Roll of Honour.

Mohr made other recommendations. The Australian Service Medal was to be issued for all service personnel, including land-based RAN personnel who had served in the FESR for periods of more than thirty days. This recognised that there had been Australian personnel serving in Malaya before the FESR was formed and that their duties continued after the independence of Malaya. The RAN radio operators who had worked alongside Army and RAAF operators in signals intelligence work — same duty, same place, same exposure to 'danger' — had not been entitled to the same entitlements because of a bureaucratic oversight in allotting them. Mohr recommended that this be redressed. The case of HMAS *Vampire*, which had had the misfortune to spend her days on Confrontation service shuttled between Borneo, where her service fell one day short of the requirement, and the Singapore and Malacca Straits where she fell seven days short of qualifying, led to a recommendation for the award of the appropriate awards to recognise her combined fifty-three days of operational service.

Finally, those Australian personnel who had been seconded to the RMN during the period including Confrontation should have their service recognised by their allotment to the FESR. Although this step had been agreed in 1965 by the Department of Defence and the Repatriation Commission, administrative action to make it so had not been taken. This decision also carried flow-on benefits in eligibility for medals.

The case put to the Mohr Review by the Consultative Group was thoroughly prepared and competently argued, and resulted in recommendations for the overturning of almost all the barriers that had been placed in the way of naval veterans when they sought their entitlements.

That would have seemed to be that, except for the post-Review resurrection by Defence of issues with the eligibility of naval veterans of the Emergency for the award of the NGSM, even after the Minister had publicly accepted the Review's recommendations. The charts and deck logs were brought out again in the Personnel Executive under the umbrella statement that 'General Mohr's recommendations and conclusions need to be read in conjunction with the considerations to understand their full meaning'. This exquisite piece of bureaucratic double-speak emerged from the office of the Head of the Defence Personnel Executive in July 2002, and rightly drew the attention and counter-fire of Admiral Hudson. Defence's backtracking was quickly squelched by application to the Minister, which effectively drove the stake through the heart of this monster. The Government accepted the Mohr recommendations and by December 2002 the instruments of allotment were issued by Defence. The *allotment* of RAN ships for service in Malaya was formalised in legislation in an amendment to the Veterans' Entitlements Act 1986, which now contains a list of ships and the dates of their service.

But success in this review led to a new set of claims being lodged by veterans for conflicts from World War II to Southeast Asia and Commonwealth personnel and civilians. And in February 2002 the Minister for Veterans' Affairs set up yet another review, this one headed by the Honourable M.J. Clarke, another distinguished judge. A small number of naval veterans represented that their service in the FESR unrelated to the Emergency and Confrontation should entitle them to repatriation benefits, a suggestion the Review rejected.

None of this short-circuited or shielded naval veterans from the rigours of the process by which they submitted and defended their claims to DVA. The lack of official documentation continues to bedevil applications, as proof of their service in specific localities at the times claimed is extremely hard to come by. Poor record-keeping at the time and the loss or misplacement of important documents, as well as the apparently indiscriminate destruction of many of the applicable naval files, makes the veterans' task a difficult one. To give an indication of the size of the issue, by July 2006, DVA had dealt with claims from 5056 naval veterans of service in Malaya, Malaysia and the FESR, totaling over 32,000 claims of injury or incapacitation, with an acceptance rate of 53.5 per cent. [25]

Which leaves the question of why it took so long for these anomalies to be dealt with effectively by the Government and the bureaucracy. Much of the documentary evidence that might answer the question is missing or ambiguous, but the problem had its origins in a decision by Prime Minister Menzies to withhold benefits made available to Army and Air Force personnel serving in Malaya from sea-going RAN members of the FESR serving in the same theatre. If there was dissent or protest about this decision it has not emerged from the records. Menzies was the dominant political figure of the period, and it not difficult to see him getting his way by overriding his ministers and directing compliance from the bureaucracy. The Chief of Naval Staff had been in office only a matter of months and he and his Naval Board had issues on their plates which possibly seemed more pressing. As for the reason for this unfair decision, there is a tenable argument that it was to save money at a time of financial stringencies.[26]

Bureaucrats in the Treasury and Navy departments did point out the anomalies in the treatment of naval personnel, but this resulted in no apparent action at a Cabinet level, apart from the grant of taxation concessions. The 1956 FESR Repatriation Bill was, apparently, drafted without consultation with Navy — which could only have happened on instruction from on high, and the Prime Minister was quite capable of enforcing discipline when it came to the parliamentary debates. It didn't really matter whose voices were raised in pointing out the disservice the Bill would do to RAN personnel, it was going to be passed anyway. It is harder to find an explanation for the connivance of those who might have been expected to think differently over the retrospective un-allotment of RAN ships from the FESR. If, as suggested, the 'original intent' of the 1956 Act was to save money, then the Labor Party ministers of the 1990s were only too happy to follow suit. This may seem a harsh judgment, but they could have been in no doubt, having had the legislation found wanting by the courts, that there was an issue requiring resolution. They missed the opportunity of providing it, and cost the veterans another decade of denial and struggle.

As for the Navy, the whole episode casts the Naval Personnel Division of the 1950s and its successors in a poor light. Apart from the wishy-washy comments by its chief in 1958, there was no attempt at any stage to raise the issue administratively or politically. When repatriation benefits surfaced as a problem the Navy took refuge in obfuscation, and a fixed belief that the matter of eligible service in Malaya was for the RN to resolve. It failed to allot retrospectively the RAN shore-based personnel to the FESR, despite agreeing in 1965 that this needed to be done. At very senior levels it remained locked into a view that the Australian ships had not been engaged in operational service during the Emergency, a belief supported by very sloppy research which had been entrusted to relatively junior officers, and a deplorable misappreciation of the facts of naval operations in a limited war situation. This rolling mess trapped the Navy's most senior officer into inaccuracy in 1997 and into providing incorrect information to his minister.

In mitigation, Navy Office was not alone in these practices; DVA was no less guilty of relying on inaccurate information in making its judgments and did nothing to promote a re-examination of the consequences of the poor legislation of 1956 on naval veterans seeking its assistance. External sources, like official histories of the conflicts in Southeast Asia, which might have been expected to present an independent view, did not. It would have been a bold and confident public servant or naval officer who challenged respected historians like Professor Dennis, who got away with covering the

RAN's contribution to the Malayan Emergency in just over a page, and confidently made the following allegation:

> Within the context of the Strategic Reserve commitment, the anti-CT role never amounted to anything more than a token participation. It could not have been otherwise. The communists themselves had no naval capacity that threatened the security forces or the general situation in Malaya. There was no evidence to suggest that CTs were being smuggled into Malaya by sea routes ... Nor could naval power significantly enhance the activities of land or air forces, particularly in the clean up phase in which Australian forces were involved from mid-1955 on.[27]

It was statements like that which prompted the research and writing of this book; on the basis of practical and historical naval experience they just could not be true. The tragedy is that naval officers with a responsibility for determining the truth, lacking that experience or, perhaps, the will to follow up the issues, didn't bother to challenge them. The veterans who survive, and who now enjoy the just entitlements for the service they rendered to this country, owe a great debt of gratitude to the gallant band of their fellows, led in fact and in spirit by Sir Richard Peek. Despite official stonewalling and denial, and discouragement and ignorance at the most senior levels of government and the Navy, their persistence was rewarded. But the cost was high — over 5000 naval veterans of the FESR with more than 17,000 'accepted' injuries or illnesses had to wait until 2001 to gain access to the entitlements that should have been theirs in the 1950s. The other terrifying statistic is that the FESR Association estimated that only 7000 naval personnel served in the theatre: that's a 'casualty' rate of over 70 per cent.

Epilogue

ANZUK did not long survive the British withdrawal, and was dealt a death blow when the Whitlam Labor Government announced in 1973 that the Australian infantry battalion would be withdrawn in 1975. This left one New Zealand battalion in Singapore, which made the concept of ANZUK being a ready reserve for SEATO deployment untenable. The new Australian Government did not immediately remove the RAAF contingent, so IADS remained. The RAN continued to send ships to Southeast Asia and to use the Singapore Naval Base, but it was on a bilateral basis that it did so. The position of RAN Liaison Officer was established in 1976 and continues.

ANZAM was officially terminated on 10 February 1975, following the final meting of its Chief of Staffs Committee. It should, however, be proudly stated that, of all of the collection of acronyms of regional and security organisations with which Australia had surrounded itself in the 1950s and 1960s, only ANZAM had actually deployed forces in the field for active service twice, and it had decisively won both of the contests.[1]

SEATO also faded away without fanfare. The American decision to withdraw from Vietnam had led the other 'free world' partners to withdraw their contingents as well, a process which was completed for Australian forces in 1972. The spectacle of desperate Vietnamese trying to climb aboard helicopters evacuating the US Embassy in

Saigon in April 1975 effectively ruled off America's interest in being involved in ground operations on the Asian mainland. Pakistan officially withdrew from the Manila Treaty in 1973, and France in 1974; the British had already done so in all but name, by withdrawing their ground force commitment to SEATO in April 1969. The treaty organisation was officially dissolved in 1977.

With ANZAM, ANZUK and SEATO also went Australia's concept of forward defence. In fact, it had probably been a hollow shell following President Nixon's Guam announcement in 1969. With no major partners now willing to stay in Southeast Asia, the relatively few forces Australia could keep in the region — even supposing Australian governments had wanted to station them there — constituted no kind of defence at all. This marked the collapse of a diplomatic and military effort which had been going on since 1945. However, it is difficult to make a case that the era of 'forward defence' did not produce, on the whole, positive outcomes for Australia and for its Southeast Asian neighbours, the benefits of which are still being reaped today.

It is impossible to know whether the Chinese Communists ever had any plans to launch a land, sea and air assault on Southeast Asia during the 1950s and 1960s and thus whether ANZAM and SEATO had had any deterrent effect. But these alliances had ensured that Laos, Malaysia, Singapore and Indonesia had been given the opportunity to establish themselves in a post-colonial world without becoming a battlefield of ideologies, and that Thailand had become capable of presenting its own defence against encroachment. The other former French colonies in Indochina, in contrast, had become battlefields over which the West on one hand and Communism on the other had waged a series of fierce and costly wars. Stability and varying degrees of prosperity had become the norm for the former British colonies, and even for Indonesia after the aberration of *Konfrontasi*. Relations between these new nations were cordial at least within the region and with the nations which had gone guarantor for their security. That successive Australian governments and their armed forces were able to have a hand in producing such a positive outcome from twenty years of instability must surely rank as a strategic achievement of the highest order.

Ever since 1965, Australia has enjoyed close and cooperative relations with Singapore, and the massive investment of Singaporean capital in Australia we see today is a by-product of that ANZAM involvement of so long ago. It is probable that most Singaporeans are totally unaware of the fact, and it would make little difference to them anyway, but Australians would do well to remember how it was that the thriving Republic of Singapore emerged unscathed from Confrontation.

Australian relationships with Malaysia have fluctuated between friendly and less so. For a number of years there appeared to be some personal animus towards this country from important political figures in Malaysia, and this affected attitudes on both sides of the equation. But, once again, Australians would do well to reflect on their country's part in safeguarding the development of the Federation of Malaya and its expansion into Malaysia. The Malaysian Government has certainly done so, and in 2006 it announced the minting of a special medal, the *Pingat Jasa Malaysia*, to be awarded to the servicemen of Commonwealth forces who came to the aid of Malaya in defeating the CTs and Malaysia in frustrating Confrontation. It is a very welcome and touching tribute, and the medal citation reads:

> This medal is awarded to the peacekeeping groups amongst the Commonwealth countries for distinguished chivalry, gallantry, sacrifice or loyalty in upholding Peninsular Malaya or Malaysia sovereignty during the period of Emergency and Confrontation.

Australia's relations with Indonesia have been through some choppy waters since 1966, but the long-term trend has been positive and deep. Anguish on one side over East Timor and on the other over West Papua have not prevented the development of close cooperation between the two governments over a wide range of issues from trade, immigration and fishing to border security.

Australia now has a security treaty with Indonesia, reflecting not only the maturity of the political relationship but also the confidence in which each holds the other. In November 1972 the RAN and ALRI commenced a series of bilateral naval exercises, and the practice continues.

That stability of regional relationships is even more evident at the level of defence cooperation. Because, despite forecasts that FPDA would be a short-lived substitute for an alliance for military cooperation, it still operates and has become, with one or two hiccups, a strong and mature umbrella for a host of service-related activities.[2] Its longevity and growing strength have confounded the critics and even the experts. Just why his should be so is not easy to determine. Perhaps the wording of the arrangement 'to consult' rather than a more solid and unequivocal commitment has been a strength, rather than the weakness it was once regarded as. While a partner might draw comfort from the certainty of consultation, it could not be a cause of concern to a regional neighbour. For example, the Chinese premier Zhou Enlai, when asked for his views on FPDA in June 1974, was reported as being in favour because he regarded it as a deterrent to Russian meddling in Southeast Asia. Similarly, the Soviet Union had no objections because they saw FPDA as a means of keeping the Chinese out.[3]

Because it was not tied to any of the alliances involved in Western defence against the Soviet Union and its satellites, the end of the Cold War did not bring the rationale of the FPDA into question. This feature of its terms of reference has also made possible a degree of flexibility in confronting perceived threats to the security of the member nations that was not possible for more formal alliances.[4] And, remembering that the original purpose of the arrangements was to improve the capability of the armed forces of the two Southeast Asian members to defend their territories, that flexibility has been used to develop a range of exchanges and exercises of increasing sophistication and complexity. This has led to increasing confidence in the value of FPDA in improving interoperability and understanding between the partners. As the Malaysian and

Singaporean navies have modernised their orders of battle and technological capabilities, often in areas of less priority to the other partners, the student has frequently become the teacher in the defence of littoral waters.

When reflecting on the benign strategic and military environment of Southeast Asia in 2007, it is difficult to imagine the depth of concern that convinced the governments of Britain, Australia and New Zealand to join together in common cause against the perceived menace of international Communism to the region and to their own strategic circumstances. If one had not served in that theatre of operations at that time, one might be forgiven for forgetting the contribution made by Australian service men and women in protecting the region and ushering in the conditions evident today. It has been suggested, for example, that this period of Australia's naval history is too specialised to attract much interest.

For those who did serve, it took a long time for Australian governments to fully recognise and honour that service. The contrast with the attention devoted by governments, the media and the public to veterans of the Vietnam conflict underlines an odd fact about Australia, best reflected in the devotion paid to celebrating Anzac Day each year. The gallant but futile sacrifice of Australian lives in a sideshow action in 1915, which reaped only humiliation, began a scant eight months after Australian forces, spearheaded by the new Australian Fleet, won a victory of lasting strategic significance against German forces in the Pacific. Yet the first campaign, which commenced with the victory of RAN landing parties at the Battle of Bita Paka on 11 September 1914, is virtually unknown to the vast majority of Australians.

Vietnam was a military, political and strategic defeat, the outcomes of which linger in Southeast Asia and influence Western attitudes to defence commitments to this day. In contrast, the contributions Australia made to the Far East Strategic Reserve helped to deliver a stunning victory whose beneficial military, political and strategic effects are clearly operating internationally. But, as Prime Minister Howard implied, how many Australians recognise that?

This book has been written to record and celebrate the service and contributions of the men and women of the Royal Australian Navy who made that victory possible.

BRAVO ZULU

Appendix
RAN Ships of the Far East Strategic Reserve

None of the ships which served with the FESR remain in commission in the RAN — which is just as well! Their names are familiar to naval veterans of the period, who generally remember their old ships with affection, but to the layperson they are just names. This appendix has been included to provide a ready reference to, and description of, the ships in which our men served over thirty-five years ago. A fuller history and description can be found in Bob Bergin's book, *R.A.N.: Ships of the Far East Strategic Reserve, 1955–1966*.

Aircraft Carrier
HMAS *Melbourne*, light fleet carrier of the *Majestic* Class
Laid down 1941, launched 1945, purchased by Australian Government 1949. Fitted with 5° angled deck, mirror landing system and steam catapult and commissioned 1955. At 214 m long and with a full load displacement of 20,000 tons, she was capable of 24 knots (optimistically). She carried a complement of around 1350.

During her FESR service she carried an aircraft complement of Sea Venom jet fighters, turbo-prop Gannet anti-submarine aircraft and Sycamore helicopters. Later these were replaced with A-4 Skyhawk fighter bombers, S-2 Tracker patrol aircraft and Sea King anti-submarine helicopters. *Melbourne* paid off in 1982 and was sold to the Chinese for scrap in 1985.

Fast Troop Transport
HMAS *Sydney*, light fleet carrier of the *Majestic* Class

Laid down 1943, launched 1944, purchased by the Australian Government in 1947, and commissioned in 1948. Had an axial deck, no catapult and a 'batman' landing aid. With a full load displacement of 19,500 tons, and 210 m long, she was capable of 24.5 knots. She carried a complement of around 1250.

Her aircraft complement initially comprised propeller-driven Sea Fury fighters, Firefly anti-submarine aircraft and Sea Otter amphibians. In September 1951 she joined the UN forces in Korea and established a distinguished record of sorties flown and results obtained. She returned to Korea in 1954 and carried out several armistice patrols before returning to Australia for conversion to a training ship, as conversion to an angled deck and for higher performance aircraft was too expensive. She paid off in 1958 and underwent a limited conversion for a troop transport role.

Her first deployment in this role was to Malaysia but she later undertook twenty-three voyages to Vietnam in support of Australian forces there. Her last deployment was to the United States in 1971 to embark new aircraft for the Fleet Air Arm. She finally paid off in 1973 and was scrapped in South Korea in 1976.

Destroyers
The Tribal Class

Two ships of this class served in the FESR. 115 m long and displacing 1970 tons, they were capable of 36 knots. Their main armament was six 4.7-inch guns in three twin mountings and a variety of anti-aircraft weaponry. They had four 21-inch torpedo tubes and carried depth charges. They had a complement of around 260.

HMAS *Arunta* was laid down in Sydney in 1939, launched in 1940 and commissioned in 1942. She saw distinguished war service in the Pacific including the destruction of Japanese submarines, a role in the annihilation of a Japanese fleet at the Battle of Surigao Strait in 1944, attacks by kamikaze aircraft at Lingayen Gulf and support for the Australian Army landings in Borneo in 1945. After the war she served two tours with the British Commonwealth Occupation Force (BCOF) in Japan.

In 1950 she was taken in hand for conversion to an anti-submarine destroyer; her after 4.7-inch gun mount was removed and a Squid anti-submarine mortar fitted. After service with the UN armistice patrols in Korea in 1954, in 1955 she was deployed for exercise in Southeast Asia and become one of the first RAN contributions to the FESR. She was paid off into reserve in 1956 and was sold for scrap in 1969. Not willing to become Taiwanese razor blades, she sank off Broken Bay NSW while on tow.

HMAS *Warramunga* was laid down in 1940, launched in 1942 and commissioned in November the same year. She served in the Pacific supporting amphibious landings up the New Guinea coast to the Philippines, where she also came under kamikaze attack. She was present at the Japanese surrender ceremony in Tokyo Bay and afterwards served four tours with the BCOF.

This was followed by two tours with the UN forces in Korea, and she also underwent anti-submarine conversion until 1954. She joined *Arunta* in the FESR in 1955 and completed a second tour of FESR duty in 1958. She was paid off into reserve in 1959 and sold to Japan for scrap in 1963.

The *Daring* Class

Originally planned to be a class of four, these ships were based on British designs of large destroyers which emerged from World War II. They were essentially gunships, although they did carry sonar and anti-submarine weapons.

One hundred and eighteen metres long and with a light displacement of 2800 tons, they could achieve speeds of 30.5 knots.

Their main armament was six 4.5-inch (114 mm) guns in three twin turrets, and a variety of 40 mm Bofors anti-aircraft guns. The class also carried 533 mm torpedoes in five tubes and the Limbo anti-submarine mortar. Their complement was around 320.

The first of the class, *Voyager*, was laid down in 1949, launched in 1952 but not commissioned until 1957. She served three tours in the FESR and was lost in collision with HMAS *Melbourne* on 10 February 1964, taking eighty-two personnel with her.

Vendetta was also laid down in 1949, but was not launched until 1954 and did not commission until 1958. She made five deployments to the FESR, including Confrontation service, and in 1969/70 served a six-month tour with the US 7th Fleet off Vietnam. She achieved the distinction of being the only ship of the class to be employed on her primary function of gunfire support, and her performance in this role attracted much favourable comment.

Vampire was laid down in 1952, launched in 1956 and commissioned in 1959. She also undertook five FESR deployments.

In 1970 and 1971 *Vampire* and *Vendetta* were taken in hand for major modifications, involving the fitting of new radar and fire control systems, removal of the torpedo tubes and remodelling of superstructure, masts and funnels. A renovated *Vampire* served in ANZUK force for six months in 1972–73. Both ships were sent to Darwin after Cyclone Tracey devastated the town in December 1974 and both also patrolled in the vicinity of Timor during the Indonesian occupation of East Timor in 1975.

Vendetta was paid off in 1979 and sold for scrap in 1987. *Vampire* was converted to a training ship role in 1980 and paid off in 1986. She is now a museum ship at the Australian National Maritime Museum in Sydney.

In May 1964, the British-built *Duchess*, which had commissioned into the RN in 1952, was transferred on loan to the RAN as a replacement for *Voyager*. She served two FESR tours and was purchased by the RAN in 1972. In 1973 she was converted to a training ship, but paid off in 1975. She was broken up in Taiwan in 1980

Frigates
The Q Class

Five destroyers of the wartime Q Class were manned by the RAN during World War II, serving in the, Mediterranean, and the Atlantic, Indian and Pacific Oceans. The class displaced around 1700 tons and could achieve 34 knots. They were transferred to the RAN in 1945.

In 1950 a program of converting four of these ships to fast anti-submarine frigates commenced with *Quadrant*. Their bridges and superstructure were remodelled, largely in aluminium, with the removal of most of their original gun armament, and they were fitted with twin Limbo anti-submarine mortars. The redesigned ships displaced 2000 tons and their speed was reduced to 31 knots. They carried a twin 4-inch (105 mm) gun mount aft.

Quadrant emerged from dockyard hands in 1953 and served two FESR tours before being paid off in 1957. She was scrapped in 1962 in Japan.

Queenborough completed her conversion in 1954. She served two FESR tours before being paid off in 1963. In 1966 she was recommissioned as a training ship, a role she served in until paying off again in 1972. She was sold for scrap to Hong Kong in 1975.

Quiberon's conversion started in 1950 but extended to 1957. She served three tours with the FESR before paying off in 1964. She was scrapped in Japan in 1972.

Quickmatch entered her conversion in 1951 and emerged in 1955. She had five FESR deployments before becoming a training ship in 1962. She paid off in 1963 and was scrapped in Japan in 1972.

River Class

Based on the British Type 12 design, six ships of this class were built in three flights in Australian yards to replace the Q Class. 113 metres long and displacing 2100 tons, they had a speed of 28 knots and carried a complement of around 250.

Parramatta and *Yarra* were laid down in 1957, launched in 1958–59 and commissioned in 1961. They carried a twin 4.5-inch (114 mm) turret forward and twin Limbo mountings aft. Both served two tours in the FESR, including Confrontation service. *Yarra* later served with ANZUK Force. In the mid-1960s both ships were fitted with the Ikara anti-submarine missile system and Seacat anti-aircraft missile system. One Limbo mortar was retained.

In 1977 both were taken in hand for modernisation, which involved the fitting of improved fire control equipment, removal of Limbo, fitting of homing torpedoes, sensor improvements and a superstructure makeover. *Yarra* paid off in 1987 and *Parramatta* in 1991.

Of the second two ships, *Derwent* was laid down in 1958, launched in 1961 and commissioned in 1964. Similar to the first two, but commissioned with Ikara and Seacat, she was designed to operate a towed variable depth sonar. She served three FESR tours, one during Confrontation, and a further ANZUK deployment.

Modernised in 1981, she recommissioned in 1985 and in 1990 was converted to a training role. All told, *Derwent* deployed on twenty-one tours in the Far East. She paid off in 1994, was used in explosive survivability tests in 1995 and scuttled off the Western Australian coast as a dive wreck.

Swan was the other River Class to serve in the FESR. Laid down in 1965, she was launched in 1967 and commissioned in 1970. She was the first RAN ship to serve with the ANZUK Force, and in 1975 she was also the last. Paid off in 1996 she became a dive wreck off Bunbury WA in 1997.

Mine-Countermeasures Vessels

Six ships of the Ton Class were purchased from Britain in 1961. All had been completed between 1953 and 1955, and had been used for Reserve training before commissioning into the RAN in mid-1962. Displacing 375 tons and with a complement of thirty-four, they were 46.5 m long and had a maximum speed of 16 knots (optimistic). Their original armament was one 40 mm Bofors gun forward. While all carried mechanical sweep wires, MM11 electric pulse (magnetic) sweeps and acoustic and pressure sweeping equipment, *Hawk, Gull, Ibis* and *Teal* were standard minesweepers, while *Curlew* and *Snipe* had been modified for a sonar dome for minehunting. This equipment was subsequently fitted in 1968–69.

In 1964 *Hawk* and *Gull* deployed for Confrontation duties and were followed later that year by *Curlew* and *Snipe* and then *Ibis* and *Teal*. After Confrontation, *Hawk, Gull* and *Curlew* took part in deployments to Southeast Asia. By 1975 all but *Snipe, Ibis* and *Curlew* were in reserve and *Hawk* was broken up and the other two sold. *Snipe* and *Ibis* paid off in 1983 and 1984 respectively, before being broken up. *Curlew* continued in service until 1990, when she was sold.

Bibliography

Archival Records

National Archives of Australia

A816 Department of Defence Correspondence Files, 1935–1958.
A1068 Department of External Affairs Correspondence Files, 1933–1971.
A1209 Department of Prime Minister and Cabinet Files, 1957–.
A1308 Department of Treasury, Correspondence Files, 1941–1963.
A1813 Department of the Navy/Department of Defence Correspondence Files, 1959–1974.
A1838 Department of External Affairs Correspondence Files, 1914–1993.
A1945 Department of Defence Correspondence Files, 1946–1985.
A2031 Defence Committee Minutes, 1926–1989.
A3211 Department of Foreign Affairs and Trade, Correspondence Files, 1961–.
A4311 Department of Foreign Affairs and Trade, 'Cumpston Collection' 1901–1961.
A4359 Department of Foreign Affairs and Trade, Australian Embassy Jakarta, 1947–1985.
A4638 Cabinet Office, 1949–1951.
A4940 Menzies and Holt Ministries — Cabinet Files C, 1949–1985.
A5477 Department of the Treasury, Consultant Reports.
A5619 Cabinet Office, 1949–1972.
A5799 Defence Committee Agenda, 1932–.
A5868 Cabinet Office, Second Gorton Ministry, 1969–1969.
A5954 Department of Defence 'The Shedden Collection', 1937–1971.
A6768 Department of External Affairs Correspondence Files (East Asia Top Secret), 1941–1952.
A7942 Defence Committee Papers, 1936–1985.
A8447 Department of Defence, Chiefs of Staff Committee, 1939–.
A8580 Department of Defence Correspondence Files, 1946–1966.
MP691 Department of Defence Policy Files, 1951–1959.
MP729 Department of Army, Secret Correspondence Files, 1939–1960.
MP1049 Department of the Navy Correspondence Files.
MP1185 Department of the Navy Correspondence Files, Secret and Confidential.
MT1131 Department of the Army, Army Personnel Files, 1952–1962.

Australian War Memorial

AWM 78   HMA Ships Reports of Proceedings.
AWM 121   Directorate of Military Operations and Plans Files.
AWM 207   Records of Administration of ANZUK Force, 1969–1975.
AWM 208   Records of Units under command of ANZUK Force, 1969–1974.
AWM 263   Official History of Australia's Involvement in South East Asia Conflicts, 1949–1975, Peter Edwards.
AWM 269   Official History of Australia's Involvement in Southeast Asia Conflicts, 1948–1975, Records of Peter Dennis and Jeffrey Grey.
SO 2803   Interview with Commodore A.N. Dollard.

United Kingdom National Archives

ADM 1/23646   HMS *Alacrity* Report of Proceedings.
ADM 1/26140   Joint Operations against Communist Terrorists in Malaya.
ADM 1/29144   Reinforcement for the Far East Fleet.
ADM 205/69   First Sea Lord's Correspondence.
ADM 205/74   First Sea Lord's Correspondence.
AIR 20/6595   Policy in Malaya.
CO 968   Defence: Original Correspondence, 1941–1963.
CO 1022   South East Asia Department: Original Correspondence, 1950–1956.
DEFE 7/1560   Malaysian Naval Operations and Overflights, 1963.
DEFE 7/2221   Malaysia: Organisation for Control of Operations.
DEFE 11/777   Western Malaysia.
DEFE24/98   Report on Naval Operations in East and West Malaysia.
DEFE 25/170   Indonesian Confrontation.
DEFE 48/167   Maritime Patrols.

Monographs

Aldrich, Richard J., and Hopkins, Michael F., eds, *Intelligence, Defence and Diplomacy: British Policy in the Post-War World*, London: Frank Cass, 1994.

Bailey, Mark, *Aspects of the Australian Army Intelligence System During Confrontation and the Vietnam War*, Canberra: Australian Defence Studies Centre, 1994.

Bergin, Bob, *The RAN in the Far East Strategic Reserve, 1955–1971*, South Australia: Self-published, 2006.

Bergin, Bob, *RAN Ships of the Far East Strategic Reserve, 1955–1966*, South Australia: Self-published, 2006.

Blue, R.S., *United and Undaunted: The History of the Clearance Diving Branch of the R.A.N.*, Sydney: Naval Historical Society of Australia, 1976.

Bridge, Carl, ed., *Munich to Vietnam: Australia's Relations with Britain and the United States Since the 1930s*, Melbourne: Melbourne University Press, 1991.

British Parliament, *Arrangements for the Employment of Overseas Commonwealth Forces in Emergency Operations in the Federation of Malaya After Independence*, London: Her Majesty's Stationery Office, 1957.

Brookes, Andrew J., *Photo Reconnaissance: The Operational History*, London: Allen, 1975.

Burrell, Henry, *Mermaids Do Exist,* Melbourne: Macmillan, 1986.

Carroll, John R., *Out of Sight Out of Mind: The Facts of the Royal Australian Navy's Logistical and Support Role in Vietnam*, Heathmont, Vic.: The Grey Funnel Line, 1999.

Chin Kin Wah, *The Five Power Defence Arrangements and AMDA*, Singapore: Institute of Southeast Asian Studies, 1974.

Chin Kin Wah, *The Defence of Malaysia and Singapore: The Transformation of a Security System, 1957–1971*, Cambridge: Cambridge University Press, 1983.

Chin, Peng, *My Side of History: Recollections of the Guerrilla Leader who Waged a12-Year Anti-Colonial War Against British and Commonwealth Forces in the Jungles of Malaya*, Singapore: Media Masters, 2003.

Clarke, John, *Report of the Review of Veterans' Entitlements*, Canberra: Department of Communications, Information Technology and the Arts, 2003.

Clutterbuck, Richard, *The Long, Long War: The Emergency in Malaya, 1948–1960*, London: Cassell, 1966.

Collins, John, *As Luck Would Have It: The Reminiscences of an Australian Sailor*, Sydney: Angus & Robertson, 1965.

Darby, Phillip, *British Defence Policy East of Suez, 1947–1968*, London: Oxford University Press, 1973.

Darwin, John, 'Britain's Withdrawal From East of Suez', in *Munich to Vietnam: Australia's Relations with Britain and the United States since the 1930s*, ed. Carl Bridge, 114–29. Melbourne: Melbourne University Press, 1991.

Dee, Moreen, ed., *Australia and the Formation of Malaysia, 1961–1966: Documents on Australian Foreign Policy*, Canberra: Department of Foreign Affairs and Trade, 2005.

Dennis, Peter, and Grey, Jeffrey, *Emergency and Confrontation: Australian Military Operations in Malaya and Borneo, 1950–1966*, Sydney: Allen & Unwin, 1996.

Donohue, Hector, *From Empire Defence to the Long Haul: Post-War Defence Policy and its Impact on Naval Force Structure Planning, 1945–1955*, Canberra: RAN Maritime Studies Program, 1996.

Edwards, Peter G., *Crises and Commitments: The Politics and Diplomacy of Australia's Involvement in South East Asia, 1948–1965*, Sydney: Allen & Unwin, 1992.

Foster, John, *'Hands to Boarding Stations!' The Story of Minesweeper HMAS* Hawk, Loftus, NSW: Australian Military History Publications, 2003.

Frame T.R., *Pacific Partners: A History of Australian–American Naval Relations*, Sydney: Hodder & Stoughton, 1992.

Grazebrook, A.W., 'Vice-Admiral Sir John Augustine Collins, KBE, CB, RAN', in *The Royal Australian Navy in World War II*, ed. David Stevens, 135–45. Sydney: Allen & Unwin, 1996.

Greenwood, Gordon and Harper, Norman, eds, *Australia in World Affairs, 1961–1965*, Melbourne: F.W. Cheshire, 1968.

Grey, Jeffrey, *Up Top: The Royal Australian Navy and Southeast Asian Conflicts,1955–1972*, Sydney: Allen & Unwin, 1998.

Grey, Jeffrey, *A Military History of Australia*, Melbourne: Cambridge University Press, 1999.

Grove, Eric, 'British and Australian Naval Policy in the Korean War Era', in *Reflections on the RAN*, ed. Tom Frame, James Goldrick and P.D. Jones, 245–74. Kenthurst, NSW: Kangaroo Press, 1991.

Hack, Karl, 'Corpses, Prisoners of War and Captured Documents: British and Communist Narratives of the Malayan Emergency, and the Dynamics of Intelligence Transformation', in *Clandestine Cold War in Asia, 1945–65: Western Intelligence, Propaganda, Security and Special Operations*, eds Richard Aldrich, Gary Rawnsley and Ming-Yeh Rawnsley, 211–41. London: Frank Cass, 2000.

Harkness, Harry, *Onus of Proof*, Pialba, Qld.: Self-published, 2003.

Harper, Norman, *A Great and Powerful Friend: A Study of Australian American Relations Between 1900 and 1975*, St Lucia, Qld: University of Queensland Press, 1987.

Hawkins, David, *The Defence of Malaysia and Singapore: From AMDA to ANZUK*, London: Royal United Services Institute for Defence Studies, 1972.

Horner, David, *Defence Supremo: Sir Frederick Shedden and the Making of Australian Defence Policy*, Sydney: Allen & Unwin, 2000.

Jackson, Robert, *The Malayan Emergency: The Commonwealth's War, 1948–1966*, London: Routledge, 1991.

James, Harold, and Sheil-Small, Denis, *The Undeclared War: The Story of Indonesian Confrontation, 1962–1966*, London: Leo Cooper, 1971.

Jackson, Franklyn, *Defence by Committee: The British Committee of Imperial Defence, 1885–1959*, London: Oxford University Press, 1960.

Komer, R.W., *The Malayan Emergency in Retrospect: Organisation of a Successful Counterinsurgency Effort*, Santa Monica, Ca: Rand Corporation, 1972.

Lowe, David, ed., *Australia and the End of Empires: The Impact of Decolonisation in Australia's Near North, 1945–1965*, Geelong: Deakin University Press, 1996.

Mackay, Donald, *The Malayan Emergency, 1948–60: The Domino That Stood*, London: Brassey's, 1997.

Mackie, J.A.C., *Konfrontasi: The Indonesian–Malaysia Dispute, 1963–66*, Kuala Lumpur: Oxford University Press, 1974.

Mackie, J.A.C., *Low Level Military Incursions: Lessons of the Indonesian–Malaysian 'Confrontation' Episode, 1963–66*, Canberra: Strategic and Defence Studies Centre, Australian National University, 1986.

McDougall, Derek, 'The Malayan Emergency and Confrontation', in *Munich to Vietnam: Australia's Relations with Britain and the US Since the 1930s*, ed. Carl Bridge, 130–39. Melbourne: Melbourne University Press, 1991.

MacLean, L.D., *ANZIM to ANZUK — an Historical Outline of ANZAM*, Canberra: Department of Defence, 1992.

Methven, Philip, *The Five Power Defence Arrangements and Military Cooperation Among the ASEAN States*, Canberra: Strategic and Defence Studies Centre, 1992.

Mohr, R.F., *Review of Service Entitlement Anomalies in Respect of South-East Asian Service, 1955–1975*, Canberra: Department of Defence, 2002.

Murfett, Malcolm, *In Jeopardy: The Royal Navy and British Far Eastern Defence Policy, 1945–1951*, Kuala Lumpur: Oxford University Press, 1995.

Nesdale, Iris, *Action Stations: Tribal Destroyers of the Royal Australian Navy*, Adelaide: South Australia Branch, HMAS *Warramunga* Veterans' Association, 1989.

Nott, Rodney, and Payne, Noel, *'The Vung Tau Ferry' (HMAS Sydney) and Escort Ships: Vietnam, 1965–1972*, Melbourne: General Aviation Maintenance, 1998.

O'Ballance, Edgar, *Malaysia: The Communist Insurgent War, 1948–1960*, London: Faber, 1966.

O'Keefe, Brendan, and Smith, F.B., *Medicine at War: Medical Aspects of Australia's Involvement in Southeast Asian Conflict, 1950–1972*, Sydney: Allen & Unwin, 1994.

O'Neill, Robert, *Official History of Australia in the Korean War, 1950–53*, Vol. 1: *Strategy and Diplomacy*, Canberra: Australian War Memorial, 1981.

O'Neill, Robert, 'The Korean War and the Origins of ANZUS', in *Munich to Vietnam: Australia's Relations with Britain and the United States Since the 1930s*, ed. Carl Bridge, 99–113. Melbourne: Melbourne University Press, 1991.

Ovendale, Ritchie, *The English-Speaking Alliance: Britain, the United States, the Dominions and the Cold War, 1945–1951*, London: George Allen & Unwin, 1985.

Ovendale, Ritchie, *British Defence Policy Since 1945*, Manchester: Manchester University Press, 1994.

Pemberton, Gregory, *All the Way: Australia's Road to Vietnam*, Sydney: Allen & Unwin, 1987.

Reese, Trevor, *Australia, New Zealand and the United States: A Survey of International Relations, 1941–1968*, London: Oxford University Press, 1969.

Reynolds, Wayne, 'Imperial Defence After 1945', in *Australia and the End of Empires: The Impact of Decolonisation in Australia's Near North, 1945–1965*, ed. David Lowe, 119–35. Geelong, Vic.: Deakin University Press, 1996.

Richelson, Jeffrey T., and Ball, Desmond, *The Ties That Bind*, Sydney: Allen Unwin, 1990.

Rolfe, Jim, *Anachronistic Past or Positive Future: New Zealand and the Five Power Defence Arrangements*, Wellington: Centre for Strategic Studies, 1995.

Royal Malaysian Navy, *Serving the Nation*, Kuala Lumpur: Royal Malaysian Navy, 2004.

Royal United Services Institute of New South Wales, *'Konfrontasi' — Indonesian Confrontation of Malaysia, 1963–1966, Seminar 12 April 1994*, Sydney: Royal United Services Institute, 1994.

Short, A., *The Communist Insurrection in Malaya*, London: Muller, 1975.

Smith, E.D., *Counter Insurgency Operations: 1 — Malaya and Borneo*, London: Ian Allen, 1985.

Smith, Neil C., *Mostly Unsung: Australia and the Commonwealth in the Malayan Emergency, 1948–60*, Melbourne: Smith, 1989.

Stevens, David, *In Search of a Maritime Strategy: The Maritime Element in Australian Defence Planning Since 1901*, Canberra: Australian National University, 1997.

Stevens, David, *Maritime Power in the 20th Century: The Australian Experience*, Sydney: Allen & Unwin, 1998.

Stevens, David, ed., *The Australian Centenary History of Defence*, Vol. III: *The Royal Australian Navy*, Melbourne: Oxford University Press, 2001.

Stevens, David, and Reeve, John, eds, *Southern Trident: Strategy, History and the Rise of Australian Naval Power*, Sydney: Allen & Unwin, 2001.

Waters, Christopher, *The Empire Fractures: Anglo-Australian Conflict in the1940s*, Melbourne: Australian Scholarly Publishing, 1995.

Waters, Sydney, *The Royal New Zealand Navy*, Wellington: Department of Internal Affairs, 1956.

West, Nigel, *SIGINT Secrets: The Signals Intelligence War, 1900 to Today*, New York: William Morrow, 1986 (also published as *GCHQ: The Wireless War, 1900–86*, London: Weidenfeld & Nicolson, 1986).

Wilkins, John M., *Short History of Naval Intelligence and the Royal Australian Navy Intelligence Department*, Melbourne: Self-published, 2001.

Journal Articles

Andrew, Christopher, 'The Growth of the Australian Intelligence Community and the Anglo–American Connection', *Intelligence and National Security* 4 (1989): 218–29.

Barclay, G. St.J., 'In the Sticky Flypaper: The United States, Australia and Indonesia, 1959–1964', *Naval War College Review* 34 (1975): 67–80.

Barnes, Ken, 'The Defence Signals Directorate — its Roles and Functions', *Australian Defence Force Journal* 108 (1994): 3–7.

Blenkin, Max, 'Military/Konfrontasi', *Indonesia Papers* 213 (1994): 5–7.

Cooper, Alastair, 'At the Crossroads: Anglo–Australian Naval Relations, 1945–1971', *Journal of Military History* 58 (1994): 699–718.

Edwards, Peter G., 'The Australian Commitment to the Malayan Emergency 1948–50', *Historical Studies* 22 (1987): 604–16.

Farrell, Brian P., 'What Do we Do Now? British Commonwealth and American Reactions to the Separation of Malaysia and Singapore', *Australian Defence Force Journal* 170 (2006): 16–38.

Hack, Karl, 'British Intelligence and Counter-Insurgency in the Era of Decolonisation: The Example of Malaya', *Intelligence and National Security* 14 (1999): 124–55.

Keating, Gavin, 'The Five Power Defence Arrangements: A Case Study in Alliance Longevity', *Australian Defence Force Journal* 170 (2006): 48–61.

Kramers, Peter J., 'Konfrontasi in Borneo, 1962–1966', *Military Review* 70 (1990): 64–74.

Lee, David, 'The National Security Planning and Defence Preparations of the Menzies Government, 1950–53', *War and Society* 10 (1992): 119–37.

Lee, David, 'Australia and Allied Strategy in the Far East, 1952–1957', *Journal of Strategic Studies* 16 (1993): 511–38.

Lee, David, 'Britain and Australia's Defence Policy, 1945–1949', *War and Society* 13 (1995): 61–80.

Moulton, J. L., 'The Indonesian Confrontation', *US Naval Institute Naval Review* (1969): 144–71.

Stewart, Brian, 'Winning in Malaya: An Intelligence Success Story', *Intelligence and National Security* 14 (1999): 267–83.

Thomas, Andy, 'British Signals Intelligence After the Second World War', *Intelligence and National Security* 3 (1988): 103–10.

Weir, S.P., 'Bookshelf: Emergency and Confrontation — Australian Military Operations in Malaya and Borneo', *Duty First* 8 (1999): 5–13.

Electronic Records

Defence Signals Directorate, *DSD — Past and Present*, read 7 June 2001 on website http://www.dsd.gov.au/evolution2.html.

Interviews and Correspondence

Denis Appel, interviewed by author 15 March 2007.

Commodore Hari Arasaratnam RMN (Rtd), interviewed by author 8 February 2007.

Commander J.A. Bate RAN (Rtd), interviewed by R.A. Howland 21 October 2002.

Ray Brown RAN (Rtd), correspondence with author 17 May 2007.

Chief Petty Officer Jack Callander RAN (Rtd), correspondence with author 2 June 2007.

Petty Officer Joe P. Chelliah RMN (Rtd), correspondence with author 17 April 2007.

Rod Clarey, interviewed by author 29 May 2007.

Ex-CPO Electrical (WE) John Dobson, interviewed by author 28 May 2007.

Commodore Alan Dollard DSC RAN (Rtd), interviewed by author 10 July 2007.

Rear Admiral W.J. Dovers CBE DSC RAN (Rtd), interviewed by author 16 November 2001.

Commander W.T. Fox RAN (Rtd), correspondence with author 4 June 2007.

Elizabeth Gordon, interviewed by author 23 April 2007.

Rear Admiral G.R. Guy Griffiths AO DSO DSC RAN (Rtd), interviewed by author 4 April 2007.
Graeme Hanisch, interviewed by author 22 April 2007.
Lieutenant Commander D.E. Hiron RAN (Rtd), interviewed by author 26 April 2004.
Commander J. Hume RAN (Rtd), interviewed by author 28 May 2007.
Laurie Jones, interviewed by author 28 May 2007.
Captain Tee Chuan Khoo RMN (Rtd), correspondence with author, various.
Commander Lam Ah Lek RMN (Rtd), interviewed by author 3 May 2007.
Captain John Lancaster RAN (Rtd), correspondence with author, 19 July 2007.
Captain H. MacGowan RAN (Rtd), correspondence with author 13 March 2007.
Commodore P.D. McKay RAN (Rtd), interviewed by author 16 March 2007.
Glen McMahon interviewed by author.
Lieutenant Commander G.H. Miller BEM RAN (Rtd), interviewed by author 3 April 2007.
Ex-WO Gerry Mitchell BEM RAN, interviewed by author 1 May 2007.
Robin Moyle, ex-RAN, interviewed by author 28 May 2007.
Commodore P.K. Nettur RMN (Rtd), interviewed by author 3 May 2007.
Captain Ian Pfennigwerth RAN (Rtd), interviewed by D.H. Ruffin 8/9 November 2002.
Kevin Pickett, interviewed by author.
Michael Olden, correspondence with author 9 February 2007.
Paul Procopis, correspondence with author, 30 April 2007.
Commander Pat Spence RAN (Rtd), interviewed by author 24 May 2007.
Commodore M.B. Rayment AM RAN (Rtd), interviewed by author 18 December 2006.
Commander Ken Schmack RAN (Rtd), interviewed by author 11 June 2007.
Ex-LEM (WE) Bernard Verwayen RAN, interviewed by author 17 April 2007.
Commander A.K. Wait RAN (Rtd), interviewed by author 29 August 2002.
Commander Ron Whitmore RAN (Rtd), interviewed by author 4 May 2007.

Endnotes

Introduction

1 Grey, *Up Top*, 24–70.
2 O'Keefe and Smith, *Medicine at War*.
3 Prime Ministers message, '16th Minesweeper Squadron Reunion Social Club Unveiling of a Commemoration Plaque at the Australian War Memorial', 30 June 2006.

Chapter 1 A Decade of Post-War Planning

1 National Archives of Australia (NAA) A5447, Item M1/1050 to M4/1954 — COSC Appreciations, COSC minute 25/50, September 1950: 'Australia's Strategy in Relation to Communist Expansion in the Pacific, Southeast Asia and the Far East during the Cold War Period'.
2 McLean, *ANZIM to ANZUK*, vii–viii, provided a list of other contemporary security concerns for Britain, fourteen in all.
3 Manne, *Age*, 3 August 1998.
4 Recruitment of sailors for the RAN from 1940 onwards had been on a temporary 'hostilities only' basis. As a result, in July 1945 there were only 3706 permanent service ratings in the Navy. This number was quite insufficient to man the ships already in commission, and severely compromised planning for the post-war order of battle. The War Cabinet approved an emergency recruitment program to bring the naval strength up to 7500 by July 1946. [NAA A5954, Item 1645-1 — Post-War Defence Policy, Agendum 434/1945.]
5 NAA A5954/69, Item 956/2 — Australian Defence Policy: Relation of Singapore to Basis of Australian Defence Policy.
6 NAA A5954, Item 956/2 — Australian Defence Policy: Relation of Singapore to Basis of Australian Defence Policy. In the Minutes of the 258th meeting of the Committee of Imperial Defence held on 6 April 1933, the Australian High Commissioner in London, Stanley Bruce, emphasised the importance of Singapore to Australia's Security.
7 NAA A5799, Item 109/1947 — JPC Agendum 109/1947, 'Strategic Importance of Singapore'.

8 NAA A816, Item 14/301/371 — Directive for the Guidance of the Defence Department and Department of External Affairs: Defence Policy and National Security, 15 February 1946, 9.

9 NAA A5954/69, Item 1662/1 — British Commonwealth Conference 1946: Briefing Paper 'Defence and Security'.

10 MacLean, *ANZIM to ANZUK*, 2–3.

11 NAA A5799/15, Item 125/1952 — Responsibilities of ANZAM Chiefs of Staff in Relation to the External Defence of Malaya, Attachment to CNS letter of 10 June 1952.

12 NAA A5954/69, Item 1631/1 — Strategic Planning in Relation to British Commonwealth Defence: Basis for Planning the Defence of Sea Communications in the ANZAM Region: COSC Agendum (50) 68 of 17 February 1950, 3. This was a significant step for the RAN, which formerly had had no strategic planning responsibilities of any kind. [Cooper 'At the Crossroads', 699–718.]

13 Minutes 206/57 of State-Army-Navy-Air Force Coordinating Committee (SANAAC), 18 May 1948, quoted in Cain, 'Missiles and Mistrust', 12

14 Ovendale, *The English-Speaking Alliance*, 59.

15 Frame, *Pacific Partners*, 86–87.

16 Donohue, *From Empire Defence*, 82–84. The Radford–Collins agreement was essentially a formal confirmation of what had been agreed as early as 1948 between Admiral Ramsay, Radford's predecessor, and CNS Collins.

17 Murfett, *In Jeopardy*, 90.

18 A contrary view is put by the leader of the Communist Party of Malaya, Chin Peng, who made the claim that the Australian Foreign Minister, Dr H.V. Evatt, showed interest in providing assistance to the British as early as August 1948. However, he conceded that it took two years for any assistance to eventuate, and seven years before Australian troops joined the battle. [Chin, *My Side of History*, 248–53.]

19 It was felt that the hard work that Australia was putting into the development of the Colombo Plan (1950) might be placed in jeopardy by too willing a toeing of the British line on Malaya. [O'Neill, *Strategy and Diplomacy*, 38.]

20 NAA A1068, DL47/5/1 Part 1 — JIC Appreciations: Defence File, JIC Appreciation 6/1949.

21 NAA A4638, Item Set 1 — Fourth Menzies Cabinet Decisions, Decision 97 of 2 May 1950.

22 NAA A4638, Item Set 1 — Fourth Menzies Cabinet Decisions, Decision 97 of 2 May 1950.

23 Stevens, *Royal Australian Navy*, 160–62.

24 The Battles were to take nearly five years to complete, and the *Daring* program was delayed and then reduced to three ships. [Grove, 'British and Australian Naval Policy', 249–50.]

25 On 20 December 1948 CNS Collins advised First Sea Lord Fraser that 'Owing to a lack of manpower and materials we shall only do about 75 per cent of what was planned'. [UKNA ADM205/69 — First Sea Lord's Correspondence.]

26 *Melbourne* was not delivered until 1955; HMS *Vengeance* on loan served in her place in the interim.

27 United Kingdom National Archives (UKNA) ADM 205/74 — First Sea Lord Correspondence, CNS Australia letter 6 October 1950.
28 AWM S02803, interview with Commodore A.N. Dollard.
29 NAA A6768, Item EATS 25 — East Asia from Commissioner Singapore, Annual Conference of British Representatives 23–26 November 1951.
30 NAA A1209/23, Item 1957/4686 — Defence of Malaya: Force Requirements, Joint Planning Staff Report 46/1953.
31 NAA A1209/23, Item 1957/4686 — Defence of Malaya: Force Requirements, Joint Planning Staff Report 46/1953.
32 NAAA1838, Item TS654/8/3/2 — Regional Defence Arrangements: Five Power Staff Agency.
33 NAA A4940, Item C2414 — 'Defence and Development — 1950–1953'.
34 The specific matters addressed are listed in MacLean, *ANZIM to ANZUK*, 6.
35 NAA A5799, Item 66/1951 — Defence of Malaya: Visit of Joint Planning Team, Report of Joint Planning Committee.

Chapter 2 The Malayan Emergency

 1 Short, *The Communist Insurrection*, 19–25. The reference gives a detailed background history of the Communist Party of Malaya and its role in the MPAJA.
 2 Short, *The Communist Insurrection*, 104.
 3 The MRLA had members from other ethnic origins, but most non-Chinese activists were bandits rather than terrorists. The Chinese population was the subject of a struggle between the Party and the *Kuo Min Tang* (KMT) with its roots in Nationalist China. [Short, *The Communist Insurrection*, 208–21.]
 4 The British faced a grave shortage of Chinese-speaking officers to deal with an essentially Chinese-rooted insurgency. Stewart, 'Winning in Malaya', provided an interesting account of the work of the Chinese Affairs Department in increasing the flow of anti-MRLA intelligence.
 5 However, Chin, *My Side of History*, 321–22 recounts one extremely successful attack on his headquarters by the RAAF bombers in March 1953.
 6 UKNA FO 371/69698, correspondence dated 17/18 August 1948.
 7 NAA A1068, Item DL47/1/19 — JPC Report 29/49 of 15 December 1948.
 8 NAA A5954, Box 2292 — Assistance to Malaya 1948, press release 471 of 18 July 1948.
 9 *Melbourne Age*, 7 July 1948.
10 O'Neill, *Korean War*, Vol. 1, 48–49.
11 NAA A1838/2, Item 411/3/3/1/2, memorandum of 14 July 1950.
12 NAA A5954, Item 2296/4 — Aid for Malaya File 2: Report by Military Mission.
13 Australian War Memorial (AWM) 269, Item B/13/9 — Emergency & Confrontation: Military Mission to Malaya: McBride letter to Prime Minister of 15 December 1950.
14 NAA A5954, 1682/3— Prime Ministers' Conference London 1951. Australian Participation in Cold War Operations in Malaya, Appendix D: Defence Committee Minute 203/1950. Military Mission to Malaya and List of Needs of Far Eastern Land Forces.

15 UKNA AIR 20/6595 — Policy in Malaya, Air Ministry message A.2680 of 29 March 1951.
16 NAA A5954/69, Item 2296/4 — Aid For Malaya, File 2: Report by Military Mission, 12.
17 Mackay, *The Malayan Emergency*, 106.
18 Smith, *Counter Insurgency*, 35.
19 UKNA ADM 1/23646 — HMS *Alacrity* Report of Proceedings 26 April to 8 May 1952.
20 UKNA CO1022/317 — Supply of Arms to Bandits in Malaya.
21 UKNA CO 1022 — External Aid to Malayan Communists, Intelligence report for period 1–15 April 1952.
22 Chin, *My Side of History*, 351, 327.
23 Hack, 'Corpses, Prisoners of War and Captured Documents', 226. The statement was attributed to Chin at a workshop held at the Australian National University, Canberra, on 22 and 23 February 1999.
24 UKNA CO1022/250 — Cooperation between Singapore and the Federation of Malaya in Dealing with Communist Terrorists. The MRLA chain of command in 1951 showed the Third, Fourth and Ninth Regiments, estimated to number 900 CTs in Johore. [Smith, *Counter Insurgency Operations*, 20.]
25 NAA A1209/23, Item 1857/4152 — Strategic Basis of Australian Defence Policy 1953, Defence Committee minute 368/1952 of 8 January 1953.
26 Komer, *The Malayan Emergency in Retrospect*, 41–45.
27 NAA A5954/69, Item 2292/4 — Malaya 1949–November 1952 File 3, 'The Police of Malaya', dated 26 May 1952.
28 Thomas, 'British Signals Intelligence', 104, noted that the signals intelligence station near Colombo maintained a ship–shore link from 1947, and suggested that this was to ships monitoring signals off the Malayan coast.
29 Two submissions to the Mohr Review make this point. The first appears in a personal submission made by Commodore M.A. Clarke AM RAN (Rtd), and the second in the submission made on behalf of its members by the FESR Association.
30 FESR Association records — A.D. Moffatt submission to Mohr Review undated.
31 NAA MP691/1, Item 3712/4/28 — Korea and Malaya — Special Overseas Forces, Navy Office letter of 31 August 1953.
32 NAA A1838, Item TS682/22 Part 1 — Commonwealth Strategic Reserve in Far East, Lord Alexander letter of 29 June 1953.
33 Edwards, *Crises and Commitments*, 162–64.
34 NAA A2031/8, Item 4/1956 — ANZAM Defence Committee Memorandum 4/1956.
35 Grey, *Up Top*, 25, 29, Table 2.1.
36 NAA A816/56, Item 19/321/34 — FESR Directive to HMA Ships, 1956.
37 NAA MP1185/10, Item 5245/22/10 — FESR: Deployment of HMA Ships.
38 AWM78, Item 40/4 — HMAS *Arunta* Report of Proceedings June 1955. In a note against this passage, the Director of Plans has written, 'I informed him of the reasons for this before his report was written', but he did not indicate what the reasons might have been.
39 NAA MP1185/10, Item 5219/53/4 — Urgent Military Preparations Required in Malaya.
40 NAA MP1049/6, Item 5063/37/2 — HMAS *Anzac* Breach of Discipline, address to ship's company 16 November 1955.

41 Short, *The Communist Insurrection*, 371–72. Grove noted that this activity was 'fairly constant' but agreed with Short that many of the missions were in the nature of harassment. [Grove, *Vanguard to Trident*, 150–51.]

42 Other forces involved included three infantry battalions, seven special units (jungle-trained police patrols) and a force of ex-CTs. The operation was successful, not so much in killing CTs but in breaking their morale and persuading them to surrender. [Short, *The Communist Insurrection*, 489–92.]

43 Photo reconnaissance was also useful in spotting areas of food cultivation in the jungle. [Hack, 'British Intelligence', 148 and Footnote 23.]

44 AWM78, Item 34/4 — HMAS *Anzac* Report of Proceedings, September 1956.

45 AWM78, Item 300/4 — HMAS *Quickmatch* Report of Proceedings, January 1957.

46 NAA MT1136/1 Item 4019/124/1150 — Report on Death of AB Spooner, HMAS *Melbourne* letter 28 April 1957.

47 NAA A816/56, Item 19/321/3Y — FESR Directives to HMA Ships, 1956.

48 A Ministry of Defence minute of 13 November 1951 noted that one frigate, six minesweepers and two motor launches were engaged, with additional forces being raised by the Malayan Government. The estimated annual cost of the operations was £600,000. [UKNA DEFE 7/240 — Malaya: Defence Expenditure.]

49 AWM78, Item 34/4 — HMAS *Anzac* Report of Proceedings, September 1956.

50 AWM78, Item 40/4 — HMAS *Arunta* Report of Proceedings, October 1955.

51 AWM78, Item 34/5 — HMAS *Anzac* Report of Proceedings, June 1957.

52 AWM78, Item 34/5 — HMAS *Anzac* Report of Proceedings, July 1957.

53 Brown, *Memoirs,* Chapter 8: HMAS *Quickmatch*, Part II, 3.

54 FESR Association submission to Mohr Review, J. Carlyon letter of 17 July 1999.

55 NAA A1209, Item 1958/5029 — Directives to RAN Ships with FESR.

56 Clarke Submission to Mohr Review, ACNB Message DTG 130731Z March 1958.

57 AWM78, Item 298/5 — HMAS *Queenborough* Report of Proceedings, January 1957.

58 AWM78, Item 343/6 — HMAS *Tobruk* Report of Proceedings, June 1959.

59 NAA A5799, Item 23/1956 Supplement 1 — Future Defence Arrangements with the Federation of Malaya and Singapore.

60 Smith, *Counter Insurgency*, 34. The CTs were active again in a minor way during Confrontation.

61 FESR Association to the Mohr Review, A.D. West letter of 7 June 1999.

62 AWM78, Item 343/5 — HMAS *Tobruk* Report of Proceedings, October 1956.

63 AWM78, Item 343/5 — HMAS *Tobruk* Report of Proceedings, August 1957.

64 FESR Association submission to Mohr Review, KN O'Brien letter undated.

65 AWM78, Item 40/4 — HMAS *Arunta* Report of Proceedings, August 1955.

66 AWM78, Item 343/5 — HMAS *Tobruk* Report of Proceedings, October 1956.

67 The *Attack* Class patrol boat project was not commenced until September 1965, its genesis — apparently — was experience gained in Confrontation, rather than the Malayan Emergency. [Stevens, *Royal Australian Navy*, 199–201.]

68 Dennis and Grey, *Emergency and Confrontation*, xv.

Chapter 3 The Calm Before the Storm

1 NAA A1209, Item 1957/5293 Part 1 — Commonwealth Prime Ministers Conference London 1956: Minutes and Memorandum, ninth meeting 4 April 1956.

2 British Government, *Arrangements of the Employment of Overseas Commonwealth Forces*, 2.

3 The British Government agreed to provide defence assistance in cash and kind to the Malayan Government of £13 million over the five years 1957–61. To this was added around £8 million worth of buildings and property. [Hawkins, *Defence of Malaysia*, 17.]

4 NAA A1945, Item 15/1/1 — Future of ANZAM Part 1.

5 The first meeting of this group had been held in Bandung, Indonesia, in 1954.

6 NAA A1838, Item TS682/21/3 — Operational Planning for the Defence of Malaya.

7 NAA A1838, Item TS687/7/2 — ANZAM: Internal Threat to Malaya.

8 Singapore gained internal self-government on 3 June 1959, with Britain retaining the external affairs and defence powers.

9 NAA A1838, Item TS682/22 Part 7 — British Commonwealth Planning: Commonwealth Strategic Reserve, Australian Commission letter of 24 January 1957.

10 The Australian Cabinet decided on 22 February 1957 that Australia needed well-equipped mobile forces with which to react to any fast-developing emergency, and that it was more likely that Australian contingents would be fighting under the umbrella of an American-led reaction force. [Lee, *Australia and Allied Strategy*, 532–33.]

11 NAA A1209, Item 1957/5983 — ANZAM Planners' Report: Review of Malayan Defence Requirements up to the End of 1956.

12 It was not until 1962 that all these insurgencies had been stamped out, the last being the *Darul Islam* religious movement in East Java.

13 NAA MT1131/1, Item A323/1/1057 — Enquiry to Minister re Indonesian Students at RMC.

14 Dee, *Formation of Malaysia*, Document 21, 35–36. The Australian Foreign Minister's concerns with the proposal centred on Malaya's ability to administer the two Borneo territories and the issue of 'the vigorous and energetic population of Singapore'.

15 Indeed, the Malaysian Government fully intended to place restrictions on the wider use of the Singapore bases. Wrangling continued until July 1963, when agreement was reached that they could be used 'for the preservation of peace in South East Asia'. [Hawkins, *Defence of Malaysia*, 19.]

16 Hawkins, *Defence of Malaysia*, 20.

17 Dee, *Formation of Malaysia*, Document 27, 46. At a meeting in February 1963 the Defence Committee reaffirmed the importance of the Singapore bases but noted that support for Malaysia might well bring Australian forces into conflict with Indonesia.

18 NAA A1813/49, Item 312/201/15 — Intelligence Lectures for Ships Proceeding to FESR.

19 Dee, *Formation of Malaysia*, Document 29, 48–51.

20 In November 1961 the Indonesian Foreign Minister said in the UN, 'When Malaya told us of her intentions to merge with the three British crown colonies of Sarawak, Brunei and British North Borneo as one federation we told them that we had no objections'.

By September President Sukarno was claiming that Indonesia would 'crush' Malaysia. [Mackie, *Konfrontasi*, 200.]

21 NAA A1945/39, Item 162/3/21 — FESR Directive for HM Ships, 1963.

22 NAA A1945/40, Item 162/3/42 — Employment of RAN Ships in Borneo Waters.

23 Dee, *Formation of Malaysia, 1961–1966*, Document 20, 34–35.

24 Sukarno's term was *ganjang*, which means to devour, or to eat raw. He referred to 'munching Malaysia and then spiting it out'. [Moulton, 'Confrontation', 154, footnote.]

25 UKNA ADM1/29144 — Reinforcement for the Far East Fleet in General and Limited War.

26 NAA A1945, Item 65/1/46 — Joint Planning Committee (Far East)) Minutes of Meetings.

27 NAA A1838, Item TS687/9 Part 1 — ANZAM: Examination of Indonesian Policy, Annex to UK COS 302/63.

28 Dee, *Formation of Malaysia*, Documents 47 and 48, 80–82.

29 Between 1 August and 20 November 1963 there were 69 armed incursions across the border into East Malaysia: 58 of the raiders had been killed and 20 captured. Commonwealth casualties had been fewer than 10. [Moulton, 'The Indonesian Confrontation', 155.]

30 Dee, *Formation of Malaysia*, Document 39, 62–63.

31 Dee, *Formation of Malaysia*, Document 74, 113–14.

32 Dee, *Formation of Malaysia*, Document 119, 167.

33 NAA A1838, Item TS687/9 Part 1 — ANZAM: Examination of Indonesian Policy.

34 Dee, *Formation of Malaysia*, Document 135, 192–93.

35 Dee, *Formation of Malaysia*, The Kennedy Mediation Talks, 217.

Chapter 4 A Malayan/Malaysian Navy

1 This was not the first Malayan naval venture in support of the RN. The 31,000 ton RN battleship *Malaya*, commissioned in 1916, was paid for by contributions by the nine Malay rulers of Malaya.

2 RMN, *Royal Malaysian Navy*, 3.

3 Kept (R) Khoo, correspondence with author, May 2007.

4 UKNA ADM 1/26140 — Joint Operations against Communist Terrorists in Malaya (Operations NASSAU and REX).

5 Kept (R) Khoo, correspondence with author, May 2007.

6 UKNA CO 968/664 — Transfer of RMN from Singapore to the Federation of Malaya, COS (57) 266 of 9 December 1957.

7 NAA A1836, Item TS682/21/3 — Operational Planning for the Defence of Malaya, Australian High Commission KL letter 201/8/4 of 27 September 1957.

8 NAA A1838/269, Item TS696/6/3 part 1 — Defence of Malaya: Malayan Armed Forces, Annex A to DCC (FE) (60)) 240 of 14 February 1958.

9 UKNA CO968/664, Transfer of Royal Malaysian Navy from Singapore to Federation of Malaya.

10 Commodore Arasaratnam, interview with author, 9 February 2007.

11 NAA A1945/28, Item 162/1/7 — Malayan Request for Australian Naval Advisers — RAN

Officer to Command Federation Navy.

12 The High Commissioner was to reap the benefits of this support personally in 1965 when, after being invited to cruise on board the first Malaysian frigate, KD *Hang Tuah*, to Trengganu, he got into difficulties while diving off a beach, was rescued unconscious from the sea by the RMN and flown by the ship's helicopter to Kota Baru, where he was resuscitated. [Khoo, correspondence with author, 6 July 2007.]

13 Arasaratnam interview.

14 Commodore Nettur, correspondence with author, 9 February 2007.

15 Rear Admiral Dovers, interview with author, 16 November 2001. Dovers was reprimanded by the Fleet Commander for his 'rude' response of 'No' until he pointed out that the single word was merely the answer to the question posed.

16 Dovers interview.

17 Arasaratnam interview.

18 Nettur correspondence.

19 NAA A1838, Item TS682/21/3 — Operational Planning for the Defence of Malaysia, Australian High Commission letter 201/8/1/2/ of 22 August 1963.

20 Commander Fox, correspondence with author, 4 June 2007.

21 Commander Whitmore, correspondence with author, 29 April 2007.

22 NAA A1838, Item TS682/21/3 — Operational Planning for the Defence of Malaysia, Ministry of Defence's Ordinary Estimates 1963.

23 Captain John Lancaster, correspondence with author, 19 July 2007.

24 Petty Officer Joe Chelliah, correspondence with author, 17 April 2007.

25 Lancaster correspondence.

26 Chelliah, correspondence.

27 Commodore Rayment, interview with author, 8 December 2006.

28 Rayment interview.

29 Four Ton Class minesweepers, four Ham Class inshore minesweepers and seven seaward defence launches plus the Vospers. In November 1964 a *Loch* Class frigate was transferred by the RN and named KD *Hang Tuah*. [Moulton, 'Confrontation', 146.]

30 AWM269, Item B/3/1/3/1 — Defence Committee Minutes and Defence Committee Agenda 1964: Indonesia, Report of Australian Defence Mission to Malaysia of 10 March 1964.

31 Captain MacGowan, correspondence with author, 22 February 2007.

32 MacGowan correspondence. The ship, KD *Selangor*, finally completed refit in March 1965. In the interim, MacGowan commanded two other RMN vessels.

33 Arasaratnam interview.

34 Kept (R) Khoo, correspondence with author, 29 June 2007.

35 Arasaratnam interview.

36 The construction of the new Malayan base for the RMN continued to be put back and did not in fact become fully operational until the early 1970s.

37 Tom Edgerton, correspondence with author, 5 May 2007.

38 Ex-LEM (WE) Bernard Verwayen, interview with author,16 April 2007.

39 UKNA DEFE 24/98 — Reports on Operations in East and West Malaysia 1964–1966.

40 On 8 October 1963 two RMN patrol craft intercepted a pair of Indonesian gunboats

attempting a pirate raid on Malaysian fishing craft in the Malacca Strait. The Indonesians withdrew without fighting. RMN ships were active in the Malacca Strait on 9 and 10 January 1965, intercepting two attempts by Indonesian parties to get ashore in Negri Sembilan State. [Moulton, 'Confrontation', 155, 165.]

41 The assistance also included the provision of training for RMN officers and sailors in RAN schools. [NAA A1945/28, Item 245/1/7 — Malayan [*sic*] Request for Defence Assistance, Defence Cabinet Submission: 'Defence Assistance for Malaysia'.]

42 MacGowan correspondence.

43 MacGowan correspondence.

44 Nettur correspondence.

45 'Ed' is the Commodore's preferred corruption of the nickname given him by his term mates at the Royal Australian Naval College when they translated his initials — AND — into the French 'Et'.

46 Commodore Dollard, interview with author, 10 July 2007.

47 MacGowan correspondence.

48 Dollard interview.

49 Dollard interview.

50 Khoo correspondence.

51 Rear Admiral Griffiths, interview with author, 4 April 2007.

52 Griffiths interview.

53 Griffiths interview.

54 Griffiths interview.

55 Commander Hume, interview with author, 28 May 2007.

56 Mitchell interview.

57 Mitchell interview.

58 Edgerton correspondence.

59 Commander Spence, interview with author, 24 May 2007.

60 Spence interview.

61 Edgerton correspondence

62 Edgerton, correspondence.

63 Edgerton correspondence.

64 Spence interview.

65 Lieutenant Commander Miller, interview with author, 3 April 2007.

66 Miller interview.

67 NAA A1813/49, Item 311/201/306 — RMN: Training of Apprentices in Australia.

68 NAA A1813/49, Item 311/201/239 — RMN: Proposed Syllabus for Training in Australia as CDs. Before this training could be offered, the RAN had to get clearance from the RN and USN for Malaysian students to use standard Allied training and procedure manuals. The clearance process was surely aided by the fact that the commanding officer at *Rushcutter* was none other than John Lancaster, fresh from commanding KD *Malaya*.

69 Commander Lam Ah Lek, interview with author, 16 May 2007.

70 Miller interview.

71 NAA A1813/49, Item 311/201/306 — RMN: Training of Apprentices in Australia, Navy

Office letter of 2 July 1969.
72 Graeme Hanisch, interview with author, 22 April 2007.
73 Hanisch interview.
74 Griffiths interview.
75 Griffiths Form AS 206 — Confidential Report on Officers, 1 January – 30 June 1969.
76 Rayment interview.
77 Rayment interview.
78 Griffiths interview.
79 Hume interview.
80 Miller interview.
81 Hume interview.
82 Rayment interview.
83 McKay interview.
84 Miller interview.
85 Arasaratnam interview.
86 Miller interview.
87 Rayment interview.
88 Verwayen interview.
89 McKay interview.
90 Miller interview.
91 Hume interview.
92 Captain C. Slater, correspondence with author, 27 June 2007.
93 Rayment interview.
94 Slater correspondence.
95 Miller interview.
96 Griffiths interview.
97 Slater correspondence.
98 Gerry Mitchell, interview with author, 1 May 2007.
99 Spence interview.
100 Edgerton correspondence.
101 McKay interview.
102 Kept Khoo, correspondence with author, 7 June 2007.
103 Miller interview.
104 AWM208, Item 26 — 9 ANZUK Signals regiment; Australian Technical Mission to Malaysia.
105 Rayment interview.
106 Arasaratnam interview.
107 Khoo correspondence.

Chapter 5 Indonesian Confrontation
1 In 1962 Indonesia claimed a 12-mile territorial sea drawn from base lines connecting the outermost points of its claimed territory. A second claim was that the Java, Banda and Molucca Seas were now Indonesian internal waters. These were disputed by the Commonwealth as being contrary to international law, but ships were directed to stay

clear of Indonesian-claimed waters as far as possible. [UKNA DEFE 7/1560 — Malaysian Naval Operations and Overflights, 1963.]

2 'We have no evidence that the Indonesians have pressure mines. Furthermore, they have so far shown little interest in mine warfare. However, so long as the Russian naval influence prevails we should assume a small mining threat'. [UKNA ADM 1/29144 — Reinforcement for the Far East Fleet in General and Limited War, Flag Officer-in-Charge Far East Fleet letter FEF 32 OPS 2 of 10 October 1963 to Vice CNS.]

3 The ALRI order of battle in 1963 is shown in Grey, *Up Top*, 44, Table 3.1. According to the Indonesians in 1961, the purchases from the USSR were in preparation for a war. [Harper, *A Great and Powerful Friend*, 301.] The war in the offing at that stage was the dislodgment of the Dutch from West New Guinea.

4 Barclay, 'In the Sticky Flypaper', 73.

5 The occupant of the post had to be a British officer, since he would be receiving Sigint that could not be shown to Malaysians. [UKNA DEFE 7/2221 — Malaysia: Organisation for Control of Operations, COSC DP 104/63 (Final) of 18 October 1963.]

6 Commodore Robertson — former Leader of CinCFE Joint Planning Staff Team A — interview with author, 6 August 2002.

7 AWM121, Item 4/7 — Operations Borneo/Malaysia, COMFEF Message DTG 111439Z September 1964.

8 Three PR Canberra aircraft were available in the theatre, and occasional overflights over the Riau Archipelago and the islands off North Sumatra were authorised by CinCFE. [UKNA DEFE 25/170 — Indonesian Confrontation, Vice Chief of Air Staff letter VCAS.5448 of 8 October 1965.]

9 NAA A1945/40, Item 248/1/14 — CinCFE Meetings.

10 This strategy was almost ruinous financially and militarily to the UK. 'I think we were all set to lose Confrontation, because it was costing the Brits an arm and a leg'. [Robertson interview.]

11 NAA A1945/39, Item 71/1/120 — Record of Conversation between CinCFE Sir Varyl Begg and Sir Arthur Tange, 21 October 1964. These plans were revised and renamed SPILLIKIN and HEMLEY respectively.

12 NAA A5954/69, Item 1671/21 — Conference of Defence Ministers, June 1951. DSB and the associated service intercept units had strengths of 249 and 179 respectively. These figures do not match those provided by the agencies themselves in NAA A816/1, Item 41/301/170 — Staffing JIB and DSB, 'JIB and DSB Review of Staffing' of 4 September 1951. JIB had only 91 of 115 established positions filled and the situation at DSB was 124 filled out of 160. The Review was produced to bolster the case for accelerated recruitment before the Public Service Board.

13 NAA A1838/269, Item TS666/57/8 — JIC (M) 8 — Australian Intelligence Organisations. JIC Minute 180 of 11 July 1957 noted that the language school had been most effective in training Mandarin Chinese translators.

14 NAA A8580/1, Item Z1/11 — JIO Report to PM on JIB and DSD (1955), letter X8/35 undated from Minister of Defence to Prime Minister.

15 NAA A8580/1, Item Z1/11 — JIO Report to PM on JIB and DSD (1955), letter X8/35 undated from Minister of Defence to Prime Minister.

16 Robertson interview, and interview of CMDR Nicholls by the author, 11 February 2003. Bailey gave an account of the bugging of the Indonesian Embassy in London as the basis of the penetration of Indonesian diplomatic traffic. [Bailey, *Aspects of the Australian Army Intelligence System*, 11.]

17 Robertson interview.

18 JIC (A) submitted a report (17/1961) on 20 September 1961 on Indonesia's arms acquisitions. This was accompanied by a technical intelligence report, 'Technical Capability of the Indonesian Armed Forces', in which the difficulties faced by Jakarta in terms of its readiness and technical standards was revealed. [NAA A1838/269, Item TS690/2/2 Part 1 — JIC (A) Report on Acquisition of Armament by Indonesia.]

19 1945/41, Item 146/1/16 — Indonesian Military Capability, JIC (Aust) (64) 40 FINAL November 1964.

20 NAA A1838, Item TS687/9 Part 5, Folio 243.

21 As Joint Planning Committee Report 35/64 of 16 March 1964 explained, the RAN was only able to respond to the Malaysian request with two instead of four minesweepers because of manpower constraints, maintenance difficulties and concern for the dilution of RAN minesweeping capabilities. [AWM269, Item B/3/1/3/1 — Defence Committee Minutes and Defence Committee Agenda 1964: Indonesia.] This decision was changed in April as a result of a request from Cabinet that two more minesweepers be made available for Confrontation.

22 NAA A1209, Item 1961/1243 — Direction for the British Commonwealth FESR — Review 1961, Supplementary Directive for the Employment of Commonwealth Forces on Operations Against Infiltrators from Indonesian into Malaya and Singapore.

23 Captain Pfennigwerth interview by D.H. Ruffin, 8/9 November 2002.

24 AWM78, Item 290/5 — HMAS *Parramatta*, Report of Proceedings, June 1964.

25 Robertson interview.

26 AWM121, Item 408/A/1 — ANZAM Defence Committee: Intelligence, Annex A to JIC Report No. 4/1964, December 1964.

27 RUSI (NSW), *Konfrontasi*, 1963, p. 3.

28 James and Sheil-Small, *The Undeclared War*, 93–97.

29 Central Intelligence Agency Records Search Tool, CIA-RDP80B01500R000100040014-5, memorandum for Mr Carver, 1 August 1974. As late as 1974 the CIA regarded the Sabah dispute as a possible *casus belli* in Southeast Asia.

30 NAA A1813T19, Item 1617/205/70 — *Yarra* Encounter with PN Patrol Boat.

31 Foster, *'Hands to Boarding Stations!'*, 82.

32 Foster, *'Hands to Boarding Stations!'*, 56, and AWM78, Item 374/5 — HMAS *Yarra* Report of Proceedings, July 1965.

33 Lieutenant Commander Hiron, interview with D.H. Ruffin, 24 June 2004.

34 HMA Ships were given special approval to return fire directed at themselves or at other ships in Malaysian waters only in the vicinity of Tawau. [NAA A1813, Item 1605/201/19 — Borneo Operations: Employment of RAN Ships of the Strategic Reserve, ACNB message 27 January 1965.] In April 1966 HMAS *Hawk* exercised that right in response to Indonesian harassment of boat traffic by mortars. [AWM78, Item 136/3 — HMAS *Hawk* Report of Proceedings, April 1966.]

35 A good impression of the nature of patrol duties in Tawau can be found in NAA A1945/42, Item 162/3/46 — HMA Ships Reports of Proceedings, Enclosure (2) to HMAS *Ibis* letter I.PR of 10 November 1964.

36 AWM78, Item 315/2 — HMAS *Snipe* Reports of Proceedings 1964–1965, September 1964.

37 AWM78, Item 374/5 — HMAS *Yarra* Report of Proceedings, June 1965.

38 NAA A1945/72, Item 162/3/46 — Reports on Operations by Australian Ships Attached to FESR, HMAS *Ibis* letter I.PR of 10 November 1964.

39 Foster, *'Hands to Boarding Stations!'*, 78–79.

40 Commander Adrian Wait, correspondence with author, 20 July 2007.

41 NAA A1945/42, Item 244/3/76 — COMFEF message DTG 140224Z MAR 66 and DOBOPS message DTG 111222Z APR 66.

42 AWM78, Item352/7 Part 1, HMAS *Vendetta* Reports of Proceedings, 1964–1966.

43 Graeme Hanisch, interview with author, 22 April 2007.

44 Hanisch interview.

45 Hanisch interview.

46 Miller interview.

47 AWM78, Item 374/5 — HMAS *Yarra* Report of Proceedings, June 1965.

48 UKNA DEFE24/98 — Report on Naval Operations in East and West Malaysia 1964–1966.

49 Smith, *Counter Insurgency*, 64–67.

50 There were apocryphal stories of British helicopters landing cargo nets full of Indonesian heads at Kuching airport, tokens for which the headhunting Ibans and Dyaks could claim their bounty money. The British were said to have later substituted a set of ears as the qualifying token.

51 Grey, *Up Top*, 59. A fuller explanation of what the Sarawak patrols entailed is found in NAA A1945/42, Item 162/3/46 — HMA Ships Reports of Proceedings, Enclosure (2) to HMAS *Ibis* letter I.PR of 10 November 1964.

52 NAA A1945/72, Item 162/3/46 — Reports on Operations of Australian Ships Attached to FESR, Enclosure 2 to HMAS *Ibis* letter. I. PR of 10 November 1964.

53 Waters, *Royal New Zealand Navy*, 21.

54 Hiron interview.

55 AWM 78, Item HMAS *Ibis* Reports of Proceedings, September and October 1964.

56 Pfennigwerth interview.

57 These reports and summaries were also distributed to Australia. They form much of the basis of the JIC (A) Note 1/1964 of 27 April 1964, 'The Situation in the Borneo Territories', which was produced in support of the recommendation that Australia respond positively to the Malaysian request for assistance. [NAA A1945/43, Item 245/3/11 — Commonwealth Military Assistance to the Defence of Malaysia: File 5.]

58 UKNA DEFE24/98 — Report on Naval Operations in East and West Malaysia 1964–1966.

59 Australian Fleet Tactical Instructions (ACB 0348), P. 26-28.

60 A number of the infiltrators and saboteurs were subsequently captured, but the Indonesian Ambassador to the United Nations admitted to the Security Council in

September 1964 that infiltration of Indonesian 'volunteers' had been going on 'for some time'. [RUSI (NSW) *Konfrontasi*, 1964, p. 8.]

61 UKNA DEFE 48/167 — Maritime Patrols, comprises an operational analysis of the effectiveness of patrolling in the Singapore Strait.

62 The incident in Semporna in Sabah in March 1966, in which a member of the crew of HMAS *Hawk* turned automatic weapons on his own ship, demonstrated that bullets not only penetrated the aluminium but also dislodged spalls of the metal to create another projectile hazard to those in the vicinity. [Foster, *'Hands to Boarding Stations!'* 62–63.]

63 Foster, *'Hands to Boarding Stations!'*, 21–24. The omission of these items from early deployments represents a failure of intelligence — and of imagination.

64 Commander Wait, interview with author, 29 August 2002.

65 AWM78, Item 136/3 — HMAS *Hawk* Report of Proceedings, March 1966 and Foster, *'Hands to Boarding Stations!'*, 7–8.

66 Adrian Wait, correspondence with author, 10 July 2007.

67 AWM78, Item 339/1 — HMAS *Teal* Report of Proceedings, December 1964.

68 NAA A1813T19, Item 1623/202/28 — Incursion into Indonesian Waters by HMAS TEAL, Australian High Commission Singapore letter 820/1 of 14 December 1964.

69 It was not the last exploit by *Teal*. On the night of 23/24 February 1965 she captured a boatload of nine armed infiltrators in the Malacca Strait. In all, this one ship accounted for 22 infiltrators. [Wait interview.]

70 Wait interview.

71 UKNA DEFE 24/98 — Reports on Operations in East and West Malaysia 1964–1966.

72 NAA A1945/40, Item 245/3/9 — Australian Forces for Defence of Malaysia, Defence Cabinet submission 126 of 8 April 1964. Commonwealth naval forces were at a high state of alert for attacks on ships by underwater swimmers. One such suspected attack in Singapore Naval Dockyard was foiled on 4 June 1965. [AWM78, Item 374/5 — HMAS *Yarra* Reports of Proceedings 1964–1965.]

73 AWM121, Item 408/A/1 — ANZAM Defence Committee: Intelligence. The high command was responding to intelligence like that contained in JIC (FE) Report 4/1964 of 18 December 1964, which stated that 'Indonesian and Indonesian-inspired seaborne and possibly airborne infiltrations will continue'.

74 UKNA DEFE 48/167 — Maritime Patrols.

75 Intelligence on a possible incursion across the Strait and an Australian frigate's operational deployment resulting from it are described in NAA A1945/42, Item 162/3/46 — HMA Ships Reports of Proceedings, HMAS *Yarra* Report of Proceedings, April 1964, 2–3.

76 Commonwealth intelligence had identified up to 6000 ALRI Marines in the Riau Archipelago and had begun to develop a contingency plan to deal with the anticipated seaborne assault on Singapore. [Robertson interview.]

77 Robertson interview.

78 NAA A1945/41, Item 146/1/16 — Indonesian Military Capability, Annex A to CinCFE 88/64, 'The Internal Security Threat to Malaya and Singapore from Indonesia'.

79 UKNA DEFE 24/98 — Report on Naval Operations in East and West Malaysia, 1964–

1966, COMFEF Letter 1763.FEF.143/12 OPS of 23 November 1966.

80 UKNA DEFE 24/98 — Report on Naval Operations in East and West Malaysia, 1964–1966, COMFEF Letter 1763.FEF.143/12 OPS of 23 November 1966.

81 Foster, *'Hands to Boarding Stations!'*, 33–35.

82 NAA A1945/72, Item 244/3/76 — Shelling of HMAS *Hawk* by Indonesian Shore Batteries, SecDef minute 244/3/76 of 24 March 1966.

83 NAA A1945/72, Item 162/3/46 — Reports on Operations by Australian Ships Attached to FESR, HMAS *Yarra* Report of proceedings April 1964.

84 Commander Bate, interview with R.A. Howland, 21 October 2002.

85 Denis Appel, interview with author, 15 March 2007.

86 Appel interview.

87 NAA A1617/205/66, HMAS Yarra letter 0028/2/29 of 6 June 1965.

88 NAA A1617/205/66, HMAS Yarra letter 0028/2/29 of 6 June 1965.

89 NAA A1945/41, Item 146/1/16 — Confrontation: Threat to Malaysia, Annex B to Part 1 of JIC (FE) 165/64 (FINAL).

90 Appel interview.

91 Appel interview.

92 Elley, 'The Thoughts and Duties of a Young Clearance Diver on Active Duty in 1965'.

93 Harkness, *Onus of Proof*, 38–40.

94 Harkness, *Onus of Proof*, 143–47. His claim for treatment for post-traumatic stress disorder was later successful on appeal.

95 Rod Clarey, interview with author, 30 May 2007.

96 Paul Procopis, correspondence with author, 30 April 2007.

97 Robin Moyle, interview with author, 30 May 2007.

98 Moyle interview.

99 Kevin Pickett, letter to FESR Association, 9 July 1999.

100 It has been alleged that ALRI units became involved in order to make up for arrears of pay. [Moulton, 'Confrontation', 165.] But piracy and extortion were familiar hazards for barter traders operating into Singapore from the Riaus.

101 RUSI (NSW), *Konfrontasi*, 1964, p. 6.

102 Patrol aircraft from Changi in Singapore were normally available for five flights per week. These were supplemented by five flights by the Royal Malaysian Air Force per month for beach reconnaissance or as required. [UKNA DEFE 24/98 — Report on Naval Operations in East and West Malaysia, 1964–1966, Enclosure to DS 5/31/19/15/A, Naval Operations in Malacca and Singapore Straits, 1964–1966.]

103 Photo reconnaissance was ruled out as a source except for 'occasional' missions, as CinCFE believed overflights of Indonesian territory would be 'provocative'. [Robertson interview.]

104 The 'network' included a number of radars borrowed from the Army and the air defence radars of RAF airfields at Butterworth and Singapore. [UKNA DEFE 11/777 — Western Malaysia: 11 to 31 August 1965, COSC minute COS 144/65 of 13 August 1965: Provision of Radar Coverage.]

105 Smith, *Counter Insurgency*, 85–86.

106 Edwards, *Crises and Commitments*, 319.

107 AWM263, Item B/1/53/32 — Sunda Straits Crisis September 1964.

108 NAA A1945/39, Item 71/1/120 — Begg/Tange Conversations 21 October 1964.

109 AWM 78, Item 102/1 — HMAS *Duchess*, Reports of Proceedings, 1964–1965.

110 Wait interview.

111 NAA A1945/29, Item 133/3/27 — DSC to Lieutenant Murray.

112 During one patrol in April 1965, the frigate *Yarra* had 182 fishing boat contacts aloneon her surface plot. [AWM78, Item 374/5 — HMAS *Yarra* Report of Proceedings, April 1965.]

113 Later in the campaign more Malay policemen with a sufficient command of English were deployed in other units of the security force, down to and including minesweepers. [Foster, *'Hands to Boarding Stations!'*, 27.]

114 The onus was on the warship to keep clear of merchant shipping while not trespassing into Indonesian-claimed waters. This was not a problem for the warship as the merchant ships were fully lit, but it was an issue for the merchant skippers, or at least those who kept a proper lookout and detected darkened shapes weaving in and out of the traffic lanes, and who might be tempted to manoeuvre around them. [AWM78, Item 102/1 — HMAS *Duchess* Report of Proceedings, February 1965.]

115 Moulton, 'Confrontation', 161–62.

116 'I can remember being really impressed by that, because I'd actually seen someone apply mathematics'. [Wait interview.]

117 'The assessment that infiltration was expected proved remarkably correct for on 23 February *Teal* detected an unlit vessel nine miles southeast of Cape Rechardo.' [AWM78, Item 339/1 — HMAS *Teal* Report of Proceedings, February 1965.]

118 AWM78, Item 102/1 — HMAS *Duchess* Report of Proceedings, February 1965.

119 ACB 0348, P. 26-1–41.

120 Between April and June 1964, Malaysian and British Special Forces carried out clandestine raids against Indonesian bases on islands in the Strait. [Grey, *Up Top*, 58.]

121 NAA A7942, Item M124 — The Military Threat to the Malaysian Area up to the end of March 1967, ANZAM Defence Committee minute 6/65.

122 Dee, *Formation of Malaysia*, Document 206, 327–29.

123 Dee, *Formation of Malaysia*, Document 194, 308–10.

124 Dee, *Formation of Malaysia*, Document 292, 460.

125 Farrell, 'What Do We Do Now?', 20.

126 NAA A7942, Item M124 — The Military Threat to the Malaysian Area up to the end of March 1967, ANZAM Defence Committee minute 212/65.

127 ACB 0348, P. 26-11.

128 Dee, *Formation of Malaysia*, Document 377, 588.

129 Moulton, 'Confrontation', 170.

130 AWM 78, Item 222/8 — Report of Proceedings HMAS *Melbourne*, Report to Flag Officer Commanding Australian Fleet by Fleet Medical Officer May 1966.

131 O'Keefe and Smith, *Medicine at War*, 264–65.

132 Hiron interview.

133 Foster, *'Hands to Boarding Stations!'*, 57–67.

134   Cited in Moulton, 'Confrontation', 169.

Chapter 6 The British Withdraw
1   AWM121, Item 211/E/1 — Malaysia/Singapore End of Confrontation.
2   Moulton, 'Confrontation', 169.
3   NAA A4311, Item 675/13 — ANZAM Joint Planning Committee Other Business — Anti-Confrontation, UK COS brief 120/66 of 19 October 1966. It is interesting that this quote from an Australian intelligence appreciation should appear in a British staff paper.
4   NAA A7942, Item U25 — UK Defence Policy, ANZAM Defence Committee minute 2/67, 'Review of UK Defence Policy'.
5   NAA A1838, Item 3024/12/1 Part 1 — Singapore: Defence — Armed Forces, High Commissioner Singapore letter of 16 April 1966. This is a very high-quality report of considerable interest in describing Singaporean efforts to assert total independence from both the British and the Malaysians. It is the first to note the influence of Israel in Singaporean military affairs.
6   NAA A7942, Item M118 — Additional Assistance to Malaya [sic] and Singapore, Secretary DEA letter 3027/12/1 of 2 March 1967.
7   NAA A7942, Item M118 — Additional Assistance to Malaya [sic] and Singapore, Secretary DEA letter 3027/12/1 of 2 March 1967.
8   NAA A4359, Item 221/4/31/4 Part 1 — Five Power Defence Arrangements, Cabinet decision 614 of 28 September 1967.
9   CMND 3357 Supplementary Statement of Defence Policy 1967.
10 UK Parliamentary Debates, House of Commons, 16 January 1968.
11 NAA A7842, Item A213 — ANZAM Committee Meetings, Minutes of meeting 3 October 1968, Annex C.
12 NAA A7942, Item M104 Part 2 — Future of ANZAM, ANZAM Defence Committee Agendum 2/69 of 13 February 1969.
13 McLean, *ANZIM to ANKUK*, 33.
14 James Hume, interview with author, May 2007.
15 NAA A1838, Item 3024/12/1 Part 2 — Singapore: Defence — Armed Forces.
16 NAA A4311, Item 696/1 — Bundle of Defence Committee papers on the Situation in Malaysia and Singapore, Joint Planning Committee Report 265/68.
17 NAA A5619, Item C22 Part 1 — Withdrawal of British Forces from Malaysia/Singapore
18 James Hume interview with author, May 2007.
19 NAA A5868, Item 282 — Report on Five Power Defence Talks Kuala Lumpur
20 Hawkins, *From AMDA to ANZUK*, 35.
21 NAA A4311, Item 696/1 — Bundle of Defence Committee papers on the Situation in Malaysia and Singapore, Joint Planning Committee Report 265/68.
22 NAA A5619, Item C22 Part 2 — Withdrawal of British Forces from Malaysia/Singapore.
23 NAA A1838, Item 3024/12/1 Part 2 — Singapore: Defence — Armed Forces.
24 Elizabeth Gordon, interview with author, 23 April 2007.
25 Laurie Jones, interview with author, 29 May 2007.
26 ASEAN was formed after a meeting of the foreign ministers of Indonesia, the Philippines, Singapore, Thailand and Malaysia in Bangkok in August 1967, with the aim of fostering

economic and social cooperation amongst the nations of Southeast Asia. [Baginda and Bergin, *Asia Pacific's Security Dilemma*, 36.]

27 Chin Kin Wah, *Defence of Malaysia and Singapore*, 149–50, 153, 156–59.

28 Lam Ah Lek interview.

29 NAA A1838 Item 696/1/13 — Five Power Arrangements — Defence Cooperation with Malaysia and Singapore.

30 NAA A3211, Item 1969/1846 Part 3 — UK Defence Policy. These attitudes are revealed in a series of cables to Canberra from the Australian High Commissioner in London.

31 Chin, *The Five Power Defence Arrangements*, 5–6.

32 Chin, *Defence of Malaysia and Singapore*, 168.

33 Chin, *Defence of Malaysia and Singapore*, 137.

34 NAA A4359, Item 221/4/31/4 Part 1 — Five Power Defence Arrangements.

35 NAA A1209, Item 1969/9036 Part 1 — Malaysia/Singapore Defence Policy and Administration.

36 AWM207, Item 842-F3-1 Part 7 — Headquarters ANZUK Forces, Exercise Bersatu Padu, Headquarters ANZUK Force, Exercise Bersatu Padu, CinCFE 3540/7001/11 of 22 October 1968.

37 Arasaratnam interview.

38 AWM207, Item 842-F3-1, Part 8 — Headquarters ANZUK Forces, Exercise Bersatu Padu, press release by Minister for Defence, 23 February 1970

39 AWM207, Item 842-F3-1, Part 10 — Headquarters ANZUK Forces, Exercise Bersatu Padu, Navy Office letter1624/1/41 of 22 Jul 70.

40 Chin, *Defence of Malaysia and Singapore*, 174.

41 Speech by Malcolm Fraser on Defence, Parliamentary Debates, 10 March 1970.

42 McLean, *ANZIM to ANZUK*, 34.

43 Chin, *Defence of Malaysia and Singapore*, 148–49.

44 The new arrangement was announced on 16 February 1971. The title was chosen to remove any confusion that continuation of the 'M' in ANZAM might cause by associating the organisation with Malaysia. [McLean, *ANZIM to ANZUK*, 34.]

45 G.J. Swinden, correspondence with author, 18 March 2007.

46 Chin, *The Five Power Defence Arrangements*, 2–4.

47 Chin, *The Five Power Defence Arrangements*, 1.

48 Keating, 'The Five Power Defence Arrangements', 49. These two bodies were combined in an FPDA Consultative Committee in 1994.

49 NAA A4359, Item 221/4/31/4 Part 2 — (Jakarta): Five Power Defence Arrangements, contains a series of cables explaining both Indonesian puzzlement and assurances of only peaceful intentions towards Malaysia and Singapore.

50 NAA A1838, Item 696/1/24 Part 1 — Five Power Arrangements: Indonesian Attitude Towards

51 NAA A1838, Item 696/1/14 Part 10 — British Withdrawal: Five Power Defence Arrangements — Status of Force Malaysia and Singapore.

52 I know, because I was that flag lieutenant.

Chapter 7 The Veterans' Struggle for Recognition

1 NAA A11857, Item 63 — Secretary's papers: Budget Documents — Cabinet Submissions.

2 NAA A1209, 1957/5024, 424758 — Directives to Australian FESR — PM Dep't File, Directive for the Attachment of HMA Ships to the Far East Fleet for Service with the Strategic Reserve.

3 NAA A1209, 1957/5024, 424758 — Directives to Australian FESR — PM Dep't File, Directive for the Attachment of HMA Ships to the Far East Fleet for Service with the Strategic Reserve.

4 NAA A1308, Item 77/1/18 Part 1 — Strategic Reserve Malaya: Repatriation and Re-establishment Benefits, Treasury Finance Committee Report of 25 July 1955.

5 Quoted Major General The Honourable R.F. Mohr RFD ED RL, *Review of Service Entitlement Anomalies in Respect of South-East Asian Service, 1955–1975* (the Mohr Report), 3–5.

6 Mohr Report, 3–4.

7 NAA MP729/8, Item 20/431/164, PM&C letter 439/1/46 of 25 November 1955.

8 NAA A1813, Item 302/210/12 Part 1A, Navy Office letter of 7 February 58.

9 Quoted in Submission by Admiral M.W. Hudson AC RAN (Rtd) to the Mohr Review Part 1, 22 June 1999, 7.

10 In the 1956 debate on the FESR Repatriation Bill in the Senate, the Minister for Health representing the Minister for Defence made that statement regarding naval personnel that 'They are not regarded as being subjected to additional operational risks. They are subjected to the risks of the service for which they engage, and therefore their conditions are in accordance with the terms of their enlistment.' Note that the Minister conceded that the RAN ships were facing operational risks, even if those of the FESR were not 'additional'.

11 Vice Admiral Sir Richard Peek KBE CB DSC letter to Assistant Chief of Defence Force — Personnel 26 October 1996.

12 Vice Admiral Sir Richard Peek KBE CB DSC letter to Assistant Chief of Defence Force — Personnel 26 October 1996.

13 Mohr Report, 2–5.

14 *Commonwealth Gazette* No. 40, 5 June 1952, Item 2716.

15 Department of Parliamentary Library Research Memorandum, 'Defence Service on *Tobruk*' of 15 May 1977.

16 NAA A1308, Item 77/1/18 Part 1 — Strategic Reserve Malaya: Repatriation and Re-establishment Benefits Treasury letter 206/600/255 date illegible.

17 NAA A1308, Item 77/1/18 Part 1 — Strategic Reserve Malaya: Repatriation and Re-establishment Benefits, Assistant Secretary Treasury letter of 3 September 1956.

18 Navy Office Minute N95/528 from DGPSC-N to ACPERS-N of 3 May 1995.

19 Navy Office letter N93/22351 of 8 March 1995 from Director Naval Personal Services to RN Directorate of Naval Service Conditions — 'Naval General Service Medal Clasp Malaya'.

20 Hudson Submission, Part 2, 24.

21 The Review of Service Entitlement Anomalies paragraph 34, quoted in Hudson Submission, Part 2, 26.

22 CN Minute CN97/24073 of 16 January 1998.
23 Mohr Report, 3–22.
24 Mohr Report, 3–21.
25 Letter from Repatriation Commissioner to author, 24 July 2006.
26 Sir Roy Dowling relieved Sir John Collins as CNS only on 25 February 1955.
27 Dennis and Grey, *Emergency and Confrontation*, 69.

Epilogue
1 McLean, *ANZIM to ANZUK*, 35.
2 Chin, *The Five Power Defence Arrangements*, 14–15. At the outset the Five Power arrangements were expected to last only about five years.
3 NAA A1838, Item 696/1/23 Part 4 — FPDA: Malaysia's Attitude Towards.
4 Keating, 'The Five Power Defence Arrangements', 49.

Index

Anglo-Malayan/Malaysian Defence Agreement, 88, 221, 227, 234, 240–1
Anzac, HMAS, 54, 59, 61, 63, 65, 66, 67, 70, 71, 73
ANZAM, 22–4, 27, 84–5, 93–4, 208–9, 212, 221–3, 227–8, 274
ANZUK, 242–3, 245, 274
ANZUS Treaty, 32, 221
Arunta, HMAS, 58, 65, 281–2
British Commonwealth defence, 21–2, 42–3
British 'East of Suez' policy, 80–3, 86–9, 211, 221–2, 226–7, 238–9, 241
Brunei insurrection, 92, 153
Chin Peng, 41, 48–9, 50, 53–4, 80–1
Collins, Rear Admiral J.A., RAN, 12–13, 23–5, 30
Confrontation
– battleground described, 150–2
– Commonwealth command and control, 153–5
– constraints on Commonwealth military action, 156
– Australian forces requested, 158–9
– activities around Tawau, 163–73
– NGS at Tawau, 172–3
– operations off Sarawak, 174–9
– operations in Singapore Strait, 179–81, 183–8
– interception procedures, 182–3
– prisoner handling, 185–6
– tactical instructions,187–8
– work of clearance divers, 192–6
– heightened tension after Labis landing, 203–4
– Commonwealth tactics in Malacca Strait, 204–7
– diplomatic efforts end hostilities, 213
– summation and lessons learned, 213–15
Curlew, HMAS, 286
Derwent, HMAS, 172, 285
Dollard, Commodore A.N., RAN, 119–20, 122–3
Dovers, Rear Admiral W.J., RAN, 104–7, 110
Duchess, HMAS, 204, 228, 283
Far East Strategic Reserve
– inception of, 55–6
– RAN Directive, 56–7,
– exercises, 59
– future of, 222
– extension to Singapore, 225
– RAN deployments, 228
– termination, 242,
– conditions of service, 248–51
– denial of repatriation benefits to RAN, 251–2
– 'allotment' for service, 256–7
– concept of 'active service', 257–8

– entitlement to NGSM, 259–61, 264–5
Five Power Defence Arrangements, 236, 243–5, 277–8
Griffiths, Rear Admiral G.R., RAN, 123–5, 133–4
Gull, HMAS, 159, 169, 286
Harwood Working Party, 26, 80, 230, 245
Hawk, HMAS, 159, 164–5, 169, 170, 178, 183, 188–9, 217, 286
Hudson, Admiral M.W., RAN, 265, 266, 267, 270
Ibis, HMAS, 177, 198, 286
Indonesia, 18
– internal insurrections, 68
– Australian diplomatic engagement with, 86
– military trainees in Australia, 86–7
– Sukarno regime instability, 90–1
– 'Crush Malaysia' policy, 92
– Soviet arms for, 98
– diplomatic dilemma for Australia, 95–6
– attacks on East Malaysia, 150
– Confrontation command, 151
– BT boats, 151
– activities at Tawau border zone, 163–4, 168–9, 173
– submarine activities, 189
– landings near Singapore, 190
– activities in Malacca Strait, 202–3, 208
– withdraws from UN, 204
– Jakarta coup attempt, 212
– Australia resumes military cooperation with, 241–2
– Australian flagship visits, 245–6
Intelligence
– in Malayan Emergency, 52–5
– RAN contribution to, 52–5, 78
– Australian contribution during Confrontation, 156–8
– in Singapore Strait, 186–7
– in Malacca Strait, 206–8
– post-Confrontation arrangements, 233–4
Jerai, KD, 120–1
Korean War, 31–2, 55, 57

Mahamiru, KD, 110–11, 116
Malaya
– defence of, 16–17, 22, 27–8, 33, 35–6
– political and geographic situation, 38–40
– Bridgeford mission to, 45–8, 58
– Australian concern about, 51
– independence of, 65
– defence arrangements post-independence, 82
Malaya, KD, 115, 116, 144, 146, 229, 231
Malayan Communist Party/MRLA, 40–1
– foreign support for, 48–50
Malayan Emergency
– outlined, 41–2
– Australian attitudes towards, 43
– Australian forces committed, 45
– naval role in, 46–50
– reorganisation of British strategies, 51–2
– collapse of, 72
Malaysia
– concept first mooted, 87
– Indonesian suspicions of, 91
– ANZAM planning for defence of, 93–4
– proclamation of, 84
– defence aid to, 114
– post-Confrontation defence arrangements, 221, 224–6
– implications of British withdrawal, 235–6
– issue of *Pingat Jasa Malaysia* to veterans, 276
Melbourne, HMAS, 66, 162, 192, 196, 197, 198, 215, 228, 238–9, 245, 254, 280–1, 283
Mohr Review, 53–4, 256, 267–70
Mull of Kintyre, HMS, 199–201
Nettur, Commodore P.K., RMN, 119, 134, 136
Parramatta, HMAS, 160–1, 285
Peek, Vice Admiral R.I., RAN, 252, 255, 265, 273
Philippines
– Sabah claims, 94, 163–4, 234–5
– pirates, 133, 163, 165
– naval patrols, 164–5

Quadrant, HMAS, 284
Queenborough, HMAS, 67, 70, 284
Quiberon, HMAS, 61, 72, 284
Quickmatch, HMAS, 61, 63, 65, 67, 70, 284
Radford–Collins Agreement, 25–6
Royal Australian Navy
– post-war deficiencies, 29–31
– increase in capability, 35
– committed to FESR, 56–8
– readiness for operations, 59
– gunfire support in Malaya, 60–2
– Malayan coastal surveillance, 63–4
– showing the flag, 64–8
– presence role, 68–9
– support to RMN, 69
– development of knowledge of SE Asia,
    69–71
– impact on personnel, 73–7
– lessons learned from Emergency, 77–8
– capabilities strengthened, 89–90
– provides loan personnel to RMN, 108,
    111–12
– concern over RMN standards, 112–13
– provides 'Adviser' to RMN CNS, 123
– accepts RMN students in training schools,
    131–2
– senior responsibility for RMN ends, 134
– loan personnel responses to RMN service,
    136–147
– deploys Army and RAAF units to Malaysia,
    160–1
– first clearance diving team deployed to
    Singapore, 191
– second CDT to Singapore, 198
– maintenance teams to Singapore, 199–
    201
– lessons learned from Confrontation, 214
– health issues from Confrontation service,
    215–18
– heavy Southeast Asian deployment load,
    222
– discussion over use of Singapore naval
    base, 230–1
– revised commitment to FESR, 232

– contribution to Exercise *Bersatu Padu*,
    238–9
– responsible for ANZUK naval base, 242–3
– RAN officer takes command of ANZUK,
    245
Royal Malayan/Malaysian Navy, 69
– origins, 97–9
– roles laid down, 100
– responsibility for accepted by Federation,
    100–1
– Australian assistance requested, 103
– development of new order of battle,
    105–6
– expansion, 108
– staff development, 108–9
– contribution to Confrontation, 116–17
– Tawau operations, 116–17
– urges stronger reaction to Indonesian
    attacks, 120
– recovers minesweeping skills, 120–1
– new patrol craft, 121
– choice of first Malaysian commander,
    122–3
– development of training base, 125–7
– logistics developments, 127–9
– developments in engineering
    maintenance, 130–1
– improved operational standards, 133–4
– language difficulties in training, 141–2
– trains to attack Indonesian bases, 207–8
– developing international standing, 232
– cooperation with Singapore over basing,
    223
SEATO
– inception, 34
– exercises, 59, 60
– Malayan response to, 84, 87, 228, 237,
    274–5
Singapore, 18–20
– security concerns for, 65–6, 75
– self-government, 82
– becomes major ANZAM base, 85
– interest in Malaysia concept, 88
– naval personnel join RMN, 108

– split with Malaysia, 119, 210–11
– Republic of Singapore Navy established, 119
– confrontation activities, 179–80, 181–3, 186–7
– race riots, 209–10
– barter trade issues resolved, 212–13
– defence arrangements with, 223–6
– gains control of naval dockyard, 231
– struggles to develop navy, 232–3
Sixteenth Minesweeping Squadron, 15
– capabilities and limitations, 181–2
– commendation, 218–19
Snipe, HMAS, 111, 223, 286
Sri Selangor, KD, 119
Swan, HMAS, 285

Sydney, HMAS, 160–1, 162, 199, 216, 228, 281
Synnot, Admiral A.M., RAN, 45 107–8, 118, 141–2
Teal, HMAS, 169–70, 183–5, 204–5, 286
Thanabalasingham, Rear Admiral K., RMN, 122–4, 127, 134
Tobruk, HMAS, 54, 61, 62
– casualties, 62, 64, 66, 68, 71, 73, 254
Vampire, HMAS, 190–1, 269, 283
Vendetta, HMAS, 68, 171–2, 216, 228, 283
Vietnam War, 92, 162, 199, 214, 224–5, 227, 228, 234, 241, 274–5
Voyager, HMAS, 68, 74, 116, 252, 283
Warramunga, HMAS, 53, 58, 63, 65, 74, 282
Yarra, HMAS, 160, 164, 165, 189, 193–5, 285